FOR ALL AS FOR ONE

UPLIFTING MESSAGES FROM SPIRIT TIED IN WITH SCRIPTURE

LeRosa Leigh

FOR ALL AS FOR ONE
UPLIFTING MESSAGES FROM SPIRIT TIED IN WITH SCRIPTURE

iUniverse books may be ordered through booksellers or by contacting:

iUniverse
1663 Liberty Drive
Bloomington, IN 47403
www.iuniverse.com
844-349-9409

Unless otherwise noted, all Scripture is taken from
The HOLY BIBLE, NEW INTERNATIONAL VERSION.
Copyright 1973, 1978, 1984, International Bible Society.
Used by permission of Zondervan Bible Publishers.

ISBN: 978-1-6632-5345-3 (sc)
ISBN: 978-1-6632-5344-6 (e)

Library of Congress Control Number: 2023909753

Print information available on the last page.

iUniverse rev. date: 05/25/2023

CONTENTS

PREFACE

I am writing under the pen name "LeRosa Leigh" (Lay).

Receiving the lessons from Spirit that are included in *For All As For One* came about in this way: In my mid-forties, while attending a workshop on prayer and Scripture, I invited Jesus to come into my heart. As I said the words, "Please come in!" my heart was instantly filled with immense love flowing out to everybody without exception.

From that point on, I was drawn to spend up to an hour a day reading the Bible and spending quiet time with God. (Before that, I would develop a headache almost right away every time I tried to read it for a few minutes.) I began writing down Scripture verses that were meaningful for me along with my thoughts about them, and spontaneous prayers.

After I had been doing that for several months, a friend of mine received a "word" from the Holy Spirit, that at prayer time I should first pray quietly for a few minutes and then write down the thoughts that would come to mind. As I began doing that, spiritual thoughts and lessons flowed easily into my mind and I simply wrote them down. The messages in this book are from the first few years of following those directions.

I often wondered about the worth and validity of the lessons and understandings I was receiving, especially at the beginning. Here are some of the replies I received:

How can I know if these thoughts are from me or not?

[| Rest easy and do not fear. My words will prove themselves. A knife or a pencil cannot judge whether or not its work is good. |]

Lord, please affirm that You want me to write like this.

[| I truly do desire that you write thus. The things of the spirit cannot always be connected directly with the senses of the body. You are using a spiritual sense that can be developed.

Where do these thoughts come from? They come from Me. When you are open to Me, I can speak to you wordlessly in your spirit. My peace will be a sign to you.

Do not be afraid to write if you feel even the slightest impulse to do so. The Spirit is Breath and moves very lightly in those who are accustomed to His movements. |]

Messages from Father-Mother God/the Holy Spirit and Jesus are enclosed in brackets: [| ...lesson... |]

Some of the Bible quotes are from *The New American Bible* (NAB) because that is the only Bible that I had for many years. I used some quotes from that translation that I especially love.

Dear readers, I offer this material to you for your prayerful consideration and pondering. It is my hope and prayer that the lessons will bless and invigorate you and that they may be a light for your path. May you be inspired, also, to listen to the "still, small voice" within for affirmation, direction, guidance, and blessing.

I want to point this out: Some people have misgivings about accepting "the Will of God" for themselves because of thinking that it may not be what they would choose. I have come to understand that our will – the desire of our Soul for our spiritual good and well-being – is the same as God's Will:

"..your will is God's..." (ACIM T8.II.6.4) "There is no difference between your will and God's" (ACIM T9.I.5.3).

A message to carry with you:

God speaks to all at all times.
What God speaks is "for all, as for one."

What God speaks is that He (She, It) is always with us,
  That we are loved by everlasting love,
  That all is well,
  That there is peace, joy, and love to be found because
    God is.
  Ask and you shall receive, seek and you shall find.

Peace to all!

LeRosa

ACKNOWLEDGEMENT

Father-Mother God, Holy Spirit, and Jesus, I offer you the deepest and most profound thanks of which I am capable, along with the wish that those thanks be multiplied a-thousand-times-a-thousand times and more.

Bless You, in who You are and in who You are coming to be!

Thank you, my friends and acquaintances, along the way, for your prayers, encouragement, and support as I was doing this writing. Several people said they would like to have a copy when I was finished with writing.

I pray that the Holy Spirit will guide you and many others to read this book and other spiritually-focused material that will provide you with what you are searching for. Bless each of you in who you are and in who you are coming to be!

CHAPTER 1

FAITH AND TRUST

1.1   OF VIOLETS AND PIANOS

The African violet plants on my windowsill hold their leaves expectantly toward the window throughout the night. Although it is dark out, the plants continue reaching toward the source of light that they trust will return. That teaches me a lesson about trusting God. Darkness around us does not change the source of our good.

A piano can be compared to one's Soul, also. Discordant, soul-rending sounds can be played on a piano, as well as harmonious, joyful melodies. Whatever type of music is being played, the sounds come from within the interior of the piano's "self." The type of music being played does not affect the piano. It stands there as stolidly and safely with one type of sound as with the other

In our being in and with God, we are immovable and "unhurtable." The worst frenzy or the most alluring swan call, neither one affects us. Let come and go what may, if we are set steadfastly in God, we can trust that security and look forward to what tunes will next be played in our life or other people's lives.

Everywhere we walk, we walk in love, for we walk in God, our loving Father who has brought us forth in love. He wants us to relax away every care and anxiety into His loving arms. As the African violets on the window sill can set within a few inches of cold, stormy weather and remain safe, even so, we need not let anxiety and problems worry us. The life-giving sunlight comes to the plants right through that cold and snow. Taking in the loving light in abundance on sunny days gives the plants enough reserve energy to tide them over on the days when the sun is hidden by clouds.

The house and window can represent God's mantle of love. As we look out from the security of God's love, nothing needs to upset us. The only thing that matters is that God loves us!

1.2   ON COMING TO KNOW GOD

God is an ocean of love that carries us safely,
A bosom of love that enfolds us and places us within its heart if
    we choose to accept love,
A current of love that draws us to sympathize with hurting
    hearts and moves us to share our very selves, in turn.

As we sit on a chair, we can feel the chair and the floor holding us securely. The ground beneath is solidly supporting us, the earth held firmly in its orbit by an Unseen Hand. We can feel our breath coming and going under a sure, steady impulse sustaining life in us. Our hearts beat steadily, assuring us that we are being held in life by some Power outside of us, for we do not make our heartbeat. In unspoken words, we hear:

[| You rest securely in Me and on Me, your God. Your breathing and heartbeat are ever-present signs within you that you have been created by Me and are moment-by-moment being sustained by Me. I keep you ever-existing by keeping you ever-present in My mind and heart.

Observe the wonders of nature. Where does all the energy come from to keep things in motion, with constant rebirth and regeneration of life? Where does all the energy come from that people are learning to harness? All of this is a sign that I Am.

You carry an ever-present sign of My presence within you. Who can explore the depths of a single human mind or Soul? Which of you could begin to explore the depths of the people who now live on the earth, to say nothing about all of those who lived in the past and all those yet to live?

You cannot, because it is beyond your powers of comprehension, just as I am beyond your comprehension. You cannot fathom Me and never will be able to. I understand that. My creation surrounds you with its majesty and mystery to give a little reflection of My power and majesty and be a vehicle to carry My love to you.

However, you cannot learn much about Me even from that, so, I came to you in My Son, Jesus. Now it is for you to do your part by coming to know Me through him. Jesus is the way. Come to know him and you will know the way, you will know Me.

I am tenderness, I am love. When you experience tenderness and love towards others, you will know how I feel toward you, the workings of My heart. And when you experience rejection by loved ones – indifference, hate, spite, seemingly being forsaken by Me along with having physical pain and a strong desire for your loved ones and friends to come to know Me and you seemingly cannot help them to understand – then you even more truly know Me. To truly understand another person, you need to experience what they experience, so even your sufferings have a tinge of blessedness about them, for they make us become more truly one. |]

When we do not have the strength we need, we can ask God for His strength.

When we simply cannot understand, we can stop trying to understand and put our trust in the wisdom of God, who knows and understands all things.

When we do not have enough love to go out to a particular person, we can rest in God's presence long enough and often enough until we can go forth in love.

When material supplies have dwindled and we fear we will be left in dire need, we can go to Him who has promised *"Ask and you will receive"* (16:24b).

When we feel unloved and unlovely, we can go to Him who loves us with everlasting love and be healed.

The desire for happiness and love that we feel is God, drawing us to come to know Him. If we but be open, love will enter our hearts and heal us little by little of the hurts that keep us closed in on ourselves.

1.3   WALK WITH FAITH

[| Do not be afraid, little one. It is I. I come to you, walking upon the waters of faith. When you believe, you create the medium whereby you make contact with Me. Every cry for help that comes from someone's heart reaches My ears. An outsider may think that some particular person has no faith, but a person's crying out for help is an acknowledgment of a Power greater than him or her.

Life is simple if you take it on faith:

Created by Me for love,

Destined to be in that love forever,

Growing in love through the exercise of that love.

This world gives you ample opportunities for choosing and living in love, with the chance to begin again when you fail. |]

Lord, I believe! Help my unbelief!

[| Have courage! No matter how strong the temptations to doubt become, faith has the greater power. Courage! I have overcome the world! I have overcome the "Prince of Darkness." All of his wiles are but shadows that cannot hurt you unless you give way to fear.

Hang onto My promises. All is well and all will be well. I promise salvation and glorious freedom for everyone. You are not there to judge. You are there to love and guide others as I prompt you.

My child, live without fear. Leave it outside your gate. Live with Me, the companion of your Soul. Rest in Me and I will accomplish a great work in your Soul. And be at peace. When you achieve peace to your inmost being, you realize somewhat in the physical My presence with and in you. |]

1.4   FAITH, HOPE, LOVE

[| My child, what have you to fear? You are My child. I, the Lord of heaven and earth, hold you tenderly in My care. I will not let anything harm you. The only way you can come into harm's way is if you go off on your own, thinking you know the way yourself. Then you will run into spiritual entities, beings, that you will not be able to handle yourself, such as fear, resentment, clinging anger, doubt, confusion, and despair. At every moment, though, I am ready to come to your aid. You need only to call.

How much better, though, to spend your days in surety and peace, in spiritual union with Me! My side of the union is always open. My arms are open. My heart is open. My mind, My Spirit is open to you. You need to be open to Me, too, and the union is. You are in love, in peace, in safety. All it takes is for you to realize that, to accept it, to believe.

Do not think it is too hard to believe. I give you that grace, also, the gift of faith. You can use faith against doubt. Believe that faith can vanquish all doubts and it does and will! Hang onto faith, hope, and love. They are the three anchors of the spiritual life. They connect you with Me while you are yet living this earthly life.

The way seems long and uncertain to you, I know. That is the very means of testing that is needed to strengthen the faith and hope I have given you. How could swimmers save themselves if they did not use their muscles? If you use the muscles of faith and hope to pull you through the dark waters of doubt and confusion you will come, at last, to the shores of love and mercy.

Say: "God, I believe that You will save me,

That You will give me all the graces I need,

That You love me and care for me as much as it is possible to."

There is no limit on My love! []

1.5   DO ALL IN ME

Do You have a word for me, Lord?

[| Rest in Me, My child. That is always My word for you and all. It is an eternal word, for it pertains to what is imperative for the health of your Soul. Whatever task you are doing, rest in Me as you do it. Be conscious that power and ability to do the task are coming directly from Me, flowing from Me to you at every moment. Your physical strength, your eyesight, your mental acuity, can and ought to be, signs of My love for you. In love, I sustain you in your strength and abilities.

You never are resting in fear. I am the foundation of life and being. Fear just tricks you and masks My love and protection, so that you think you are alone and helpless. Use the word of faith that you are given. As you stand on solid ground, do you stand less solidly when you close your eyes, making you unable to see the ground?

Of course not! The ground remains solid and sure. Well, in your present condition in this earthly life, your spiritual eyes are not yet open, but you rest just as surely and solidly in My love and care now as you will come to see and know once you pass through to the fullness of eternal life. Do not fear, little one! []

1.6 TAKE MY FAITH

Father, are You mindful of me?
[| My child, you know you do not need to ask that question! My thoughts, My love, are eternal, unchanging, forever the same. My delight in you as you progress and unfold becomes dearer to My heart! I see you and hold you in love as you are coming to be. No one could have more love and care for anyone than I have for you, and it is the same for all of My children.

My heart calls out to your heart. My being is completely open to your being. As you gradually relinquish anxiety, resentment, fear, and such, and allow hope, faith, trust, and love to rule your life, we then become united more and more. There was a perfect union between his humanity and his divinity In My Son Jesus. You are called to become ever more like him. []

I read in an article on faith that "fear is wrong believing," that when we fear, we use the gift of faith to believe against God and His goodness. Help me, Lord, to grow stronger in faith.

[| My child, see how immature you are yet? Even as you write these words you fear that you will not be able to believe as you should, even though you know that fear is wrong believing. Put that mistrust where it belongs and you will do all right. It is good to mistrust *yourself,* to think that surely you will not be able to have the faith necessary to believe as you should, but you are not alone and never will be. It is My faith and strength in you that accomplishes all.

I am united with you in body, mind, and spirit for you have asked Me to be with you.

My life is within you, for you to let flow through and vivify you.

My faith is yours to appropriate.

My love is yours to unite with, that thus you may truly love with Me and as I do.

My grace is supplied at every turn: yours to use or let lay idle.

Now it depends on you, to do your part in completing the union of love that we have.

You, each of you, are My beloved. I take you, accept you, and love you unreservedly, paying no heed to the gross shortcomings in your character. Love overcomes all and overlooks all. I supply what you lack. Do not try to understand with your finite mind. Just believe with the will of your spirit. *"Everything is possible for one who believes"* (Mk 9:23b).

"You did not choose me, but I chose you and appointed you so that might go and bear fruit—fruit that will last." (Jn 15:16a). What I choose to do is done eternally. I will never reverse My choice. I take you to Me tenderly in love. |]

1.7   FOREVER THE SAME

[| I bless all, My child. The more open you can be, the greater your share of the blessing will be. When you are open to others in love, you receive My blessing through them, also.

I am in all of life: in plants, animals, human beings, angels, and saints. Life is the gift of Myself to you. It is a sign of My presence, of My reality. Cling to Me and all is well. Cling to that vine! Nothing else matters except to be open and loving and trusting, to believe in Me. All things come to him who believes. It is a power greater than death, for I have conquered death.

Continue to trust that everything that is meant to be will come about, in its own good time. Take one day at a time and live it in trust and love. Do not fear! I am with you always.

I understand that you feel your best is not good enough, that you wish you could do much more and love Me more deeply, but remember, you are a child and are meant to remain as a child spiritually. That ensures humility. *"I tell you the truth, anyone who will not receive the kingdom of God like a little child will never enter it"* (Lk 18:17).

I recognize your insecurity, but it is just a sign of a need for deep, tender love and I am giving you that. Your insecurity will lessen the longer you rest in Me, but I warn you, it will not be without a struggle. Doubts and fears will assail you mercilessly and the time may come that you wonder once again what life is all about, anyway, and whether truth can be found to which to cling.

The lesson of a few days ago is so important: No matter what comes up in the world of men, no matter what is brought forth as the answer to the riddle of life and the workings of the human mind, know that I am the base and the foundation of life. I am the way and the truth. You are secure when you rest in Me.

Your ideas about Me may change as you come to know Me more intimately, come to know more about Me, the author of life, but that does not change Me. I am forever the same, unchanging in My Godhead.

Life is in My Godhead. You see but a faint reflection of the power and activity of that life mirrored in creation. No one can give that which he does not have, not even Me, so you can rest assured that I am above and in authority over all powers and all life. Rest in Me, in the kingdom of life, in love. Live in Me and love Me. []

1.8   HEART KNOWLEDGE

[| My child, it does My heart good to have you be attentive to Me and My feelings. You cannot know Me directly using your mind, but you can come to some idea of how it is for Me through experiences that you have. That way you come to have heart knowledge, and you need heart knowledge if you want to come to truly know someone.

To know what it was like for Jesus to be abandoned by Me, a like experience is given you in one way or another, of crying desperately to Me for help and strength, with seemingly no response.

Once your heart is attuned to true love and the gifts of faith and hope are constantly renewed in you by Me, the fact that you can go on believing and hoping, despite receiving no apparent answer to your prayers, shows that you are in My care. Your existence is a sign in the physical world of My encircling love.

Being in a plane completely closed in by clouds and fog does not alter the fact that the sky is around you and the earth is below you. I Am. My love and My covenant are the bedrock that you can walk on with sureness.

My children, how I long to gather you under My wing! For those who respond to My mercy, that day will come and I anticipate it eagerly. Just hope! Trust! Keep the faith! Take from Me the grace to see each day and the events of life from the positive side.

Each day more precious Souls are saved!

Each day you are closer to the glory awaiting you!

Each day that you correspond with grace you are filled to a fuller measure with love, humility, and life,

And should you fail to cooperate with grace there is a precious lesson learned and growth in humility, as well.

At times, you may think the negative is all there is in the world. That is not My picture at all! I see a world blossoming into the fullness of My kingdom! I give you My love and My life, My children! I empty Myself that you may be full. Receive Me, and in love give yourself likewise to Me; thus we are one. I love you dearly! Yes, you! I embrace you in love! Come! |]

1.9   CLING TO REALITY

[| My child, it warms My heart to have you entrust yourself completely to Me. It is then that I can do something about problems that concern you. Pay no mind to the doubt and confusion that try to clutter your mind. You are in Me and I am in you. That is reality, your relationship with Me. Cling to My words, to truth, and you will be safe.

When doubts assail you as to whether this is real – that I am always with you and that you are being prompted by My thoughts – ignore them. Those doubts have no power over you. *"[I]n quietness and trust is your strength"* (Is 30:15c), in quiet trust and in trusting quiet. Choose to believe and your faith becomes stronger with every movement of your will in believing.

There is give-and-take in love. That is the best, the happiest way, that of giving and receiving in the freedom of mutual love. Strive with the full intent of your Soul to open yourself to that love that permeates all and is throughout all.

Having a heavy daily cross to bear has little significance in comparison to the warmth and joy you have when you abide in love. I breathe love and joy into you. Receive the peace of the Holy Spirit of love! I am with you always. Have no fear, only joy in the Lord.

You are receiving many messages and inspirations from speakers, books, and Scripture. Do not get uptight, thinking that you have to make immediate use of all those lessons. Live in the calm assurance that I will guide you by My Spirit at the appropriate time and will bring the words to mind that will be helpful. It is not you who are doing this or that. It is I who accomplish all things in everyone.

You do well to restrain fearful anxiety, but being eagerly anxious to get at a task that you feel prompted to do is often a movement of the Spirit.

The Spirit is at work in every facet of life. *"[Y]our Father knows what you need before you ask him"* (Mt 6:8b). The Spirit knows that people need accomplishments and discipline to develop self-worth so He prompts you to that which is for the good of your body, Soul and spirit and that of your family and neighbor.

If you just relax into life, into the My arms, and let the Holy Spirit carry you along, you will have a most gratifying life! Once you learn how to discern the prompting of the Spirit, do not move without the flow that comes in guidance.

I embrace you with the eternal arms of love!

I am the truth within your being.

I am your sovereign and your servant.

I am Yahweh-who-saves, Yahweh-who-cares. Bless you! |]

1.10   AS YOU LIVE

[| My child, I love you so! My love for you is so strong that it keeps you in being. As you think of the people that you lovingly carry in your heart, wish blessings for them and desire that they are blessed by Me. Since we are one in Spirit, as you bless them and wish them well, I, at the same time, bless them, also.

Continue in your efforts to see your life, the lives of others, and all of creation as existing in joy and peace, and coming ever more fully into a realization of that peace.

My precious child, I watch over you with delight, as human parents fondly watch the activities of their little child. A mother and father cannot adequately express their love and affection in words, for words fail them. Even so, words fail miserably to express My deep concern, care, and love for you and all My children. The final coming of humankind into glory with Me will be as much of a relief and time of ecstatic happiness for Me as it will be for them!

I bless your efforts to come into union with My mind and Will. Your part is just to be open and willing. Nothing that you do in other ways will help. Everything is done in and through Me:

All creation, all keeping-in-being, all love,

All good desires, all courage, and all blessings come from Me
    and through Me.

Rest and live in Me and have no fear.

Rest your head on My shoulder. Grasp My strong hand which is ever outstretched in loving help. You can only grasp My hand and receive My help by an act of faith. The spiritual cannot be reached on the physical plane. You live in the spiritual realm, though you do not come to realize that until you have spent time with Me.

The faculties of mind and Soul that were dulled by sin (supposedly lost) can be sharpened and regained by drawing sustenance from Me through faith. It is only through faith that you can make contact with Me and keep contact. Sensible spiritual experiences are with you only for a moment and then are gone, but faith is a living entity of the life of the spirit. All that has to do with the spirit is on the spirit plane. It connects you with eternal life, for your spirit will live forever. He who is sincere, willing, and open to change as grace leads him, lives in peace.

I love the pure of heart: the sincere, single-minded Souls who strive to do their best. I love the selfish person as much, but the shell of selfishness prevents that person from accepting or giving love. Should that shell get cracked by misfortune, sickness, or a touch of grace, it is for you who are fellow travelers on the road of life to introduce that person to unselfish love.

Bless you, My child! I love you and I always will. []

1.11   SEE WITH THE EYES OF FAITH

Lord, I desire to receive a word from You.
[| My child, My little one, My eternal word to you is, "I love you!" I am the Word, I am Love. I am the Word of Love. But love is essentially wordless, so here I am in pure essence, loving you.

Life can only spring from love, so your life is an undeniable sign of your being created and sustained in love and by love. You are a child of love, no matter what the particulars of your birth. You are precious in My sight! I carry you in My heart. You are safe and secure, eternally beloved, My beloved!

Every person desires to come to Me. I have placed that desire deep within their being. The longing that you feel is the desire to know Me and it comes out as anxiety in you.

Still that anxiety by affirming My presence.

Still your Soul in the knowledge of My love for you.

Command your body to be quiet in rest before Me.

That is what you are seeking from the depths of your innermost being, to be loved with eternal love. That is The End. Cease striving! Just be in Me, in My love. []

Jesus, how can we come to know the way to have greater power and victory over problems that we face?

[| First of all, humble yourself and be in the disposition of waiting. As you recalled from a previous lesson, "... *your king is coming, seated on a donkey's colt...*" (Jn 12:15b), you are merely carriers of goodness and love. You are chalices containing precious wine and must allow the thirsty to drink.

Jesus was not recognized as the Son of God as he rode into Jerusalem on the donkey's colt. If you do not have your eyes of faith and expectation waiting and open, you may not recognize Me riding on the seemingly ordinary circumstances of life. I come to you at every moment and in every possible way.

See the divine in life and your whole outlook will change from a mere hanging in there to a life that is ever more precious, fulfilling, and filled with promise! "*We live by faith, not by sight*" (2 Cor 5:7).

If you would but have true spiritual eyes with which to see, you would see the glory and preciousness of people's faith growing ever brighter, despite, and even because of, the very darkness of the world about them. You would see Me, love, finding a way into even the most hardened hearts! Let not your hope and expectations be dimmed!

The victory is ours, no matter how dark things may look to you. You are being victorious in ways that you cannot presently know. It is not for you to figure out everything with your mind. Love will conquer and love is of the heart. The very desires of your heart for peace and victory for others do battle for their cause. Let not the thought even enter your mind that there is the slightest reason for despondency.

Let the burden of the total picture rest with Me. It is yours but to do the tasks that are assigned to you and, first of all, comes the direction to let peace be with you! Peace be with you!]]

1.12   I GIVE THE GRACE

[| I am your God, from everlasting to everlasting.

You are held in love from everlasting to everlasting.
My love not only sustains but also nurtures.
You will receive growth from everlasting to everlasting.

Do not fear ever, My child! Look on every fear as an intruder who has broken in. Out with fear immediately! It has many disguises that you must learn to recognize if you are to escape its snare. What appears to be a legitimate concern for the future may very well be fear in disguise. A frantic hanging onto faith is fear of losing it.

Faith is calm acceptance by a movement of the will. That grace will always be available for you to take hold of at any time, even if it may seem to you that you have lost it. Choose to Stay in My love and you are safe!

"I do not give to you as the world gives" (Jn 14:27b). Amid your worries, problems, and calamities, I send the grace to sustain you. The way to escape them is to fly with wings of faith over the prison walls of the difficulty and rest in the sure knowledge that all is well, despite the apparent incongruity of the situation at the present moment.

I hold everything in My love: all of you and all the situations that you find yourselves in. Standing in Me, you can stand. Apart from Me, you will surely fall.

Rest assured, My child, that I will never let you fall! I may let you experience your weakness now and then, so you do not begin to trust in your person and strength; but I am ever there to catch you, lest you fall. Even should you disdain My help I stand by listening for your call.

Rest in Me, live in Me – loved by Me.

Know that I am with you at every moment.

I am present at this moment.

I am ever-present, ever-loving, ever God.

Do not strain yourself, thinking that you must learn everything about Me. You cannot. If you were to learn all about Me, where would you stand? Head knowledge is not heart knowledge. You come to know Me, the love and the desires of My heart, by being with Me, by contemplating Me, and resting in Me. Do that now. Rest in Me. |]

Lord, teach me how to love! Teach me how to pray!

[| You learn by doing, My child. When you reach out in love to someone, you are giving Me that love, and in return, I fill you with a fuller measure of love than you gave. (I will not be outdone in generosity!) Praying is spontaneous from deep within your spirit. Everyone seeks Me from the very core of their being, but if they do not know what it is they are hungry for, they can easily get led astray by the sights and delights and material things of the world.

Many are the misfortunes and worries of those who do not trust in My mercy and love. All things turn to grass in their hands. All that is not eternal will turn to dust. *"For you are dirt and to dirt you will return"* (NAB Gen 3:19c), but returning to dust, shedding your body, is a necessary part of life.

The tenacious drive to hang onto their life that all living beings experience is a sign of that life having great vitality and of a desire for existing eternally. That desire of the spirit is good and it is granted. |]

1.13   I GUIDE YOU SAFELY

[| My child, I bless you tenderly. Those times when it has seemed to you that I was far away because of your feeling so miserable physically, I have been especially close and watchful. Much precious growth has occurred. Strengthening has taken place. It takes a strong stem to withstand the winds and storms.

Trust yourself completely and implicitly into My hands. I cannot lead you astray – that is a divine impossibility – so you can rest assured and live in the assurance of being safely guided to happiness, light, and peace.

I call to you over the troubled waters, "Fear not, it is I!" Do not row the other way, thinking you can manage alone. I have the words of eternal life. I am the answer to your quest. I will lead you and teach you what you need to know and guide you to those people that I would have you minister to. Never fear how things will turn out in your life. The living and the giving will make it worthwhile. []

(I was wondering whether a prayer-sharing group I belonged to was on the path God would wish for us to be on.)

[| My child, in this, as in all aspects of your life and actions, follow My leading. You do not need to see the outcome clearly or even to see very far ahead on the way. Indeed, there is no "way" to be seen, for I am the way.

You are to see Me and love Me in each other. Trust Me to make the right ordering of all things. Come to a time of prayer without anxiety, indeed, even without words. Rest in Me.

Good night, My precious child! My blessing to you and all. []

1.14   GOD FOR ALL

[| Patience, child! Much patience, calm, and rest are needed to be truly open to receiving. What matters the daily duties or hassles of the week when compared to the life-giving truth that can be received if you take the time and rest enough to ponder it? Rain must sink in to be available for plant growth. Words of wisdom must sink into your mind and spirit to bring forth that for which they were sent.

Consider and keep nothing as being only for you. Exclusivity is a trap, whether the exclusivity of a clique of friends or the exclusivity one may come to feel in wanting to "possess Me" and claim My love as especially special only for you. You are about as far from the truth as you can get if you are entrapped in that attitude. Pray and work constantly against the inclination of exclusivity.

When you see others being specially blessed in My love and set free, filled with joy and greatly loved, let it be for you a living sign of My love for you and all.

I am at all times loving and blessing you and am open to you to fill you with joy and set you free. This only awaits your response to come to be. The truth is that all are one in Me, one in spirit with Me. The love given to one is given to everyone else, too, at that moment. I treat you as individuals, and yet you are one.

All healing, deliverance, and answers to prayer are present in My mind and spirit. It can all come to be in the physical and your mind and spirit, as you enter the consciousness of the Spirit, as you come to have the mind of Christ in you.

Only believe! It is so simple. The way is direct. I hold all in trust for you, waiting with divine impatience for you to appropriate by faith what you and others need. Only believe and act on that belief.

Follow me, I lead the way. It is the Father's will that I lose none of those He sent me. *"As the Father has sent me, I am sending you"* (Jn 20:21b). Go and sin no more: no more unbelief, no more doubt, no more fear, no more choosing self over life. Arise and walk!

Good night and peace be with you! []

1.15   SHARED FAITH GROWS

[| My child, I am always with you, with your children, with each person. When you have people in mind for whom you desire guidance, grace, wisdom, and blessings, affirm that you believe that I am with them and that I care. Doing that will help make the spiritual more concrete for them. This is how to help all: Believe in My love and care for each and all and trust Me to take care. I have your best interest always at heart. Only believe.

Your faith is not given to you for you alone. You must share your faith in the same manner that you share your love:

Love all, and wish them peace, love, and joy.

Believe and know that your believing that I love and care for each and all will somehow help sustain and uphold all.

"I waited patiently for the Lord; he turned to me and heard my cry. He lifted me out of the slimy pit" (Ps 40:1-2a). Your fai.th can lift the hapless victim out of the pit of destruction. Join your belief with the other person's belief. Share your faith and it will grow by leaps and bounds, just as your love does when you share of yourself in love. I ask faithful obedience of My servants. That means faith-filled. []

1.16   FOR ALL AS FOR ONE

[| My child, how My heart blesses you, and as you are coming to see more and more, what is true for one person in their relationship to Me is true for all. I bless all as I bless the one. Through the openness of the one to receive blessing and love, in some measure, all receive more blessing and love, for through being open, the one (who is a part of the all) helps others to be more open.

The more open you are to the goodness and love present within others the more you are open to Me, for I dwell with each and all.

Those who seek goodness will find it wherever they turn. Likewise, those who seek evil will find plenty of companionships. "Birds of a feather flock together." Like attracts like. This is true of Me, as well, so the heart that is seeking goodness attracts Me and will find goodness.

What you desire will come to pass if you do not waver in your faith. When you hear this, you may first think of it as referring to desiring good. However, those who strongly desire evil will cause evil things to come to pass, just as much as the good-hearted will bring about good. Consequently, those of goodwill must be extra strongly committed to the good to override the evil that is trying to take over. In Me, you will conquer. All who side with Me are on the winning side!

When looking for signs of strong faith, do not look to feelings. Faith is a decision to believe. It is in the will. Get some foundational truths set firmly beneath your feet and stand firmly on them.

Say: "I am. I exist. The world and creation exist, so God is."

"Only love is creative; therefore, God created me in love and I exist in His love."

"Nothing else matters, really, except this relationship with my God, for me to come to be with Him."

"God is my Savior. He has redeemed me and redeemed all. I have nothing to fear as long as I rest in God."

All is well! All is set up in My plans for good to come to all who so choose. "[T]he plans of the Lord stand firm forever, the purposes of his heart through all generations" (Ps 33:11). []

1.17   YOU ARE ANCHORED IN

[| Rest, child. Forget the cares and worries of everyday life. Forget the concern you have for your friend and let that concern be translated into love. Worrying brings about nothing good. Concern springing from love provides a pathway for good.

The help or understanding you desire for someone does not necessarily have to come through you. I use instruments and circumstances of My choosing. When you are concerned about someone, simply hold them in love with no bars to that love. In Me, you can accept each person totally in complete safety.

Continue to trust and believe! At no time while you are still in this earthly life will you have the fullness of knowledge and truth that you seek, but you can believe and trust with and in whatever level of understanding you have at any stage.

The strongest faith comes from the heart of a person who simply believes without needing proof, and without asking for any.

The Way to Me is a way of faith, hope, and trust. Faith and hope are two anchors that tie you into the spiritual life, tie you to Me. The third, the strongest anchor, is love.

The anchors of faith, hope, and love that you use to "hook into" the spiritual life are connected from the other side, too. The object of that faith and love, the reward of that hope is holding onto you with love!

I accept you as you are, child. I know that you often wonder if you are doing as you "should" spiritually, whether or not you are following the inspirations the Holy Spirit has given you. Simply be. Simply trust, believe, and love. All is worked out in the My divine plan. For you to want to know all the details of that plan is to desire to be God. You are given to know and understand what you are meant to know. Trust! Believe! Love!

Have a good day, my child! I go with you. []

1.18   I AM ALWAYS WITH YOU

[| Many are the troubles of those who try to regulate their own lives, who try to make plans and bring them about through their effort, strength, and wisdom.

"He who trusts in himself is a fool, but he who walks in wisdom is kept safe" (Pr 28:26). *"In his heart, a man plans his course, but the Lord determines his steps"* (Pr 16:9).

You can do nothing without Me, for I am wisdom, goodness, all being. You can be truly happy only when you acknowledge Me as your Lord and God when you give credit where credit is due, and open your heart, mind, and spirit to My love and care. I am present to uphold you, bless you, and bring you to freedom. I draw you to Myself in love!

My child, as you have learned, life sometimes brings surprises! [Referring to my unexpected entrance into the hospital.] Roll with the punches and do not have your heart so set on certain routines and expectancies that you find it difficult to accept change. Look around you. Everything in nature changes! Even the faces of the seemingly immovable mountains change with time.

You are a daughter of time until your time in "time" is up. Then you will join Me in My unchangeableness. You are being formed into who you are meant to be by all of the routines and changes of life, each in its own time. Through it all and throughout all, be assured of My love, care, protection, and guidance. An unseen hand guides your destiny with the skill of a master artist. Entrust yourself to Me.

Believe in and accept My love for you so that you may be saturated with love, Inundated with joy, and brimming over with hope and expectation!

Such is what I hope and plan for you!

Be healed! Delivered! Free!

[Jesus:] You had an insight the other day that things of Earth must have looked much different to me after I had risen from the dead and was free of the bonds of the flesh. Even so, you can begin now to view all happenings and this earthly life in the light of heaven.

Desire much for all. There is no limit to the granting of loving desires that can come about, that God desires to do for all. Any limiting is in the channels through whom that love and those fulfilled desires can flow. Father God must work through you even as He worked through me during my time on earth.

The seed must be germinated to grow and bring forth fruit. The desires of the heart must be held in incubation and warm love (as the babe receives protection, nourishment, warmth, and love in its mother's womb) to be brought to birth fully developed and full of life. At the same time, you must hold yourself in warm love, cradled in the security of the heart womb of Father God.

I rest in the Father. As you rest in me you rest in Him, in life.

As you rest in the Father, you rest in me, in life.

As you rest in life, you breathe in the spirit of life that comes forth from the Father, the Holy Spirit.

Do not despair, no matter how dark things may seem to you when looked at from this earthly plane. No matter how alone you may feel you are not alone. It is not feelings that count but being. What is, *is*. You are beloved of God. You are my beloved.

Live in the peace that I came to earth to give. Live in the freedom for which I died, to give it to you. Love, rejoice, and hope without limit! Bless! Give! Desire the good for all! Pray, trust, and love.

I enfold you in a crushing caress of love! |]

1.19   ONE MOMENT AT A TIME

[| My child, many blessings upon you and yours! Each person has a circle of family, friends, and interests. I bless everyone in that circle when you are open to Me. I do the same for all others, too, so there are circles of blessings overlapping and spreading hope, love, cheer, and light throughout the world!

When you try to see the spiritual in the material with your natural eyes, you will find that it seems hopeless. Life must be seen through the eyes of faith, then you will have hope and joy and promise of better things. Time is passing. The problems and thorns of this life will pass, are passing away. Take life one day at a time and enjoy the benefits and the freedom of that day. Doing this will give you the inner resurgence you need to carry you through the next day which may be more difficult.

One day at a time, and when necessary, one hour or moment at a time. In times of pain and crisis: One moment at a time. Throughout it all, I am with you, and all of nature is with you. *"We know that the whole creation has been groaning as in the pain of childbirth right up to the present time"* (Rom 8:22). All is one glorious, harmonious whole in Me, who is in all and throughout all and is all! Rest in Me that you may find peace unto your Soul.

Peace, child! Love! Rest! Joy! Let joy enter your being. "En-joy": the entering of joy. Joy is of the spirit, however, so you cannot bottle it up within yourself without stifling the flow. Let joy enter your being, then express it with your being. Inhale, exhale: You must do both to continue breathing. Joy is the breath of the spirit. It must be breathed.

You are body, mind, and spirit. That is your being: an entity that is a union of body, mind, and spirit. You can experience and express joy in and through your body, in and by your mind and spirit. When joy is expressed in some manner by a portion of your being, your whole being shares the refilling of joy that comes surging in. Make way for Me and I will enter!

Sometimes when you are feeling only moderately joyful and thankful, try this: Express joy and thankfulness in word, in song, and in sharing with others. Do this again and again, particularly with song, and you will find that the measure of joyfulness you experience will double and triple! I wait to give!

Peace! Bless you, child! Have a good day. I have charge of everything relating to your life, for you have asked Me to take charge. Do not fear, do not be anxious. Enjoy! []

1.20   FAITH CARRIES YOU

[| It is I. I come walking on the waters of faith. If you did not have faith, I would not be present to you in a way for you to know. You "know" by faith.

There are times when you are not able to be present to Me by faith directly: times of sleeping or, as you have just experienced, times of being put to sleep by drugs for surgery. Another such example would be a state of unconsciousness brought on by whatever cause. At times like these, you are unable to consciously use your mind to believe but the faith of your waking moments carries through. If you have consciously chosen to believe and trust in Me, that faith and trust hold you as you sleep or are otherwise not conscious.

Your being under anesthetic for surgery was a small dip into the experience that those have who come near death. It is scary to let go of your conscious faculties but keep strongly in mind that I am everywhere and I am all-existence. You are safe in Me no matter what your experiences may be. I hold you in love and I affirm that love a thousand times over! You have nothing to fear! []

CHAPTER 2

THE FOUNDATION OF LOVE

2.1   INVITATION FROM THE HEART

[| Come into My heart, My child. Come into My love and concern for all. Come into the life I live, a life of complete abandonment of Myself for others. Transform your heart and desires. Let Me transform your heart and desires so that you have My desires, My love. Then you will indeed have come "into My heart."

Come into My love. Accept and believe in My love for you. Accept with unflinching, undoubting faith (not needing a sign) that I Am and that I love you!

Know that *to be* is to be loved, for I am a God of love. Let love permeate your being! Let every fiber of your being respond in love, as I fashioned it to.

I am a God of love. I can issue only offspring like unto Myself. Come unto Me! Come unto love! The father of lies tries to claim you as his, but your very makeup belies that. You are made for love and were brought forth in love. Come into and unto that love!

Relax in your aches and pains and let Me bear them with you. A harness chafed under will always cause new sore spots. Pull with the team and the burden is light.

I accept you as you are at every moment. I accept you totally, now. Love is what holds you secure, and I vow to always love you and hold you in tenderness. It is OK if you are sensitive and tender in your being. That is your real being and I love you for being you. If you would do nothing else, but just be, I would love you just the same, just as much.

You do not have to find Me, My child! All you need do is be and that takes no effort! I will pour Myself into your being so that you become joyful, at peace, and full of love. You need not, should not try to take charge of that at all. Your eternal destiny is Me! You are in Me! Just remain open to Me and you are really and truly OK!

I will never leave you nor forsake you. This is all that matters. And I am with your loved ones, sustaining them, loving them, holding them, and you in My tender care.

Do not fret at how things appear. Look to the deeper reality. Trust in My care for your family, friends, loved ones, and acquaintances, for all your fellow human beings. []

"This is how we know that we live in him and he in us. He has given us of his Spirit" (Jn 4:12-13). *"For in him we live and move and have our being"* (Acts 17: 28a). Then it is also true that He lives, moves, and has His being in us!

[| I am your God and you are My child. Do not be afraid. Be, in love, with Me. Be with Me, in love. |]

2.2   TRUST ME

[| Do not fear, My children. I am with you, even as I was with the prophets of old. It gladdens My heart tremendously for you to trust Me for your needs.

Bring your needs to Me, I will supply them.

Bring your fainting heart to Me, I will revive it.

I will be to you both life and breath.

I am life and health, freedom and liberty, joy, and love.

I know your needs, your worries, and how things will turn out.

I have the blueprint of life. I decree that it be.

I am in you and you have life. I am your life. Life makes you be. As long as you are, as long as you exist, you are in Me and I am in you. My Son came to earth that you may learn this marvelous truth, that you may also be in Me, be one with Me.

"But the plans of the Lord stand firm forever, the purposes of his heart through all generations" (Ps 33:11). Each person is special,

unique, a jewel. I love you, My precious one, My jewel! Would that your light may shine for all to see!

Do not worry about the time you take to spend with Me. I "take" that time also and open Myself to you in a special way when you are open to Me.

My people, I love you! My heart goes out in compassion toward you as I see you lost in sin, lost in the things of the flesh. They are meant to lead you to love, not to be an end in themselves.

Do you not already see that no avenue of material things that you take will satisfy you? You are just left with an appetite desiring more but not knowing why you desire it.

Temper the desires of the flesh with those of the spirit. Make the material subject to the spiritual in the right ordering of things; then you can and will receive joy through material things, as you realize that out of My love for you I provided them.

Everything done in love is worthwhile for it is eternal. Giving and receiving in love are both blessed. It is in giving that you receive. []

2.3   LOVE SPEAKS

[| *"I am the light of the world. Whoever follows me will never walk in darkness, but will have the light of life"* (Jn 8:12). On your own you would not know the way. I know the way, I am the Way. Come with Me. *"Peace I leave with you; my peace I give you. I do not give to you as the world gives."* (Jn 14:27a). I give love, joy, peace, patience in adversity, and grace to overcome all difficulties.

Bless you, My child! I am leading you. I will be with you and lead you always. Even when you are not aware of My presence, I am with you. I am sustaining you. I am your strength.

Do not be so hard on yourself! If you do your best to follow My Will, you will know that whatever happens has been allowed by Me. I keep all in My all-encompassing sight.

When you rest in Me and open yourself to Me, My love permeates your being and upholds, strengthens, and gladdens you. I love you!

Cherish that thought. Let it warm and gladden you. My love is life for your Soul. Drink of My love. Open yourself to Me so you can experience Me. How I long to be one with you, for you to be one with Me!

Do not fear for the future of anyone, whether yourself, your family, or your friends. Neither fear for the unfortunate of the world. All are in My love and care. All will turn out for the best. The present sufferings carry an eternal weight of glory: They perfect you and divest you of attachment to this world.

Continue to struggle to attain discipline. Nothing that is too easily accomplished is worth much. You *will* gain victory over yourself, over your appetite. Rest in Me and learn of Me.

Every point of contact with Me is a passageway for love. You have contact with Me at every point in the physical and the spiritual. I encompass you on all sides. I permeate every particle of your being, every facet of your thought life, and your subconscious.

You are immersed, covered over, and held up in love!

You live, move, and have your being in love!

Love strengthens you, heals you, and guides you.

You are completely safe, protected, and surrounded by love.

Nothing can reach you and harm you unless you allow it to.

Learn from your experiences with anger, pride, greed, and suchlike. You are fighting to defend the home ground of love. Your life is your battleground to win the victory for love. Once you have secured your stronghold with the strong allies of trust, patience, joy, peace, hope, faith, and indomitable courage, you can take them with you to help your family, friends, and needy passing acquaintances become secure in love. []

2.4   YOU ARE LOVED

[| If the need of your heart for love is so great, think how My heart longs for and needs love! Love thrives on love. I can see the love that will be within you as you come to the close of your earthly life.

I experience that love as already present and call it forth from within you. The law of the Spirit stands: Strongly desire good and believe in it without doubt and it will come to you.

Do not worry about how the various aspects of your life will be worked out. Remember Job and try to emulate him. *"The Lord gave and the Lord has taken away; may the name of the Lord be praised"* (Job 1: 21b). Rest in Me. When you rest in Me you rest securely.

I do not need accomplishments from you. *"This is the one I esteem: he who is humble and contrite in spirit and trembles at my word"* (Is 66:2b). Mind the things of the spirit more so than those of the body. In the strength of the Lord, you shall walk. Never forget to ask for and to rely on My strength.

You are OK, My child. You are precious to Me and I would have you be precious to yourself. Your *being* is one treasure that you will take with you: It is the vehicle through which you come to Me. Through your being, I come to you. What importance do the transitory hurts and pain of this life have? You must get the void of non-loving in your being filled up. Let others love you, let Me love you. As you become strong and well in that love you will be able to begin to love others as you ought.

I love you! You are My dear one, as are all. Oh, would that you, that all, would come to know My love! Open your heart so that love may enter! Open your whole being to love's presence! All that matters is to be loved. Once love is present and living in you, you will be compelled to go out to others. It is love's nature to give. Love and the bride become one: one in loving and one in giving. []

Lord, would that I could love You more and more!

[| Just know that I love you. Rest secure in My love. There is nothing that I would not do for you. Your feeble attempts at love console and gladden My heart. "Love is of God." I *am* love. All else will pass away, but love will remain, eternal. The love with which I love you is eternal: forever the same, infinite.

It is love that upholds you, that keeps you in existence. Ponder that and let the healing effects of that spirit truth sink into your consciousness. You are held in existence because I love you so much.

Bless you, My child! Never fear. I am with you always, always loving and guiding you. I am also with all those that you are concerned about. I love and uphold them. Think joy and chase the gloom away! There is no cause for sadness. I am with you always! |]

2.5   LOVE DOES NOT PASS AWAY

I desire to come into Your heart, Father. How can I know that I am in Your heart?
[| In My heart is peace and love, child. You still look too much for material signs and sensing. When you let Me love you, you are in My heart. When you allow peace to reign in your mind and heart, you are in My heart.

In reality, you already are in My heart. Every person in the whole world is held in love in My heart, but it is not until you correspond with love that your spirit can enter fully. It is only by responding that you can become consciously aware of the reality of My love. Love is fragile, in a way. It gives way to fear and worry unless you pay heed to the realization that love is the strong man who protects the heart-home. Love is stronger than death and stronger than all "evil." I am Love. |]

Please hold me in Your love and mercy, Father!
[| My child, I hold you in love and mercy at all times. I see the best in you and all and bring it forth by My desire for it to be.

All things of this world will pass away. Pain and discomfort that you feel in your body pass away. See pain as passing and as then gone and it will be easier for you to live with for the moment that you experience it.

Life has an eternal purpose: Life is for living. Live with Me, then you truly have life. "I have come that they [you] may have life and have it to the full" (Jn 10: 10b).

Listen to the song of the birds – I sing you a love song. Nature all around you is fairly bursting with life, eagerly proclaiming that I Am. Does a tree struggle anxiously, trying to cope with past drought?

Do flowers worry whether or not they will receive sunlight and rain tomorrow,? My creation ebbs forth with life: mute, yet so eloquent!

If you are meant to bloom with some certain flower, it will come about in due time. The task at hand is to trust in Me, learn of Me and love Me, and receive love from Me and others. We go forth together in love. That love that binds us together protects us from the inconstancies and pressures of this life. Your true life is already within you. Life in this physical world, what you discern now, is a mere shadow of the life you will come into.

Would that everyone would allow Me to love them! Pray for all, pray in the name of all. Your constancy and devotion will reap great rewards. Bless you, My child! I love you! []

2.6   LOVE IS THE LIFE PRINCIPLE

[| I love you, My child, and I love My little son Jason [born with medical problems]. From all eternity, I looked forward to his arrival, as I did to yours. I hold him in My love. Trust Me to take good care of him, the best. You may think, "Trust the doctor," but it is I who take care through My doctors. For your part, trust and faith are required. Put faith and trust in Me and I can transform it into well-being for the child.

People have so much excessive activity. It should be that "God proposes and man disposes." Instead, you have made it that "Man proposes." My Will will be done despite all circumstances that may try to hinder it from being worked out. I foresee all circumstances and work everything together for the good. Only good can come from Me for I am eternal good.

Tell My people how much I love them and yearn for them to are sigcome to goodness! My desires are as prayers are said and answered.

I hear the desires of your heart. What comes through to Me with truth and sincerity are the desires that spring from love. Love is the life principle from which life flows. If you have love, you have everything. All days that in a certain sense may seem to be wasted days are not wasted if they are filled with love.

Love is a perfume that fills the home and the air around you. It is taken into the very being of those you are with, whether in person or spirit. The perfume that emanates from the preserved bodies of some of My servants is a sign in the physical world of the love that indwelt them during their earthly life.

Pray much for love. Have as the main desire of your heart that you be filled to overflowing with love. Nothing that you do for someone that you love deeply will be a sacrifice for you.

You do not have the capacity that you need for love unless you become "deep." That is brought about by your bringing to the surface, admitting and repenting, all the self-love that keeps emerging. You have a certain eventuality of love and I have a certain plan for your life that will bring about that depth of love you are destined for. Being gratefully responsive to the working of grace by the Spirit is the way to reach that goal.

Do not think about growing in love from a negative viewpoint. It is the most joyful life that it is possible to lead! The joy of the spirit runs deep, however, so do not judge for joy based on Earth's values. Look within yourself and ascertain what makes you happy: It is to love and be loved, to be open and accepting of others, and to be accepted openly and completely by them.

You need to experience how much it means to be loved and accepted so you then know how it is for others and even for Me. You have been given of My divine nature: We are one. The life of love you are being called and drawn into is a living of My life. As your heart extends in love to more and more people, it is expanding and coming into being more and more with Me. Living and being in Me is living and being in love.

I am love. Love fills all of creation.

See love in yourself, in all of creation, in all people.

The love and goodness you see in others are signs of My presence. []

2.7   BE, MY CHILD

[| Write, My child. Tell of My burning love for everyone! I love all of you so much! I love each person as much as it is possible to love them! You cannot comprehend the depth or breadth or height of My love. My love surrounds you and it is in you and throughout you. In Me, you live, move, and have your being. You live in My heart. You are precious to Me.

My love courses through your veins, it prompts your breathing and the beating of your heart. Rest and grow strong in My love. Become peaceful in My love.

I give Myself totally and unreservedly to you. I am beside you and within you. You can choose whether or not to open the depths of your being to Me but do not feel bad about your reserve. I understand. Rest in My love.

"The Lord is my shepherd, I shall not want" (Ps 23:1). Come to Me for things you want, and in Me, you can ascertain if it is a legitimate request. All that is necessary for the life of your spirit is that you be. |]

What would you have me do, Lord?

[| I would have you be. As you go about your duties and the occupation of the moment, just continue to be in My love. Be in peace, in joy, and your spirit will pick that up. Thus you will be loving, peaceful, and joyful.

Do not worry about "what you are to eat or what you are to wear," as the pagans do, those who do not know or believe in Me. You have been rescued from that life. Do not go back "down to Egypt." You are entering, are in the promised land. The surroundings are new to you and may seem strange. You need to acquaint yourself with the rules and laws of the spiritual kingdom.

"You cannot serve both God and Money" (Lk 16:13c). You cannot live in both kingdoms at once. *"I have set before you life and death, blessings and curses"* (Dt 30:19b). Choose life! |]

2.8   I BLESS ALL

[| If only people could recognize the profusion of love which is being poured out on them! If only you could see, My people, that I am giving Myself to you in nature, in My sustaining you in life, love, and virtue, in the warm personal embrace of total love and acceptance!

I bless you, My child! I bless all people on the earth, every person! I promise you that I am doing all that is divinely possible for each of you.

People do not understand My ways very well. What may appear to be a life untouched by divine grace may in reality be a life that is fruitful on all sides with graces that call for love, with lessons clearly showing how much I love and care. Do not let the darkness of doubt cloud your mind! Keep the light of faith burning brightly!

Reminder: Do not take your life and circumstances for granted. Do not begin to rest in comfort in your daily schedule and forget that your life, health, material blessings, and all that you have, is a gift. *You* are a gift, each of you: a gift I gave Myself and to each "other" in your life.

I bless your efforts and the love that you are putting into writing words of encouragement and love to your friend. However, I caution you not to take her situation on as a burden. She is a fellow wayfarer in life to whom you are lending a helping hand. She walks in with My strength and is nourished by My grace. |]

2.9   I WAIT AT THE DOOR

[| My child, I cherish you! How can words express the heartthrob of love that I feel for you, for all of My children! Taken together, all of the love that parents have for their children is only a faint expression of the reality of My love for My own.

Just be with Me. That does not take great effort. Rather it takes a relaxing of the strain that you feel in trying too hard. My mind is in you, so as you relax in Me, My thoughts can surface in your mind. Do not try to figure everything out. Just relax and let it be.

My heart is heavy, child, as I sense the great need that people have for love and direction. They are to a great extent as sheep without a shepherd, following the spirit of the world: "Get rich! Be lucky! Stay young! Do not worry about anyone else but yourself." The only thing I can do is wait until the emptiness of worldly things weighs upon the mind and heart of each person and brings them to see that life *must* mean more than that. Rest in Me, My child. |]

Father, I hunger for a word from You.

[| That hunger is put there by Me. It is a part of the working of grace by My Spirit. You are led from within in the way I would have you walk. Dismiss the anxiety that still hovers within you. It is not suitable to allow that negative spirit a place in your heart.

Many are the desires of My heart but paramount is the desire for you to come into love! Love is a place, a state of being, as well as action. In Me, you rest in love. My heart is the safe abode amidst the storm. It is open for you to take refuge in.

The desire of My heart is for your happiness. My views of circumstances, happenings, and earthly possessions are much different than yours. Come to Me more and more to rest and learn of Me, that you may absorb My divine attitude. In coming to Me you enter into life. |]

I come knocking at the door of Your heart. May I come in?

[| You are in My heart, child. Do not confuse the physical with the spiritual. I hold you in love in My heart. You could not be any dearer to Me – I say that to each person who ever lived, is living, or will yet come to be. Rest in Me: Thus, you rest in My Heart. My being is heart, love. You, all of you, rest in My heart, for in love I sustain you, protect you, and keep you in being.

There are times I embrace you to Myself closely. Would that I could do that at every moment but your attention and love are turned from Me to possessions and the affairs of the moment. You are experiencing this with your children. How you long to hold them close but you know they are not always willing to receive your embrace. When the special moments come, the embrace is that much more precious because of having had to wait so long. Come into My heart, precious one. Let's live this life together! |]

2.10   I AM YOUR FATHER

[| Drink in My love, My child. Rest in My love and let go of the last traces of fear. You have nothing to fear! Why does it have to be that you feel a certain way to have a sense of My presence? I am not here in a physical way, so the signs or sense of My presence are not physical.

I am here in the brooding silence and the noise.

I am here in the reality of being which you share with all other people and with all of creation.

I am here in peace. That peace will envelop you if you release fear and anxiety.

Just relax! You are My child. What have you to fear? Do not expect perfection of yourself and then you need not fear failure. If you decide to just do the best you can within the limits of your humanity you will not have certain expectations to live up to. I love you in your humanity. I love you as you are!

I have come to set the prisoner free. I am here to free you from bondage to self-imposed goals. In the spirit, all is freedom and light. The more you are tied to the earth by your appetite, possessions, fears for safety, and pleasure-seeking, the less free you are. Rest in Me and you are secure. Let Me be your food, your prize possession. |]

(I "leaned on Father God's knees" and rested for a while.) Thank you, Father, for being so accepting and loving!

[| I not only allow you to rest at My knees, but I also hold you to My heart. You are most dear to Me! You are My child, as truly as much as a child is the child of his or her human father. But, oh! What infinitely greater tenderness and love do I have for you! This does not mean, however, that I do not act with vigor and rigor when it is needed for your good. No matter what comes in your life trust Me to bring out of it that which is My Will.

I affirm and strengthen you from within and without. Hope! Love! Trust! Rejoice! Go forward patiently, with endurance. I am with you always. Bless you! []

2.11   LIVE NOW

Thank you, Lord, for this quiet time of resting in You.

[| I want you always to rest in Me. Rest by trusting, by believing, by loving, by having your attention fixed on Me, by letting go of the burdens you carry and letting Me carry them.

I know what to do with the events and problems of your life. They are used to bring about the fulfillment of My will. If you resist leaving all in My hands, you are just bucking the tide, because My Will shall be accomplished no matter what.

Care for one another, thus you keep each other in the bonds of love. Love need not be spoken: It is, as I Am. Love is eternal and all-powerful but it does not get its way by pushing, but rather by persuasion and gentleness. The way to a person's heart is by love. The way to My heart is love. Choose and desire the good and you will receive it. You choose love by being open to it. Desire love and love will abide in you.

My child, be not anxious. The present time is now. You are in My care and loving designs at this moment. You cannot make a future time come faster than it will. and being anxious about it can spoil the quality of that time when it does arrive.

Live in the present. This is the moment to be welcomed and cherished, for this is the moment in which I am loving you! For Me, all is one moment, but as you live this earthly life you are related to eternity by the concept of time. *"Now is the acceptable time! Now is the day of salvation!"* (2Cor 6:2b).

Rest assured of My love for you. Live assured of My love. Your desire for being loved opens your heart and Soul to love in the moments to come. The desire for love comes from Me, the author of life and love. You can be satisfied at any moment as much as possible on this earth. Just take a deep gulp (breath) of faith and breathe in My love for you. Accept that it is true.

Rest on My bosom, My child! It means so much to have a little child trust enough to lean its little head on you! That is My desire, that you trust and depend on Me as a little child does its mother and father. Rest here in My heart, in My arms! |]

2.12   CLING TO MY LOVE

[| I love you, My children! Never forget that. Keep it uppermost in your consciousness. Cling to My love and it will be the ship that carries you across troubled waters. What does the turmoil in the world around you matter? What do the headache or financial problems that you have matter? Are they not of passing significance? Trust, faith, and love are the cornerstones of your spiritual life.

Bless you, as you take time to spend with Me! Taking time to be with someone is a sign of, and a giving of, love. You need not do or say anything, necessarily, to express love. Simply being with the beloved is loving them, as well as listening with an open mind and heart to what they have to say.

I speak of My love for you. My heart is overflowing with love, good wishes, and desires for peace and blessings for you! The more you can remain open to Me, to love, the more you will experience love, peace, and blessings.

Leave all in My very capable hands. Do not worry about a thing. Simply desire good and blessing for those in need. That way you begin to bring about what you desire. I hear the desires of your heart. My ear is attuned to every heartthrob.

If only you could come to know Me and know of My love for you! When you do become willing to come to Me, then I, as it were, rest in your heart, as well as that you rest in My Heart. Yes, your heart is big enough for Me. I suit My presence to the accommodations of my guest.

As you open your heart and spirit to love ever more and more, you come to have an ever-expanding capacity to know and experience Me. I will not refuse you the love and care you need. You are safe, you are loved! Dwell securely in that truth, in Me.

Bless you, My children! I place My hand in benediction upon you and your desires for peace and good for others. Adieu! []

2.13   I TELL MY SECRET

[| My child, it does My heart good to have you trust Me with your problems and needs, with the care of your Soul and body. That is the first step toward a victorious life: Entrusting yourself completely to Me. Do not be so concerned about whether your daily decisions are "right." When there are several choices as to what to do on a particular day, simply make a choice based on necessity or your inclination, then put your whole person into that as being My will; otherwise, you will feel fragmented by your unsettled thoughts.

I have no great secrets to reveal. *My One Great Secret, which I desire the whole world to know, is that I love you dearly, every one of you!* My heart throbs with holy impatience as I await the eternal day when I will take you to My heart and we become truly one! My "beloved" are all of those who are willing to be loved and to let that love transform them.

I have much to teach you, but what is most important is for you to come into love, so that love is the springboard of your every action, the checking point of every thought. Let your desires be formed in love. If your mind and heart are filled with love, everything that issues forth from you will be from love and filled with love.

I love you, My children! That is the purpose of My life, of My existence. I Am, to be your God. You cannot imagine any extent that I would not go to for your sake! *"My grace is sufficient for you"* (2 Cor 12:9b). Trust in Me! Come into My love and return love for love. Then you will find the reason for existing, the meaning of the mystery of life.

Bless you, My children! Go in peace to love and serve the Lord. You will find Me in your brother and sister, in your spouse, in your friend, and in the people that you meet at the marketplace. Emphasize the goodness in others rather than the lack of it and your world will be better as a result. Peace! []

2.14   MADE FOR LOVE

[| I envelop you in My peace and love, dear child. How I long for you to trust Me completely, with every last trace of fear removed! The time of our being united is well worth waiting for.

You are safe and secure. I love you as dearly as I love Myself. Do not try to achieve lofty ways and thoughts that, as likely as not, would fill your head with pride. The simple, sure way is the way of trust, loving resignation, and acceptance. Let the desire to love more deeply develop ever stronger within your heart. See Me in all people, events, and blessings; in creation; in all goodness and love shown toward you. Just trust and love.

How My heart hungers for love! If I cannot receive it from those who are willing to be open to grace (and how I wish that all of My children would be), then from whom?

All your life I have led you on a quest for the meaning of life. Meaning comes into one's life when you are needed, so the specific meaning for each life varies with the needs of your loved ones and neighbors but the central meaning of life is to learn that you are needed by Me. Love thrives on love.

I need and desire your love and am not ashamed to admit it. I open My heart to receive your love and to receive you. Come, My child! I enfold you in love!

I do not always lead you upon sunlit trails, but were you to see the whole picture – how all things work together unto good – you would think differently of physical suffering. Nothing is lost that you give to Me. Even the desire to be patient and accepting of unavoidable suffering is precious to Me.

I love you! I never tire of saying that and I know you never tire of hearing it. You are made for love, made to give of yourself completely. Only thus will you find true peace and happiness.

I am with you! In quiet and in rest will be your rest and your inner healing. Do not fear! Cast fear from you out into the abyss of nothingness from which it came. It is an absence of good, of trust.

Trust in Me and I will be your strength and your salvation. I am the truth and the light. Learn of Me. I lay My hands in blessing upon you. I know your faults and shortcomings but love you even with them. They can separate you from Me only if you cling to them. Take My hand! Let's go forward together! []

2.15   I AM HERE

[| My child, I know the desires of your heart. Those that were planted by My Holy Spirit will come to fruition. They need to be in someone's heart and spirit to come to pass.

Do not look upon the life of the spirit as being complicated, with a lot of dos and don'ts.

Simply be. Simply love.

Simply hope. Simply trust. Simply believe.

Simply be free, in simplicity and without fear.

I Am. Is there anything you need to fear? Nothing can separate you from My love. I am in the clouds, in the color surrounding you, in the energy of life, but most of all I am here in your heart and you are in My heart.

Rest My child. Trust that you are receiving health and blessing and are being freed from anxiety. I anoint your Soul with the unction of the Spirit.

Time may seem interminable when you do not feel well or when you are crushed with worry for a loved one and for the many you have taken into your heart. Ponder often that I am with you. I care! Just as your heart goes out in love and concern for your fellow travelers on the road of life, so My heart goes out to each of you with infinite love and concern. I care! I cast My lot with you. I am with you in the struggle through thick and thin.

The victory is ours! Continue to side with Me and you have the victory over hurt, illness, and problems. You can continue in My strength but on your own, you would fail. Rest in Me. Accept each moment in union with Me.

My heart is overjoyed when some of these truths begin to penetrate your consciousness and you accept the grace I give you to conform your mind and will to them.

I want you to see that I am always speaking to you, that any time you recollect yourself enough you can become aware of that. I speak to everyone at all times – not necessarily in words. I speak My love, My tenderness, peace, and joy. The very fact of having contact with Me through your desire to be with Me opens you to receive from Me.

My heart goes out to everyone with the fire of divine love! I embrace you, My children, each of you, even you who consider yourself unworthy to come near Me. I am near you, even in your very Soul.

Turn to Me before it is too late! You can get so caught up in the snares, worries, and pleasures of this world that you think there is nothing else. The love of your loved ones and friends can be a sign to you that there is more than the physical element to life. Consider how much you need love and friendship. If you have ever been without it for a time, you have experienced the emptiness in your spirit. I am in that love and friendship for I am Love.

I love every one of you, no matter what your attitude toward "religion" may be. I, your God, am in all of life. I am not bound by the ideas that this person or that one has about Me. I embrace each of you with life! love! joy! peace! I am closer to you than your very self. I await your discovery of Me. I place Myself in your path that you may certainly find Me. Come to Me, My child []

2.16   AVAILABLE ON MY TERMS

Lord, I open my mind and heart to what You have to say.
[| I speak love. I am Love, so My whole being speaks love.
I speak peace and freedom from fear.
I speak the fullness of life and joy.

No gnawing hunger and unquenchable thirst when you are united with Me. If you still have hunger and thirst, ask yourself from whence it comes and what you hunger and thirst for.

"Hunger and thirst" may be smoke screens blown in by the enemy to divert your attention from a full resting in Me. I am the fullness of life. When you have found Me you have found life. It may be that you are misinterpreting your body signals. Being anxious about something leads to a desire to satisfy that anxiety, but that is not true hunger and thirst. It is unrest.

"I came that they [you] might have life and have it to the full" (Jn 10:10b). I came that you may have rest for your Souls and health for your bodies. Trust me and trust My love for you! *Yes, for you.* You are the apple of My eye.

I am not too busy to listen to your every word, to attend to your every need, to answer your beck and call. I am available but on My terms: He who gives, receives. To him who has much – kindness, patience, love – more will be given. Reach out your hand and I will grasp it. Begin with what effort you have and I will shore up that effort with My strength.

Those who have trust, hope, faith, and hunger will be given:
The fulfillment of that hope,
The object of that faith,
Satisfaction of that hunger.

If you can become completely pliable in My hands, I will do all in you: I will give you the hunger and satisfy it. You are not going it alone. I am with you: loving, protecting, nourishing, and strengthening you. I am all things to the one who will turn to Me. I am the fulfillment of your desires. I am Love. |]

2.17   BELIEVE AND TRUST

[| You can trust Me, My child. I am your God. My love permeates, surrounds, upholds, and strengthens you. It gives life. Were My love not flowing into you, you would no longer be! Ponder that. Trust Me. I care! Entrust everyone to Me that you desire to help. In due time, your desires will be fulfilled.

Do not doubt My presence and My love. Having a fleeting temptation to doubt is not doubting. You must not let that unworthy spirit take up dwelling within you. Keep your faith alive by affirmations of belief and trust and, to shore up your belief in My love for you, know this: No unworthiness of yours or even outright sin can take you out of My love. Love is My very Being. I am love and cannot cease to exist. Love is eternal and I love you eternally.

I accept you and love you as you are. I do not say to you, "Become a little better and I will love you more." I love you as much as possible right now, at every moment! A person can only change for the better by being nourished by unconditional love, and by total acceptance of who he or she is and the way he or she is at any given moment.

You may have reservations about your love for other people. You may love some people because of their having concern for you. Or, you may feel unable to love some people because of personality defects that they have. Do not try to come to a full acceptance of others by yourself. You cannot do it! Only by taking time to dwell in My total, unconditional love for you and continually calling it to mind, can your heart begin to respond to others in like manner.

I am the great healer, the strength you need, ever-present, inexhaustible supply: *Love.*

I am complete acceptance, merciful forgiveness, the fountain of hope: *Love.*

I am the eternal promise of a better day: *Love.*

I am your God: Love. I am here. I am yours. *I am Love.*

As a mother hen gathers her chicks at an approaching storm, I would gather you under My wings! Come into the protection of My love! Bring your neighbor, your friend, that stranger. My arms are open! My heart is open! []

2.18   I AM

Lord, do You have a word for me, for us?

[| My child, I am the Word. My existence, My being, speaks love, tenderness, and acceptance to you and all. "Actions speak louder than words," it is said. What I have done and am doing for you speaks louder than words of My love for you. You cannot be aware of all that I do for you. The larger part of it is in the spiritual realm.

For everyone who desires it,

I am your protector, your guide, your strength.

For all, no matter what each one's attitude,

I am total acceptance and total love.

Those times when it seems to you that I am the furthest away, I am often the closest, for it is when you are in need that you are open to receiving. Those times when it seems to you that you have all you need in your self-sufficiency, you are closed and cannot receive of Me.

Do not worry about a thing, especially about how you will come to Me. I am the way. I am here. There is no search needed. I hold you in total love. Bless you, My dear ones, My "other selves!" Do not fear, for I am with you.

I love you! My love for you is such that it makes us one. My life is in you. I am in you. Do not think of Me as a person with a body. I Am before the world began. I am love. If love is in you, then I am in you. I am with and within you.

Who can put love into words? My being with and within you is the greatest proof of My love that you can have. I give My very essence to you. The power of divine Love can be operative if you are an open channel and are obedient to Love's wishes. Bless you, for your willingness and openness! Bless all! []

2.19   EXISTENCE IS PROOF

[| My child, ever My child. Nothing can change that. You were conceived and brought forth from My heart in love. The fact that you exist is proof that you exist in love. When you bless and affirm your existence, your being, you bless and affirm the source of your being. Taking glory in nature, letting its beauty and calm sink into your very being, is a means of opening yourself to Me, the source, creator, and sustainer of all.

Turn to Me, My people, that you may have Life! I long to give, I need to give! This inherent quality of My being explains why some receive many spiritual gifts. Those who are open to receiving will receive much. I give all I can to each and all: I give My very self.

I am united with you in reality, in spirit. Your actions in the spirit are your actions, surely, but they are Mine; we are that closely united. The life that you live, I live with you, for I am within you in every particle and fiber of your being, both your physical and your spiritual being, for your being is one as we are one, God and creature. You breathe the very breath of God. Could you continue if My life energy were to withdraw?

You do not see these things very clearly now for you see as in a darkened mirror, a glimpse now and then. You are trying to see with your mind's eye, whereas it is with the eye of faith that you will perceive the light of reality. The love you carry in your heart will see you through the dark way.

You can choose to carry the light of joy with you. Let it shine in all circumstances and situations. Claim the good that can come from heartbreak and disaster and be joyful about it. By doing this, you are on the way to winning the battle against evil in your life. |]

Lord, I desire to truly know You!

[| My child, knowledge comes from being with, not from learning about or even from listening to the one you love, though that can help. We will always be together. Nothing can separate you from My love, so time itself, the passing of days spent in My presence, will gradually bring greater "fulfillment" to your spirit.

By contemplating thoughts of My love you become more open and take love in with your spirit. At the same time, I tenderly ask you to give Me your love to drink, for I, also, thirst.

Love is giving and receiving. If you try to do only one or the other, you will feel unbalanced, unfulfilled, empty, hungry, and thirsty. Give and receive love in a balanced way and your life and spirit will become balanced. This is how to allow the light of love to shine brightly within you. Bless you, My little one! Go forth in love and peace and joy to light up the world! Remember, I am with you! []

2.20   LOVE IS AN ETERNAL COVENANT

covenant 1 a binding or solemn agreement to do or keep from
    doing a specified thing; compact (Web 334)
[| My children, I love you very but I cannot give as much of Myself and blessings as I would wish, for I am limited by your limited capacity to receive. However, we have all of eternity in which I give Myself ceaselessly to you. I look forward to your giving yourself more and more to Me in return, for I know that then you will be truly happy!

Trust Me, for I am worthy of all trust. I give Myself as a seal of My covenant of love: Take and eat. Take and drink.

Many are the rewards of those who give themselves to Me and diligently work at living up to that covenant. A true covenant is unbreakable because it is eternal, so at the moment the binding promise takes place, it takes effect for all eternity.

All covenants of faith between two human beings before Me are echoes, copies, of the eternal covenant I have made with you, My people. I will never abrogate My promise to bless and keep you, for I cannot. My covenant with you, our covenant, has love as its binding force and love is unconquerable, unbreakable.

Once I have given My love, it is given. It remains always and forever, filling you with life. I give you My love at the moment of creation, for you spring forth from love and in love. You continue to exist because love is. Love is always and forever.

Do all and be all that I would have you be, in My love. Keep your mind open, for you have much more to learn – you will never cease learning – and much growing to do. Becoming "little" is one aspect of the growth that must take place within you, not meaning that you should shrink in importance but that you come to know the truth of who and what you are. Nothing can change that, either. You are eternally who and what you are.

When you try to live on a level that is not consonant with that truth and reality which is the essence of your being, you cause harm to your person and spirit. Say and have an attitude of: "I am who and what God made me. I accept myself as I am. I embrace myself and heal the rifts in my own inner personal relationship."

"You have heard that it was said to the people long ago, 'Do not murder, and anyone who murders will be subject to judgment.' But I tell you that anyone who is angry with his brother will be subject to judgment" (Mt 5:21-22a). Those who are angry at themselves are intent upon self-destruction. You cannot have one truth in the spiritual without that truth coming out in the bodily counterpart of your spirit, in your body.

You also must accept your spirit, your Soul, as I made you. If you desire to accomplish great things in your spirit but are not meant or created (not destined) for that, you injure and tear your spirit, with the resultant strain necessarily surfacing materially, as well.

Should the baby's breath – a flower with delicate white blossoms – feel the urge to become a rose and compulsively drive itself inwardly to try to do that, what would come of it? It definitely would not bloom as a rose, for it cannot. Whatever bloom would result after all that turmoil would be crippled and dwarfed, and surely the plant would not bloom in happiness and freedom.

You are meant to bloom in happiness and freedom! Accept and welcome the joy of life, the joy of being who you are! That intrinsic being is yearning to be and come forth! I am drawing the real you forth as I envision your ever-unfolding creation. I hold you tenderly in My love, My little flower! |]

2.21   LESSON ON LOVE

[| My child, come into My heart where all is calmness and tranquility! Evil things that happen take place outside of My heart and cannot hurt you if you stay with Me. Being "in My heart" means to stay and be conscious of My love.

Love nourishes and protects. Love defends its own.

Love never holds quarrels or metes out judgment.

Love is open and gracious, not confining – it leaves you free to leave if you should choose to do so.

Love fills the whole world. It is present not only in the hearts and Souls of those who are willing to love and be loved but also in all of space and time, and in all created things, for they are created and given in love, the only principle upon and from which I act.

Love transcends time. It is. Love precedes you and is before, ahead of, you. It covers you from above and lifts you from below. It is the very substance of your being, the stuff of which all is made.

You came forth from Me and you are, even as I Am.

You exist eternally in Me, from Me.

You are light from My Light, love from Love,

Creature from Creator.

You are My beloved. I am your beloved. |]

2.22   CARRY LOVED ONES IN YOUR HEART

Lord, what can I do to help my husband?
[| Take him into your heart. |]

I do that, Lord. Please hold both of us in your heart!
[| You must then always rest in My heart since you carry such precious cargo. Everyone that you truly care for and give yourself to, you carry in your heart. Then by close contact with Me and by opening yourself through self-denying discipline, you become a channel of love and nourishment to those hungry, hurting Souls. You provide intra-spirit feeding. in actuality, a life-saving lifeline.

Be who I would have you be. I am calling you to obedience and discipline. You have made good progress, there is more to be made. Do that and I promise you a share in My joy and peace.

I will be the cure for your ills,

The balm to ease your worries,

A sure guide for your faltering feet.

I will be your Lord, your life, and your love if you will have Me be.

My child, peace! Your growth in understanding and maturity is necessarily slow, as growth in the physical world is. There is a time and a place for everything, even lessons to be learned. You would miss much and botch things up if the lessons were brought to you too fast. []

What can I do to help my husband with all the negative feelings and inner hurt he is carrying?

[| Everything that I do, the guidance that I give, is for your good as well as the good of others. I do not bless one to the detriment of the other. The blessings you have been receiving are for your husband, too.

You have not been an open channel of love before this. You have been blocked by hurt, doubt, confusion, fear, pride, and self-centeredness. As I bring healing and a realization of My love to you, the way is being opened for healing and love to flow to your husband, as well. Continue to carry him in your heart.

Some people are as a young child before birth, unable to sustain themselves yet. They must be in a safe womb-of-love environment where they can assimilate the love nourishment that they need for survival. This is understood to include physical touching and caring, as well. Give your husband love and care as I gave you love and care in your time of dire need when you would have perished without it.

The real hurt is in the spiritual, the remedy is in the spiritual. Trust and believe! Picture others well and whole as they are coming to be! I bring everyone to wholeness as they rest in Me.

Rest in Me, at all times consciously united with Me and with each other. For this, you were brought into being and into the place that you are at. []

2.23   ENTER AND LIVE

Lord, I confess my sinfulness, my helplessness.
[| It is not a sin to be helpless. That is truth, inherent in your being. The more you recognize and accept your helplessness, the more you are coming into Truth. Saying that you are helpless is another way of stating that you are only able to receive, that of yourself you are nothing and can do nothing.

Rejoice in your innate need to receive for it is I, your God, who fills the void of your being! I satisfy every need. I am God for that purpose: to give. You, My people, are My prize possession and prize creation: You are fashioned to receive Me into your very being.

I become your life if you will have Me. This entails not only that you be open to receiving Me but also that you clear out the clutter that blocks Me out of your heart and life. If you are filled and satisfied with materialism, with physical eating and drinking, and with accomplishments that are sought as a means of building up your ego, then I cannot enter and live in your heart.

Lift your arms to Me in your helplessness and I will gently lift you into My arms, into My heart. Enter and live! |]

My God, bless you! I open myself to love as best I can. Please heal me and purify me so that I can love and receive love freely.
[| My beloved child! I hold you tenderly in love. Let this flow of thoughts be the overflow of the love with which I deluge you and wrap you around.

Love is always there within you, within all, but it may be as snow on a mountain that is frozen and unmoving, not bringing vitalization to anyone. When warming up takes place, a thawing out of cold reserve towards other people, the love can begin trickling down to water your Soul and that of others. Return of love from others melts the reserved love even more and it can become a stream of living water going out to water the earth!

Do not fear to give your heart to others. You do not need to, indeed, you should not first judge others to see if they are worthy of your love. When you love others, it is My love going to them in and through you. My love accepts everyone as worthy of being loved, for My love makes them worthy! I would not have you be a judge who is partial to only certain types and classes of people. I came for all, not just a select few. []

2.24 YOU MUST GUARD THE DOOR

[| My child, I hold you tenderly in love. I accept you as you are and draw you forth as you are coming to be. Nothing can harm you, nothing can hinder your growth unless you allow it to. I do not allow any evil influence to penetrate your being, but you have charge of the door of your heart, also.

Your heart is somewhat like the Temple at Jerusalem. I dwell in your heart in the center of your being, in the Holy of Holies, the secret place that is the center and being of life. Naught else can enter there: not pain, not misfortune, not sin, not judgmental words, not your best friend, no matter how much you love them and share with them. The center of your being is Mine alone – I am the Lord your God.

That part of your heart that you share with intimate friends is like the next inner section of the Temple. Your general association with the physical world is characterized by the outer court where everyone may enter.

Giving entrance into your inner heart to just anyone can have dire consequences. I put a natural reserve within you as protection and have instilled a warning device within you that triggers when your peacefulness is tampered with. When you meet someone who makes you uneasy, it may be a valid warning that you should not associate with them or it may be a sign that something is amiss within your spirit. Come to Me in the inner recesses of your heart and I will make it plain to you what is causing the restlessness.

Rest in Me, My child! Come, choose the better part! It will not be taken away from you. You can rest in Me in the inner recesses of your heart and still go about the activity of the moment. The way to do this is to let it be only the activity of the moment and not a consuming activity that holds your mind and attention with thoughts of the past, present, and future.

You are in charge of time only moment by moment, now. All other "time" rests in Me. I bring time forth only moment by moment. It is here a moment and then gone. There is no past as a place. The "past" was a time of being (existing), and being is only at the present moment.

You carry memories and feelings of unpleasant and perhaps traumatic experiences which can affect the quality of your being now. When you rest in Me, I temper and mold the effect of those experiences, whether "good" or "bad" and make them redound to your spiritual good.

Your future in time has not yet come to be. It is a waste of energy to worry about the future. The future is not a person or a power. It does not exist. There is only the present *now* coming to be, moment by moment.

Do not fear! When you let go of fear it slides right off because it has no means of holding onto you. Fear is only with you and within you when you hold it there. Why allow fear entrance to the Tabernacle of your heart? I would have only peace and joy within you. I wish to be the light of your life! Fear is darkness, a dark cloud, a heavy curtain that keeps the light out. Do not fear. I am with you. I love you! []

2.25   THE MYSTERY OF LOVE

Father-Mother God, please come into my heart.
[| My child, gladly I come! The weakest heart is not too humble a dwelling for Me. Do not consider yourself unworthy. Your existence is proof of your right to have fellowship with Me. I do not create and then abandon.

Rest in Me for a while. Many would gladly rest in Me if they could they but come to an awareness of My love for them! Many do not know of My love, even of those who are consecrated to My service. That is not the way I would have things be. My Will is for this life to be joyous coming into full being and expression of love.

The only way I can reach most people is through human love:
Parent to son and daughter,
Son and daughter to mother and father,
Man to woman; woman to man,
Dear friend to dear friend.

Who of those who have ever truly experienced love would deny that love is a mystery? The mystery present in the love is My presence, My love, pervading human love. Divine love is present in human love making it divine. Through human love, I can touch hearts and bring meaning to life.

My people, you are so dear to Me! Would that I could gather you under My wings as a hen gathers her chicks! Would that I could hold you in My arms in your moments of suffering as a devoted mother empathizes with her hurting, frustrated child!

Come to Me, My son, My daughter! I open My heart to you. It is a haven of mercy, a place of safety, a stronghold against which the forces of darkness have no play.

My heart is open. Come in!

My heart is compassionate.

Rest in My love and understanding.

I am non-judgmental. The only judging I do is that I judge you worthy of My mercy. It is your sins that condemn you. Let go of your sins and they let go of you. They have no lasting claim on you. You were made to love and to be loved.

Love covers a multitude of sins. Let My love cover you like a blanket, keeping you safe, warm, and secure! Come and experience rest for your Soul, your body, and your mind!

You are one-in-being though three-in-entity, as I am three-in-one. All of the physical creation mirrors the truths of the spiritual kingdom. That is why opening yourself to nature has such a beneficial effect: You open yourself to Me in so doing. []

2.26   THE BEDROCK OF LOVE

[| Rest in Me always, child. Know that I love you: Let that be the bedrock upon which you sit and stand and have your being. All truth, goodness, and love spring forth from love. Become, and stay rooted and grounded in love and you have nothing to fear.

There is a saying, "There is nothing to fear but fear itself." The element of truth in that statement is that fear is very destructive. It eats away at the core of your being. It says you are not worthwhile, but your being is the most worthwhile thing there is!

Fear puts fear in your heart that you will fail.

Love says, "Be united with Me and you cannot fail."

Fear says, "Worry about the future. Dire happenings may come about!"

Love says, "Do not fear for the future. You are safe in Me." In love, you have nothing to fear!

My child, I am with you always. Do not be hard on yourself when you find it difficult to realize My presence. Clouds and smoke screens of darkness swirl about endlessly and sometimes you become entrapped in them for a time.

Faith, hope (trust), and love will take you up and away, out of the quagmire of doubt and darkness, as a helicopter goes up and away. Get all three working in unison and you have a powerful force to come over and out of your spiritual difficulties, to overcome them. Say often, "My God, I believe in You! I put my hope and trust in You! I love you!"

Bless you, child, this day, this place, this moment.

Bless your comings and goings, your ins and your outs.

Bless you, in your ups and downs and on the flat, dull level of everyday life.

Consecrated, it is no longer dull and useless, and lifeless.

Love transforms all things. Love makes living worthwhile. Note: Drop the "i" in living and leave a space for receiving, "o," and your living becomes loving!

Go in peace! I am with you! Let *us* go in peace! |]

2.27   COPY OF THE DIVINE

Good morning, Father God! Bless You!

[| My child, it warms My heart to receive a greeting and acceptance from you! As I have told you before, even I have needs, for the cycle of love must keep going.

Love is never spent and gone. It is given away, to be, in turn, given away to another, and in turn, to be received again by the giver.

Could you conceive of a more marvelous plan? But this is not just a plan that I have set up. it is My very nature. The inner workings of My divine life are evident in the physical workings of the universe.

You do not need to travel to reach Heaven. Heaven is here. Wherever you are that you call here, which is always the place you are at, you are in Heaven. To be sure, you are not aware of this to any great extent, but My grace is bringing about awareness, all in good time, within each of you. Times when your present life no longer seems to make sense are times of your coming closer to a realization of and a readiness for Heaven.

When you rest in Me you are in heaven. The greatest desire of My heart is for you to come into union with Me, that you may be in heaven. Believe Me, it is well worth the effort and the cost!

Take My hand and let Me walk with you on the way. Come to Me, that I may be your way. Come to Me that you may find rest, that you may be in heaven with Me. United we stand. Divided, you fall. Open yourself to My peace, rest, and assurance. []

Lord, I believe! Help my unbelief!

[| My child, at all times I am ready to help your unbelief by being with you and within you. I help it by continuing your life and breathing. Your existence is proof of My existence. Your being able to love is proof that I love. Your being able to continue to hope against all odds is proof of hope's reward, proof that I exist and that I sustain you through that lifeline of hope.

A life given up on is no longer worth living. Through my gift of hope, you continue to have a reason for living and thus your life is worthwhile. If all you could do is exist, it is ample enough reason to live. []

CHAPTER 3

ABOUT LIFE

3.1   RECEIVE SPIRITUAL FULFILLMENT

[| *"All that the Father gives me shall come to me, no one who comes to me will I ever reject"* (Jn 6:37b). You can relax completely, My child, down to the last little nerve fiber in the depth of your being. Just believe! I am Truth. All that I say is true and you can trust your very life upon it. I do love you. I wish the very best for you. I desire that you become free, whole, and gladsome! Lay aside your former ways, be converted, and live!

"What good is it for someone to gain the whole world, yet forfeit his soul?" (Mk 8:36). What does your extra eating gain for you? Just extra pounds and a continuation of the insecurity you are seeking to alleviate. *"Come to me, all you who are weary and burdened, and I will give you rest"* (Mt 11:28).

Turn to Me with your whole heart! Break the fetters that tie you to the material world! Once you are free you will still work with and in the material element, but at My bidding and in freedom. Victory over your appetite that you strive for is a key victory. Do not let it be a stumbling stone. I am one with you. Turn inward for strength.

I know the desires of your heart, I know your needs. They can be supplied in a spiritual way that will fill up what is lacking in your human relationships. You can bring that spiritual fulfillment into your relationships and then it is there, making your life a whole unit.

"Say to them, 'As surely as I live, declares the Sovereign Lord, I take no pleasure in the death of the wicked, but rather that they turn from their ways and live.'" (Ez 33:11a). I do not desire hunger, thirst and a

feeling of rejection in My people, but rather for them to be healed and filled, that they thus may live.

Life is good and worthwhile. Life is a sharing of My very self, for I am eternal life. Faith and hope spring from Me, for I am the rock of faith and eternal hope. Once you know Me you will have love and you can thus love others, for I am love. Drink deeply of the wellsprings of divine life! I am with you, the eternal fountain of life. []

3.2   HEALING AND REST

Lord, I have so many needs and questions! Please heal me!
[| RJust rest in Me as much as possible. You see how nature grows slowly but surely. Healing comes in the same way: slowly but surely in proportion to your faith and trust and obedience to My words.

I say unto you, "Come to Me and find rest." You must rest from your worries, cares, and indecisions for healing to take place. If what you need at any given moment is a place of rest, I am that to you. If your need is for a friend, I am a friend. Whatever you sincerely need, I fill that need. There is nothing I would not do for you, for I love you so much.

Do not be afraid. I keep repeating this but it is most necessary. If you have fear it dominates you so there is no room for joy and gladness. Strive to be free, gladsome, and wholesome.

You are alive because I am in you. I, your God, permeate every part of your body, and My life is your very soul, your life. How I long for you to truly know Me! I am happy that you are coming to have a little basic understanding through your reading and pondering. Do not be afraid. Open yourself to love. Open yourself to Me.

Be quiet within yourself now as you rest in Me. Do not be afraid. I am here. Doubts that cross your mind cannot change the reality of My presence. I am your life.

As you breathe, it is a sign of My presence.

As you think, it is a reflection of My mind.

All that you do, you do in Me, the principle behind all action.

You exist in Me. I Am Who Am.

My beloved one, I speak to you and to everyone who will listen to Me. You are special to Me. You are exactly as I would have you. Bless yourself as well as bless others. Affirm yourself, as well.

You have strength in My Spirit to overcome all obstacles and difficulties. Going through a difficulty with a brave and trusting heart makes you the master of that difficulty. It no longer has the power to bend and control your life.

Take courage, faith, hope and all your other spiritual allies with you, then you will not be fearful and alone. When you have faith in Me and hope in Me, you are in Me and you have strength and protection. When you open yourself to Me you are open to love, and love conquers all.

Bless you, My child! And blessings upon all who walk in the way! Blessings upon all who will receive it. []

3.3   BE FREE IN THE SPIRIT

Lord, what would You have me know, have me do?
[| I would like you to be like Me in every way you can. Strive to detach yourself more and more from material things and worldly accomplishments. These only hinder your spiritual advancement. Pray for more desire for the things of the Spirit. Open yourself to My Spirit. Let yourself be moved to compassion. Do not harden your heart; being one with others in love means caring about everything that happens to them.

Be unencumbered and free! Lack of a sense of freedom holds you down emotionally and spiritually. You are free to feel, love, enjoy, and ponder, to be! You are free to be yourself, to become that self that you desire to be. No outward circumstances can hold you back if you mount on the wings of the spirit. In the spirit, you can go over, around, or through problems as simply and naturally as Jesus passed through the closed doors in coming to his frightened apostles.

Be receptive and open, then I can come to you and abide with you. I cannot come in My fullness to a closed spirit, to one who limits My love, power, and healing strength by the narrow confines of worldly wisdom. Do you not long for perfect freedom, for the fullness of joy? I know you do and I bless your desires. They are put there by Me. I have a perfect plan for everyone's life. That plan has had to be adjusted and altered according to people's whims and fancies, but everything is working out for the greater good.

"*'For my thoughts are not your thoughts, neither are your ways my ways', declares the Lord."* Is 55:8). You cannot possibly understand, so do not try to! Leave all in My hands for that is where all things are being worked out. []

3.4   I KNOW YOUR DESIRES

[| My little one, you have nothing to fear! I am with you and always will be. I know the desires of your heart for good to come to be – I planted them there. I know the willing desire with which you turn to Me and bless you for it! I can do nothing for a person who is not willing. Be thankful for this gift of an open spirit, which is a gift even though the desire comes from within yourself.

Many are the desires of your heart. I know them all. Let your desires rest in Me. Only that which is good, holy, and blessed comes from and through Me. See life as having passed through My hands and having been blessed as it comes to you. Do not worry that your joy in Me and spiritual truths will cease to be a source of joy.

In Me is all joy and hope.

In Me are everlasting life and everlasting joy.

Rest in Me. Rest in joy.

Trust Me who am wonderful counselor, bosom friend, and willing confidant!

Leave all in My hands. I know of your struggles and that you can get nowhere spiritually by yourself. Is it not wonderful to have One who understands all, who accepts you despite everything?

I appreciate your gratitude. It is said, "Love makes the world go round." Well, it is gratitude that makes love go on. Love feeds on gratitude and on the desire of the beloved to grow in love. Give Me your love such as it is. It is precious to Me! When you give Me your love, gratitude, and understanding, I, in turn, can go out to others more powerfully in love, just as it is with you. Bless you. My child! []

3.5   JOY IS THE KEY

[| My child, you are anxious and concerned about many things! When you have something to attend to that merits your attention and concern, see about it with joyful, loving concern, rather than with anxious concern. There is a world of difference.

"What good is it for someone to gain the whole world, yet forfeit his soul?" (Mk 8:36). What profit is it to you if you can amass a mountain of achievements if it pertains little to the welfare of your immortal Soul? That is why it is so necessary to stay attuned to My Will. When you realize that you have stepped out on your own without My blessing, come back to Me with a sincere heart and try again to live in obedience to Me.

Everyone must live in obedience. It can be no other way. *"Then he went down to Nazareth with them and was obedient to them. ... And Jesus grew in wisdom and stature, and in favor with God and men"* (Lk 2:51a, 52). Gifts and virtues that you are given are but seedlings. They must be nurtured and developed by effort. No, it is not easy. You will fall back many times, but what counts is to begin again. You will have gained patience and humility in the process, and your very struggle is an exercise of the virtue of long-suffering, patience.

Perseverance consists of never giving up. Are you praying for perseverance? Just resolve to never give up, to always go on one more time. That which is easily achieved is little appreciated. That is true in the spiritual world, as well. How long must you continue trying and struggling? Not long, and, no matter how long it has been, afterward it will no longer seem long.

The key to lessening the seeming endlessness of the struggle is to take out the struggle aspect by allowing your life to be transformed by love. That which is done for the beloved is not hard and not long, for love is willing to endure anything for the sake of the joy of the beloved. If the struggle is "joy-full" it cannot at the same time be "pain-full." Do all in joy, and the drudgery no longer exists!

Your life can become a glorified life simply by letting the wonder of My love touch and transform you.

My children, how I long for you to have this abundant life! It is My very life to give of Myself to you. My desire is for your happiness and eternal good! What can I do for you that will touch your hearts? Study love. Study the Book of Life. Come to Me! []

3.6   LIVE WHAT YOU BELIEVE

"...I am with you always" (Mt 28:20c).
[| Yes, My child, I am here, I am always here. I await you. I look forward to this time together.

Keep faith. The flame of faith must be kept burning for all to see. It may seem to you that your life does not touch many, but the example of your faith influences a great many. Through seeing your faith, others can begin to let hope be enkindled in their hearts that maybe there is something to this belief in Jesus, in God.

Do not let the worry and burden for others weigh you down. You must have holy joy no matter what. I give you that joy. The joy that I give is unlike any that the world can give. If you desire to receive My joy, do not partake of earthly joys to fill yourself up. Earthly joys are given that you may rejoice ever more in Me, your Father, who am the giver of all good things.

Don't fret. A fret is a childish worry. Leave all things in My hands and that includes your sanctification. If you expect others to trust themselves and their affairs to Me, do the same with yourself and your concerns. Do not be a demigod, deciding that you can take care of this or that yourself. It is hypocritical for you to say you believe something and not live it to the fullest.

Go forth in obedience to love and serve. These days of your earthly life are precious to Me. They are the days of your giving and you must give if you are to receive. All things balance out:

For every desire, there is fulfillment.

For every space, there is that which fills it.

For every hope, there is the result of that hope.

For every giving in love, there is corresponding receiving.

Every time of rest brings strengthening.

Every doubt dismissed and every fear allayed brings a resurgence of faith and joy.

Joy is freedom from fear. You can be free by so choosing. Fear has no real claim on you. It has tried to chain you down and tie you up in knots, but Jesus defeated fear finally, once and for all, on Calvary. He met fear face to face with the worst it could affect and went through it, breaking its power and its claim on humanity.

You are My child. You can rest in Me, free from fear and concern! I am your all. Know that I am with you always. I am with you as you go about your duties. Do all in love. []

3.7   LET ME GUIDE YOU

[| Bless you, My child! Why are you fearful and tense? Everything is in My divine control. Follow the leading of the Holy Spirit and all will be well. You cannot begin to carry the weight of concern for having everything turn out well in the world and for the sake of those that you know and love. It is for you to carry trust in Me and to be joyful in being. Keep yourself in peace. Stay open to Me who brings you the peace that the world cannot give.

I love you as I love all! Each relationship is unique, as each snowflake is unique. one of a kind, special. I give all to all: all of My love, all of My patience, all of My mercy. But My love is never-ending, so you receive all that you possibly can receive at all times. You receive in proportion to your capacity and that grows in direct proportion to your giving of yourself. |]

I was wondering about how I had been praying.

[| Do your best and I will work with you. I acknowledge your sincerity and your desire to follow the guidance of My Spirit. Place yourself in My hands and you need not worry whether a certain element is from yourself or not. I work through you, so I cause the inclination to rise naturally from your heart.

I bless your efforts. Praying for others brings blessing both to them and to you. Do not worry about the overwhelming need for prayer for others' needs. I am aware of all those needs, and your desire to help is love going out to them. That in itself is helpful for their spirits.

There is a vast spiritual world that you are only beginning to get fleeting glimpses of. Continue in My love. It is My love that rules the spiritual universe, the kingdom of God. You do not need to understand it with your human mind. It is for your Spirit to come to know spiritual matters and your spirit "knows" with the heart.

Unite your desires with My desires, then let the desires of your heart lead you, for your heart, cleansed and free, is the abode of My Holy Spirit. Wake up and live! Continue to grasp all the kernels of divine truth and light that you can. I will use you marvelously if you remain faithful and humbly try to live in My grace.

You read recently, "The more received, the more indebted." It is that way with Me, too: The more received, the more indebted. The more you open yourself to Me in love, the more indebted I am for that love. Relax now, My child, in My love and mercy. My love covers all your sins and shortcomings. Peace! |]

3.8 TRUST AND REST

[| I come when you are quiet and peaceful. You need not be anxious about how to bring Me to you. I am here with you always. Simply turn to Me by a desire, a look, a word, a glance of faith. You do not need to put thoughts and feelings into words. I know the desires and needs of your heart. You trusting Me to supply those needs is the element I watch and hope for. It magnifies My heart to receive trust like that of a little child!

Fear and tension are still taking a toll on your body. Do not be afraid to open yourself to Me exactly as you are and exactly as you feel. I open Myself to you. []

Father, if only I could believe one hundred percent! If only I could know! I desire to know the truth, to know You.

[| My child, you are so impatient! Life unfolds moment by moment so that you can savor each step of the way. These days are in reality precious days, for when you live in the darkness of faith, you reap choice blessings for yourself, your loved ones, and the world.

A plant emerging from the seed eagerly stretches itself up to come out of the darkness into the light. It yearns to come to full stature and bear fruit. All in good time. Some plants have a short life span, others grow slowly over a great length of time. Each corresponds to a like Soul in its spiritual growth.

Another lesson to help guard you against the effects of spiritual pride: Each time you see a plant, whether common grass or a choice specimen, ask and ponder, "Where does it get the life? Where does it get the light? The nourishment? The pruning? The care it needs? The power to grow?"

You simply are as the plant is. You are a being who exists in Me, because of Me. You are led, fed, and shaped by Me. You live in My heart, in My love. Showers and times of pruning are all acts of love so that you may reach your finest level of beauty and fullness as you so desire in the depths of your being. Rest in Me. Be in Me. Stop trying to be you're a gardener for yourself! You are because I Am. []

Father, I hunger! I thirst!

[| I am filling you and satisfying your thirst. I am the Rock in the Wilderness from which flows life-giving water. The food and drink that I give is spiritual food. You receive nourishment every time you turn to Me. You are accustomed to the interchanges of the world and hence may not recognize what I am doing for you.

Every trimming of the self is a new growth of the "spiritual man." You may put yourself in readiness but it is I who do the work of stripping away the old self. As one layer is laid off, you soon become aware of another layer that separates you from true freedom of spirit.

But, just as in living your earthly life, if you only look ahead to the next stage of your life and do not wholeheartedly accept where you are at, you miss the living, so it is in the spiritual order. If you only see what further needs to be done and corrected spiritually, you fail to recognize where you are at and so you miss the being of the present moment.

By accepting your life wholeheartedly and by opening yourself to love, you combine the physical with the spiritual in the way it was meant to be. You combine living and being.

Me being in you and you being in me, that is heaven!

That is why I am here, that heaven may be! |]

3.9   I CALL YOU TO LOVE

[| I say this to each of you: My precious child, you are special to Me! Do not fear that My love for you will grow slack. I am eternal God, eternal love. Come receive of Me that your love may be eternal, also. I am the fullness of love. You are in Me. You breathe love, move in love, and are healed by love. You are sustained body and soul by love. Rest in Me and let Me rest in you.

I am happy that some of these spiritual truths are beginning to enter your consciousness. All in due time. I have claimed you from before the beginning of time. You are Mine. I hold you in love and call you to love. I call all to love, and everyone who has a heart of goodwill will respond and come to Me. |]

Lord, help me realize my littleness so I can come into Your arms to be held, refreshed, and strengthened.

[| My child, open your heart to Me. When you come into My heart, your heart must be open so that our hearts may merge into one. That is how you receive My strength, understanding, and love. I come to you and bring My gifts.

I am Blessing, endurance, strength, patience, and love. When you possess Me, you possess all. Do not fret that you are not good enough. That is not the way to divine life, that you become good through your efforts. Be open to Me that I may come and sup with you. I love you so much! (Whoever you are who is reading this, yes, I mean you!)

Your divine shepherd can be everything for everyone. Just open your needs to Me and I will fill those needs. Do everything in and for Me. As you glorify Me by your faith and trust, I, in turn, bless you.

Your human life, your existence in this world, has the purpose of giving you experiences of love in a physical way so that you may come to know pure love. The sufferings and experiences that you go through are designed to form in you the gifts of the Spirit: compassion, mercy, selflessness, and patience. My ways are so far above your ways that it takes examples in the physical for you to be able to come to reality in your spiritual life.

Check that snares of the antichrist have not begun to choke off faith and trust in your life. His ways are insidious. Depend not on your judgment but scrutinize all you do by the Spirit. Uneasiness about an action is a sign of your peace being disturbed. Set all aright.

Bless you, child, for believing in Me and trusting Me! Thank you for your love. It is precious to Me. |]

3.10   THE SON, THE FATHER

[| (The Son:) My child, it is not yet meant to be that you are freed from the worries, fears, and doubts that beset mankind. You have your path to follow and it is for a purpose, but you can breathe the pure, fresh air of the Kingdom even now. Continue to cling to my word. Let it sink in and bring about the purposes for which I sent it.

The Father and I are one. When you converse with me, you are loving us. You rest in the bosom of the Father, even as I do. You are so used to the meaning that those words have in the physical sphere that it takes time and contemplation for you to come to realize their reality in the real world of the Spirit. []

[] (The Father:) Yes, My child, you are in Me. I Am, and all else is in Me. I am all good, all holiness, all grace. I am divinity, supremacy, and divine order. In Me are all wisdom, holiness, and truth. Just depend on Me with childlike trust and all is well. In Me, you are in love, as well as in mercy and justice. You are safe and secure in My arms.

Oh, would that you would love Me as I so desire and need! Would that you would come to know Me and share with Me as a friend! I love you, My child, and I always will. I am always near you and with you. Unite your heart with Mine. Open your heart to receive and infilling of grace so we may become one. As a hen gathers her chicks, I would gather you to My bosom.[]

3.11   I CHOOSE YOU TO BE WHO YOU ARE

[] I love you, My child! Do not forget that. You are precious to Me. I have chosen you to be you, with the exact degree of all the qualities that make you the person you are. There is much potential there if you will but yield to My molding. I desire you to be the person you are. My wish for you is that you come to accept yourself as you are, physically, morally, and spiritually.

You are in the process of becoming one with Me. It is not surprising that at times you go through moments of doubt when all this seems unreal, for your ties to the physical world are so strong. But that is being changed. Your being is being opened to My life ever more and more.

Do not lose heart! You are dearer to Me than all the world! One precious Soul is of infinitely more value than the whole created universe. I hold you in My arms, dear one. I hold you until the last of the anxiety that binds you is dropped away. []

Lord, I open my heart and whole being to Your love. Thank You for loving Me!

[| I am never happier than when one of My children, acting in blind faith, makes an act of will to believe in My presence, to believe in My love, and to open himself or herself to My love!

Enter, dear child, into the recesses of My heart! You will not be immune from suffering, but when filled with love, you will no longer mind discomfort and annoyance. Love suffers all, gladly. Rest in My love. []

3.12   I WILL BE YOUR STRENGTH

[| My child, courage! I am with you, I am your strength. My grace to overcome doubt and temptation to despair will always be sufficient. I do not give you so much strength however that you begin to think you can rely on yourself. In Me, you will find your strength. Those who do not turn to Me but arrogantly trust their own devices and disdain the spirit's call to turn to Me for help will be left to their plight. Then, the experience of failure will be a lesson well learned.

Why do you continue to harbor doubts about the truth of My reality? Cast them out and be free! The fact that there is searching in your Soul is a sign of the existence of supernatural life. Just be, and the hours and days will not weigh so heavily on your spirit. You are meant to *be:* to be obedient, compassionate, patient, joyful, loving, peaceful, and trusting.

When a being fulfills the purpose for which it exists, there is resultant peace. You are My child and are meant to be, destined to be, one with Me. Contrary searching is from your discordant nature, twisted from its original form by the effects of sin.

Come to Me, I will give you peace!

Come to Me, I will give you rest!

Open your heart to Me! Truly open it! Cast out the last traces of doubt of My existence, of My infinite holiness and goodness, of My love for you and My providence. You have nothing to worry about and that is the truth. []

3.13   HANG IN THERE!

[| My child, bless you for your efforts! Hang in there! The reward far outweighs the cost. In reality, you are not giving up anything when you give up yourself, for you are nothing without Me.

I am your true self. My being gives substance to your being, so if you are not open to and united with Me you are but an empty shell.

You need not be afraid to give yourself, and give of yourself, in love, for in so doing you are truly living. How precious it is to Me to see the joy that fills your heart, and your determination to hang onto that joy; for that is all I exist for (the main purpose of My existence), is to give of My joy, strength, peace, and love to you! That joy within you is My very life!

My child, I care for you deeply! (I am real – just disregard those hovering thoughts of doubt.) Let yourself be loved to wholeness, to maturity.

I have been eagerly anticipating each of you, and have had long to "wait." I, too, must follow the rules that are set up for the world. All in due time. What a welcome awaits you as you enter the arms of love! Foresee it in your mind's eye and that expectancy will be a source of strength for the way.

My heart is filled with tenderness toward you, toward your loved ones, toward all the unfortunate ones of this world – indeed, toward all! I bless your efforts to bring your thoughts and actions into obedience to Me. I bless your families!

I will be with you, in love, in truth (I truly will be). I give you My blessing, I lay My hands in benediction upon you! Cheers! []

3.14   BE WHOLE

[| My child, I know that the ups and downs and problems of this life weigh you down. I know how it is for you as you live this earthly life. The life within you is Me, part and particle of My being. I am closer to you than your very self.

As you pray and desire to know Me, to be one with Me, you separate yourself from yourself by thinking of Me as outside of you. It is like you formerly did when you thought about yourself as a young child, as being out and away from yourself. The emotional pull on the spirit from doing that is hard on your spiritual energy. It affects the wholesomeness of your being.

When you come against yourself within your person with feelings of rejection and do not accept who you are and what you are like, you likewise do damage to the vitality of your spirit. "...a house divided against itself will fall" (Lk 11:17c).

You must be your own best friend for you are with Me, united in spirit within yourself by your very life. To disdain yourself is to attack your very life, your being, your existence. You must hold yourself in utmost love, united with Me as you are, for I hold you in utmost love! To do otherwise is to pull yourself away from Me. It causes a dichotomy in your spirit.

The Holy Spirit is the spirit of wholeness, unity, and oneness. It is He who binds us together. Thus, you are in the very life of the Trinity when you are open to yourself, to Me, to love. You then "know God" and "are known."

You must be whole to bring wholeness to others. You cannot give that which you do not have. You are trustees of the life I have given you. Your life is in your person. To attack your person with negative, disdainful thoughts is to come against the life I entrusted to you. It is like a dog chasing its tail. You won't get anywhere that way!

I like you the way you are. Why can't you? We go forward from where we are. What good would it do a plant to bemoan the fact that it is still so little? All of one's energies must go into the growing effort and not be lost on self-recrimination. []

3.15   RELATING TO TIME

Lord, please make it clear what you have been trying to tell me about time, about the past and the future.
[| My child, you are in Me and I am in you. There is no other place that you are or possibly can be. As you have been traveling back in spirit (thought) to a former time, you have been picturing space travel; you have been picturing yourself out and away from your person. As you think back, you must keep yourself within yourself at whatever age or time you are bringing to mind. Also, the time itself is not out and away from here; the place you were is out and away, yes, but not the time.

All of "time" is present to Me. I hold all of it as a unit. Instead of picturing the past as a long road back and the future as a long road ahead, picture what is reality: I Am, and in Me, all these events take place in order, as is ordained. But, the time element of these events must be kept together as a whole unit. This is similar to thinking through a story from beginning to end: There is a time element in a story, but the details of the story stay all packaged neatly together in your mind; you just bring it to mind in sequence.

I hold all events that take place in time in My mind. As I bring about the telling of the story in reality in the physical world, you are a participant in it. You are "My story" that I am telling to the world as your life progresses. When slides are shown on a screen, the image of each slide becomes present and real for a moment. The image "goes into the past" but it does not go to a place. That moment is just held in Me, a fragment of the whole of time. []

3.16   THE WILLINGNESS AND THE EFFORT

[| Do not let yourself get entrapped by a set of prayers or even Scripture verses that you feel you "should" or "must" say every day. I know the desires of your heart. As you lift those desires to Me – that is, let Me take charge of them – they are prayers without words. Prayer without words is the most sublime prayer for it is the universal language of all. There is no language barrier in unspoken prayer.

I bless you and your "prayer sisters." In unity, there is strength, for when you are united, you are in the one Spirit, My Spirit. The good in each person and all will check any lesser good that may try to manifest itself. Continue to desire the opportunity to meet, share and pray together. The stronger the desire, the more sure the realization of that desire. |]

Lord, I don't feel as attuned to You as I would like to be.

[| My child, I love you, and love suffices to accomplish all. Continue in the stance of love and faith that you took by and in your will. You are thus choosing life, and good results must follow.

The less capable you feel the more I can make use of you for My work. Only the willing must be there and the measure of effort asked of you. It is I, not you, who accomplishes all things in all. You need not have an understanding of all the workings of the Spirit, either. Desiring to have that could arise from arrogance and from a desire to dominate. |]

3.17   FROM LOVE TO LOVE

[| My child, I bless you and empathize with you. I have compassion for you and all.

It is time to reaffirm your stand, and your choice, of how to approach each day. Nothing else matters except My Will. No matter what the problems, if you are in My Will you have nothing to worry about. I order all things.

"Peace I leave with you; my peace I give you" (Jn 14:27a). When you are done with a project or a duty, leave it in My hands, and, in return, I give you peace. It is the same for all as it is for you: You only can do what you can, given the circumstances and the situation, and you must leave it at that. You will have done your part in that situation for that particular day or time. Remember, you are not in charge, I am. []

Lord, what would You have me do?

[| I bid you, drink in deep draughts of the joy and exhilaration of spring. Return to My presence as often as you can as you go about your duties. Do not be concerned about the lessened importance to you that the trivial duties themselves have. That is to be expected as you get more into the Spirit. You are to compensate for that lackluster by filling up the doing of the duty with love and devotion.

The fulfillment of duty is to do it in love. Go from love to love in your activities, not from doing this to doing that as ends in themselves. Rest when you are tired. Rest is a time of receiving and you must balance your giving and receiving. []

Lord, I love You! Would that I could love You more! Would that I could love You with perfect love!

[| United with Me, your love is perfected. The tiny flame of your love enters the burning fire of My love. Your love comes from My love. Love is a gift, as is life. All that you have and are is a gift, derived from My very being.

I realize that you are not yet what you should be, but you are not to dwell on that overly much. Your failure to achieve certain spiritual goals that you have set for yourself is in itself good for your spiritual well-being. Desire and strive to be all that I would have you be rather than what you would choose.

My child, I come against all forces of darkness in you and around you. My presence is light. If it seems dark for you, perhaps you have slipped too far into the level of the senses. What you choose to have, that you have.

Choose joy! Choose love!

Choose faith and hope!

Choose peace and freedom from fear!

You have no cause to fear for yourself or for others whom you are concerned about. The way is open to all. Your desire for the well-being of others puts them on the way and in touch with life. Fear for them short circuits that. []

3.18   GIVING AND RECEIVING

[| My child, I bless your attempts to be in a prayerful state. Unite your being with Me – it will mean much. There must be both giving and receiving: I, the Giver, you, the receiver. Then, in turn, I the Receiver as you give Me your love, gratitude, and faithfulness.

Not much of a connection is needed to bring about this love-and-mercy exchange. A desire on your part will do it. It is as with a plant: A single rootlet reaching into the earth will bring about growth and, from that, the development of stronger, more secure roots and resultant luxuriant growth.

Rest in My love! I know all about your concerns and desires even before you tell Me about them, but it means much to Me to have you share them with Me, to trust and confide in Me. It may seem to you that your whole life is a "way of the cross" because everywhere you look and turn there are problems and crosses.

Many of those you can avoid. You take on unnecessary activities at times. That busy social work that I have not sent you to do becomes a cross, for you take it up from a false sense of duty rather than in love and obedience. Anything that you have undertaken that you cannot come to joyful freedom about should be examined as to whether you are My Will in that regard.

I bless your efforts, but I am trying to teach you that it is not so much your efforts that are important (not your deciding to accomplish something) as your willingness to cooperate with My efforts: to be a channel of My love and peace for those to whom you are asked to go in particular and a sign of peace for all who observe you or come in contact with you.

Do not forget that I am with you. I fill up where you are lacking, so the weaker you are – the more you see and acknowledge your weakness and call on Me to be your strength – the stronger I can be in and through you.

You are troubled and anxious about many things. Only one thing is necessary. Choose the better part. Have you given yourself to Me one hundred percent? What attachments to worldly goods, to your personal opinion, do you see in yourself? I know that you are unable to do something about this on your own, so My grace is proffered at all times. Please take it! I need those who are willing to be used, who are willing to serve. []

3.19   WHEN TRULY OPEN

[| My child, I give you My love, My very self. When you are open to Me, we merge into one:
   It is your mind but My thoughts,
   Your body but My strength,
   Your desiring but My accomplishing,
   Your loving, with My love. []
   Heal me, Lord, I pray, and deliver me of all my fears!
[| I will watch over you and guide you. Have no fear. Fear may try to "have" you, but if you do not go along with it, it can have no control over you. When you allow fear or other undesirable spirits to enter your "castle," you are letting your spirit merge with it. You become one with it with untold disastrous effects. You are created, destined, for union with Me, your God. Every unworthy spirit hinders the coming about of that union.

Coming into union with Me is a natural spiritual growth process, just as your body grows in a natural growth pattern. Do not be alarmed when you see countless discrepancies and shortcomings in yourself which are thwarting your full union with Me. I see the fully realized union that is coming to pass (all in good time) and I am not worried. My faith is bringing it about.

That is the way the future is present to Me: I see it by faith. I know it will come to be because I choose it. This process can only be hindered by your choosing unworthy thought patterns and activities that are contrary to love. Only love can bring about a union that is good, holy, and pure. When you allow fear or suchlike to enter you, you are in an unholy alliance. Those unholy spirits destroy rather than build up the object of their union.

I do not want to hereby instill fear in you, only caution regarding that makes you not feel peaceful. You cannot afford to let down your guard.

Be ever conscious that I permeate all of physical space and all of the thought and spirit world. No matter what people may come to know about the mysteries of the spirit world, which may appear to be very frightening and disconcerting, you have nothing to fear. I am the creator and controller of all.

When you rest in Me you rest securely upon a solid foundation. I will order all things for the greater good. Should your life turn topsy-turvy, do not be unduly concerned. I am just getting your priorities and those of others straightened out.

Rest in the peace of My heart, child! It is the balm and the cure for all ills. Those you hold a burden for – bring them into My peace by desiring and willing it. []

3.20   I WILL NOT BE OUTDONE

[| My child, bless you for your openness and love! You can trust Me for all things. I am faithful and true. I cannot be outdone in generosity. The more you give to Me in service, care, dedication, and love, of necessity the more I will give to you.

Receiving magnifies My capacity to give in return – if that were possible – but that is the closest you can come to an understanding of this, put in human terms. Praise and blessing magnify Me and I thus become "more magnanimous." I give My very qualities to those who bless and praise Me. What am I to give if not that which is My very life? for nothing exists outside of Me.

The reason that desire must be present first before you can receive is that desire is openness. You cannot receive it if you are not open. In My love, I plant the seeds of desire for spiritual gifts, for those things to come to pass that are in My will for your greater happiness, for your sanctification, and that of others. |]

Lord, please guide me. Do You have a word for me?

[| Yes, trust and follow. What have you to fear? I am the divine shepherd. I see all that ever was and all that will be. I know what needs to be done in your life and the lives of others. Do not press the fulfillment of your desires prematurely. Wait for My leading so the ground will be prepared and fruit may result.

Rest in Me in faith, love, and trust. Rest, as a child in its mother's arms (not questioning if it is safe, for it surely is). Rest not on outer forms but on the inner presence. |]

3.21   ALL IN GOOD TIME

[| My child, I realize it is hard for you, for all of you, to change your perspective and ideas about life from a predominantly physical orientation to a realization of the spiritual interspersing and regulating everything. All in good time. You do not need to be in a hurry and under pressure to come to know the laws of My universe. I am revealing them to you as needed and as the time is right that you must know them to deal with situations.

Most of all, remember that you are in My love! I surround, embrace, sustain and hold you in love! Being ever conscious of My love makes you impermeable to the darts of depression, unwarranted sorrow, anger, resentment, and despair. Nothing else matters except that I love you! Love conquers all, attains all It unites us.

What else to write? Write that I love you! You cannot hear that often enough. When reality is expressed, it affirms and strengthens that reality for you in your mind and person. Being conscious of My love and consciously letting the truth that I love you penetrate your mind, body, and spirit bring healing to your mind, body, and spirit. It loosens the fear that grips you (often unawares by you) and replaces it with trust.

The main thing to remember and do is to keep in mind My love for you and thus you are then walking in it. I bless you, fill you, nourish you, guide you, accomplish all for you and all, in and by My love. Love conquers all. Love accomplishes all. Love created a world and love is bringing it to fruition. Love holds that world and you in it to its heart. All exists in My heart, in My love.

3.22   ONLY FROM ME

[| My child, I greet you with love and with compassion! Yes, I have compassion on all, even on those who, according to outward appearances, do not need compassion. All would fall and fail miserably were I not constantly there, lifting you and being the strength within you, all unaware by you. When I let you slip so you can see your inherent weakness you see that you do need My help and turn to Me.

I would have you turn to Me at all times for strength and help. There is no other source from which to gain it. You cannot be a provider unto yourself (to try to do so would be like for an animal to feed on itself for sustenance). Your whole being rests in and on Me.

I know this is a difficult lesson to learn, for all appearances are to the contrary. Let your relationship to the earth be a sign to you of your need for My support: You will never be supportive of yourself away from the earth, both for having a physical foundation and as a source of nourishment and life-giving, life-sustaining water.

Bless you, My little one! May you always remain just that: My little one, trusting and open in love. Go in peace! |]

3.23 BE WHO YOU ARE MEANT TO BE

[| I accept and love you as you are, My child. I made you as you are. I love you as you are. Inherent in your being is the force of life that is bringing you ever more into being who and what you are called to be. You cannot be other than what you are foreordained to become. A species stays pure and true to its inner formation.

Your growth stays true to the divine blueprint stamped on your Soul. Should you thwart the natural growth and try to force yourself into another pattern and plan of growth, you may end up with a caricature, a cartoon figure barely resembling the real you. Trust Me to take charge of the master blueprint! Your greatest hope and satisfaction will come to be by being compliant with My will in your life.

Breathe a sigh of relief as you realize you do not need to worry about the present supply, the daily directions, or the future outcome of your life! Leave all in My (very capable) hands. Cannot I who brought life forth be trusted to fashion it in an equally marvelous manner?

Do not strain yourself to be or to accomplish something unique that in your mind's eye is desirable. Let Me do the fashioning and the upholding of life. Rest in Me for all, trust Me for all.

Do not let the cares and worries of the physical world entrap you. Neither let the frivolities, pastimes, and things of the senses take over your attention. When all is done as for Me your attention is on the good and you can safely mingle in the affairs of the world.

You need spiritual discipline, however, for you can so easily become entrapped in the enticements that the world and the flesh have to offer. Living in and for the body only you can never be satisfied. Your thirst and need then seem insatiable for you are trying to satisfy the spiritual with the physical.

Your real need is in the spirit. You need Me and I "need" you because I love you. I need to love. Your need for Me is the need for love. That is all that will satisfy. Ironically, love demands a denial of those parts of your nature that the physical urge would lead you to indulge. Hunger for food that cannot seem to be satisfied by eating is a spiritual hunger to be fed by the Word of God. It can be satisfied by turning to Me and away from the constant satisfaction of your appetite for food. []

3.24   BE TRUE TO YOUR CALLING

[| Trust in Me, My children! I love you and would not let you go astray! He who seeks Me with a sincere heart will find Me. There are many ways of finding Me. No matter what the circumstances of your life, how busy or not busy, you can find Me, for I am present to all who live in obedience and truth.

Be true to your calling, to who you are, and to who you are to become. What causes the deepest hurt to the spirit is to go against your very self by denying your being the life that is meant to be.

All life comes forth from Me. All life originates in Me and the seed will hold to the character stamped into it by wisdom, by life. No one can improve on the divine destiny planned for each Soul.

The physical component of each person is passing and can be said to be "immaterial," but it plays its part in their coming-to-be as directed by its divine author. All created life is obedient and worshipful. Only the human spirit goes in a contrary direction and causes havoc in the right ordering of things.

All supply and all peace are in Me. Through living in Me obediently and worshipfully, you receive both. People's lives are so intertwined, however, that the actions and disorders of each person's life affect other the lives of other people, with the result at times almost being chaos. But I am the master of all circumstances. I command those same chaotic circumstances to bring forth good and they do.

You can trust Me implicitly, My children! All is well! Live in joy, love, and peace in Me who am a God of joy, love, and peace! That which I have, I give. I am no niggardly giver. Come to Me to receive all: All of My life, the fulfillment of all your hopes, My eternal embrace for all eternity.

Rest in peace, be at peace. That means not letting your mind go on frenzied trips of intellectualization, down corridors of "What if?" and "Is this true?" You rest in and on Me, the bedrock of peace.

"Peace I leave with you; my peace I give you. I do not give to you as the world gives" (Jn 14:27a,b). I give you My heart. I would gladly be annihilated even, for your sake, if it would need to be – that is how much I love you and desire your good!

Rest peacefully in My love. Rest in sureness and strength, My little dove. I bid you farewell – that you fare well – and I know you will, for as a doting mother, I come along! I will never leave you nor forsake you. Be at peace in Me. []

3.25   ENTRANCE INTO THE KINGDOM

[| My children, many are the heartaches of those who put their trust in money and possessions and even of those who put their trust in other people without reference to a Higher Power. All that is of this world will disappoint you if it is used for its own sake alone, and for the sake of satisfying the self. Strange as it may seem, the self, your person, is only satisfied by denying yourself the very things that you seem to crave.

All is light and peace in the Lord, in the kingdom! You could be without any of this world's goods and still be mightily rich in spiritual treasures.

Everything you take to your heart as being precious to you lays a claim on a portion of your heart's desires. When that ownership is on a material level, your heart becomes tied to the material level. When you claim fame, honor, self-righteousness, vindication (getting even), and suchlike as your treasures, each of those things puts a noose around your heart and prevents you from rising to a higher, more selfless level.

It is too bad that the self has become so puffed up and infatuated with its reflection! It was not meant to be this way. The sting of sin has caused this and the reaction has been long and severe. The only remedy is love.

I realize that it is hard for you to give up the self and the self's desires. Do it a little at a time and steadily. Keep chipping away at the old block, guided by the grace I give you and in My strength. In that manner, you surely will be victorious.

Look to Me that your face may be radiant with joy!

Look to Me as the Father that I am:

Lord of Life, yes, but Nurturer of Life most of all.

The life of the Spirit within you must be given a chance to grow! When you are united with Me you receive nourishment and grow to become like Me. Giving up selfing desires is a freeing up, not a hardship as it first appears to be.

Come into the freedom that I would give you! In coming into freedom from self, you come into Me, the Father of all life. Then you truly have life and have it abundantly! Follow the way that Jesus taught, in faith, trust, and blind obedience. *"[B]lessed are those who have not seen and yet have believed"* (Jn 20:29b). Blest are you, and will you be, for your believing! Trust Me! Come! |]

3.26   I WILL GUIDE AND FEED YOU

[| My people, forget not the past, what I have done for you. I brought you out of the land of Egypt. ("Egypt" is the smelting pot of all the devious ways and entrapments of the world, the flesh, and the senses.) All have been or still are there.

I have called you out of Egypt! Have you heard Me? Do you hear Me? I call you to come with Me to a land flowing with milk and honey! It may take a while to get there. You may have to make many laps around the mountain – lessons may need to be repeated many times till you are pliable and obedient enough to learn.

As Moses guided his people under My command and direction, I guide you by My Holy Spirit. I feed you with manna in the desert, with bread from heaven.

Turn to Me, My people, and live! Let Me carry you over the rough spots and, in the searing heat of the day, let Me be your shield. I will protect you and cover you with the hovering wings of the Spirit. []

3.27 THE SPIRITUAL EVER GUIDING

[| My child, bless you! I love you! I hold you close! I am closer to you than your very self although you cannot be aware of that. Your life and stance during this earthly life must be one of faith, not of physical certainty such as your body person and your natural mind crave for. I know it seems to you that it is going the long way around to try to introduce spiritual truths through lessons and examples in the physical, but, as I have told you before, you would be unable to understand any other way.

Many are the worries of those who live for the pleasures of the world. They have a constant headache, nothing can satisfy them. Do not be quick to judge, however. Never judge. There are those people who have an ample supply and even an oversupply of this world's goods, who seem genuinely happy. *They may be.*

Do not presume to judge that people have the heart of a hoarder and that, "Surely, they are not happy, because how could they be happy when they live for their worldly wealth?"

Do you know the heart of man? (Do you know your own heart?) There are those of My servants whom life sets in the way of wealth. That does not make them "bad." It is in the attitude of the heart where the difference lies. Some people can live in comparative luxury without undue attachment. Others live with almost nothing and are unduly attached to the nothing that they do have.

Leave the judging, guiding, and discipline to Me. Attend to your duties and the call of the Spirit within you. I would have you be who and what you are meant to be. Live in My love. Live in My love. Let love so permeate your mind, spirit, and body that you become one with it. I would have you be loved, and how are you to receive if you do not take love into yourself?

Be patient with yourself, my child, and with others! All work together in marvelous divine order, despite appearances to the contrary. My Spirit works in the spirit, quietly, unobtrusively, surely, and steadily, fashioning My creation. each of you, into masterpieces. You are, you become, "pieces of your master," identical duplicates that somehow become the real thing, for those who are open to My Spirit becomes so imbued with It that the receiver and the gift become merged into one.

This may sound complicated to you, but it is not. Simply love and be open to love. Open your heart to all, even to that neighbor who has everything and whom you find yourself envying. Your openness may be what that individual needs as the next lesson and help as they search to find the meaning of life.

Gratitude consecrates your ownership of material gifts (which come from Me) and gratitude, in turn, may lead you to pass those gifts on to someone else. What it all comes down to is peace. Whether you have much or little, try to let it be immaterial to you. What counts is that you have My love! You have the life I have given you. You have the potential and possibility of living that life in joy and peace. You have Me as your God and Father. I would be your peace. May I indwell even your material goods?

Is it not My trees, My flowers, My grass that you see around you in nature?

Is it not My mountains, My rock, My sand, My earth upon which you walk?

From whence do you get the material to make your plastics, fine veneer, and bricks?

At what point does the basic ownership change?

Are not your furniture, your house, your car, and your clothing, gifts from the Giver?

Do you see how I ask that I may dwell in your material possessions? I ask that I may dwell in them by consciousness on your part that they are gifted to you by Me, with consequent swelling up of gratitude in your heart ever more and more as the truth of that sinks in and takes root in your being.

Gratitude blesses both the receiver and the giver. It magnifies your heart and opens the way for peace. In this way, material possessions can be a pathway upon which I can bring you to Me. Bless you, and your possessions! I know that you need all these things and in love, I bring them to you and hold them in being.

Is there a little nudge in your heart saying, "Perhaps I do not need all these things?" I leave that up to you. I bid you carry love in your heart and let it have its way.

Bless you, My child! I lay My hands in benediction upon you and in response to your desire, bless your loved ones and your world. |]

3.28   COMING TO BE, TOGETHER!

[| My people, My heart goes out to you! If only you could see by faith your marvelous coming-to-be that is coming to be!

You are all tied together spiritually, for you are all My children. You all have the One Life within you. Habits, entanglements, weaknesses, and enticements that have been passed along from generation to generation are now yours to do battle with. By your victory over these entanglements, you cut the chain that binds your forebears. Related as you are by family ties, and family roots, what affects one must affect all. "No man is an island." You sink or swim together.

If you wish to bring healing to those who have gone before, bless them! Blessing magnifies goodness. There is only so much "room" in each person. As you magnify the goodness in others by blessing them, you at the same time diminish the strength and power of their weaknesses, until finally that cord of weakness that binds them snaps and they are free, as a rubber band flies away when it breaks. I am a God of blessing and nothing makes Me happier than when that blessing can flow out in abundance!

Do not worry about those you are concerned about. Worry denotes a lack of faith and lack of trust. Carry them in your heart – which is what you do when you open yourself to them in love and blessing – and you can rest assured that healing, blessing, and freedom are coming to be for them and, as a consequence, for yourself and your family, as well.

This is one of the laws of the spiritual kingdom about your receiving My love and blessing: Since all of you are united by your common family bonds and as members of the one great human family, the spiritual attitudes of one affect the others to their detriment or good. You may ask, "How, then, can full freedom and peace ever come to be? Look at the many who do not love and bless."

I look at the ones who do bless. It would be wise for you to do likewise, for by giving credit to the non-blessing, you strengthen it, in a way. Love is stronger than all else. One person who loves and blesses covers the thousand who do not bless. I motivate your thoughts and movements and what will be, will come to be. Trust Me to complete what I have begun. What a marvelous divine plan it is!

Will you not open your heart to Me that I may work through you, also? Come to Me that you may be healed, and I will transmit healing and life to you and through you. Blessings, My child, My people! []

Father God, as we consecrate our families to You, I ask that Souls who are still bound in some way will be released and that their release will in turn break the bonds that bind present-day members of our families. Thank You!

CHAPTER 4

BE AT PEACE

4.1   THE LITTLE LOST LAMB

A little lost lamb scrambles here and there, not knowing where to go. Being little, it does not know its master very well yet. As the master approaches, the lamb is afraid and runs further, getting into more difficulty. The master speaks and points out the way, but the lamb does not understand.

The little lamb feels alone and frightened and if it could put its feelings into words it would say: "Why does this have to happen to me? Why can't I be safe in the fold like the rest of the sheep are? Why do I need to suffer the hurts of sliding and falling, of being pricked and torn by brambles? Who can help me? Who can get me out of this mess?"

The master approaches and gently takes hold of the frightened lamb; but it is afraid, for it does not know who it can trust. The master says over and over in a gentle, reassuring voice: "I love you! Do not be afraid. It is I, your master. Come to Me and I will carry you. I will bring you to safety."

It is not until the lamb is caught fast in the brambles, unable to help itself, or perhaps is standing helplessly on a narrow precipice and no longer able to go in any direction, that it finally allows the master to pick it up. The master swabs its wounds, gives it a drink of water, and carries it to safety in the security of the fold. There it receives daily ministration from the master and can pasture in delight.

4.2 A GUIDE FOR THE WAY

[| My child, you seem to think there is constant activity in My person, in My mind, but for the most part, all is calm, free, and unhindered in My being. I Am: It is as simple as that and because I Am Who I Am, I love, I care. I uplift you, rejoice with you, and suffer with you. Your temporal concerns are to a certain extent also My concerns, as those things are a necessary part of your life now. Just do not let those concerns become so all-encompassing that they distract you from the real meaning of life.

Live in peace. I give you My peace. I and My gift are one. If you have true peace you know that I am with you. I do not give you only "the shirt off My back," as is considered the extreme of neighborliness on earth. I give you Myself. If you have patience, joy, peace, love, humility, generosity, compassion, and a caring heart, you have partaken of Me. My Will is that you be happy, and to ensure that, I give you happiness itself, My very self.

Do you wonder why people go astray? Everyone needs a companion. Alone you will not make it. I am the unseen companion to all as they try their best to make the grade. Should you fall to the side, I do not judge or condemn. I am here to pick you up and to carry you, if necessary. Everyone needs to be carried at one time or another.

In particular, I am here to carry you over the bridge into eternity. Do not be afraid! This is reality and will not change or go away. My being with you, upholding you, interceding for you is the bedrock of love that you can count on and stand firm on. Challenge the fear that is in your heart and command it to desist from enslaving you! It has no place in your heart. You have given Me your heart, so send fear on its way into the nothingness from whence it came.

You wonder about the discomfort that you have to quite an extent. That, too, has a purpose. It is one of the fine chisels that is shaping you into perfection. It is My faithful servant, reminding you not to put stock in today and the activity of the moment. Look to the larger view: obedience to My will.

Yes, My child, I promise to save you. I have already saved you.

Cling to that promise and assurance! The way to cling to it is by exercising your faith. Each separate aspiration of faith is like the exercise of a muscle. It is the means of strengthening that faith. So, in reality, doubts that arise and need to constantly be put down by faith are occasions for strengthening.

Living a life of faith is not a static thing. Affirming your faith continuously – which you need to do as you live this earthly life – is comparable to the breathing that is necessary to keep your physical life going. You do not worry about whether your life will be continued from moment to moment by breathing. It will be. In the same way, do not worry whether your spiritual life will be sustained by your faith. It is in the supernatural order for your faith to keep pulsating (faith is alive) just like for your breathing to continue in the natural order. Breathing ends when you pass from this world into life. Faith will no longer be needed then either.

Grace is given to you and all as you need it. It is unwise to look ahead to all the tomorrows and carry those burdens and responsibilities today. Banish immediately every shadow of worry about whether you will have enough spiritual strength. Strength is given on the day of battle. A reaper receives his strength as he cuts the grain.

The main thing is, do not fear! Giving way to fear is one of the most common ways for the father of lies to gain entrance to your mind and spirit. Notice: You give the entrance.

All things are set up in marvelous divine order! Could you expect anything less of a God who has put such marvelous divine order into every atom and molecule of the visible world? Let nature be an assurance for you that all is well. Relax into the peace of My heart, child. Rest in Me without worry. []

4.3   LET GO AND LET GOD

Lord, I hunger for a word from You.
[| My word is in the Bible, My child, truly My word, though, indeed, written in the words of men. And I speak from the depths of your

heart, words of calm, an invitation to trust. *"[I]n quietness and trust is your strength"* (Is 30:15c).

The more you worry about being free from fear and anxiety, the harder it is to shake it. "Let go and let God." Your part is to trust and believe that all is well, that I have all things and all circumstances in My hands.

My supply supplies when you are lacking.

My healing unction soothes where you are hurting.

My grace supplies nourishment for growth and My love sustains you.

Your existence is proof of My love, for only love is creative and nourishing. Evil is intent only upon tearing down and destroying. Relax! Think of it, that as you breathe, you breathe peace.

My peace fills the whole world. What in this life can be so terrible as to be a good reason for despondency?

My life is within you. Is a headache so bad?

I love you! Does rejection by another merit depression?

I am with you always. Do not let passing episodes of life pull down your spirit for you are meant to soar above worries and trifles on the wings of faith and trust. Bless you, My child! []

4.4   BLESSINGS AND LOVE

[| My child, I bless you at the beginning of this New Year and, since My actions and thoughts are eternal, this blessing is forever active. This blessing has existed for all eternity, awaiting the time that you and others would be sufficiently open to receive it.

All the desires that people have ever had, all put together, do not begin to match the desire of My heart for each person's happiness and well-being! Well-being means "being where all is well," and where that is, is in My love. How I desire that you come to know, and come into, My love!

Be not anxious about the future. It is provided for. Everything is provided in My love. *"But seek first his kingdom and his righteousness, and all these things will be given to you as well"* (Mt 6:33). I leave you in My love, or rather, I hold you in My love. I know you cannot always keep that in mind but that does not change the truth of the keeping power of My love. You are safe and secure! You are loved by Me!

Calm the anxiety that eats at your heart and destroys your peace. Anxiety is like a cloud of smoke that enters a sunlit room and takes away the sparkle, beauty, and brightness that is there. Allowing darkness to enter diminishes the light.

Leave all in My hands. I already know and am directing how things will work out in your current situation. Your part is to trust and to take the next step when it is time for that step. If a blind person were to fear that there is no floor ahead of him to walk on, he would be anxious and fearful all the time! How foolish of that blind person not to trust his sighted companion who gives the assurance that the way is safe!

I, your companion – well-sighted and trustworthy – give you My assurance that all is well on the road ahead. I am walking with you to lead you on the way. Walk by faith, not by sight. Walking in faith is walking in the light! Your faith gives you sight, and light, for the next step and that is all that is necessary.

Bless you, My child! Bless your family, your dear ones, your city, our world! Peace be with you! []

4.5   REFLECTIONS

I don't need to hold anxiously onto life, physical or spiritual.
God is life. Life holds me and I can just relax and be held.
I stay in being, without any effort on my part.
I don't need to anxiously search for or hang onto the truth.
God is truth. Truth holds me and I can relax in it.
I am safe and secure in life, in truth, in God.

I do not even have the right to decide whether or not I like who I am – whether or not to accept my identity. This *is* who I am. No choice is possible. God made me and He is happy in who I am! There is no reason for me to wonder whether or not I am OK because I am! God made me OK and I am!

I continue to be who God made me. What I choose to do and how open I am to God or other people has nothing to do with the basic person of who I am. Any mistakes I make, wrong choices because of wrong judgment, do not affect my worth or being. I am who I am: a child of God, beloved of the Father.

God does not change. I am brought forth in love from the Bosom of God. That love permeates my being – indeed, it keeps me in being – and never changes. I do not need to grasp and cry and cling to love. Love holds me and I can rest in it, in God. Resting in love, I can leave everything in God's hands: the effects of past experiences, my being in the present and my continuing to be as days go by. I am safe, secure, and loved! I am me and I rest in God. I continue in being without any effort or grasping needed on my part.

As I ponder what it may be like to leave my mortal body, I do not need to be prepared to reach out frantically to take hold of something, to take hold of God, to be safe. I am now resting in God and at death can just peacefully continue resting in Him. He is my Rock, the very Substance of my being. The only way for me to cease to be and to be safe would be for God to cease to be.

Bless you, my Lord, my rock, my God!

4.6   ENTRUST ALL TO ME

[| My child, I bless you as you pray for others and bless those others through you. Then, also, I bless you from within them, through the gratitude in the spirit of those you have prayed for. Those who are open to the Spirit make possible the spreading of the joy and peace of the Spirit to others. Human channels are an efficient way to reach My hurting and despondent children for the contact takes place through a world they are familiar with.

Your hurting and aching-heart problems are in My heart, too, for our hearts are united. All who have recourse to Me appeal to My love and I take them into My heart, into My love. My just being with you is love. No words need to be spoken. Rest in My love! Drink in love in large draughts, it is a healing potion.

Be at peace, My child! You must choose peace and joy as you do love and faith. I give you the desire and the strength to do so.

You are troubled and anxious about many things. Only one thing is necessary: Live in love and trust. Pay no mind to the clamor of voices urging you to fear, to rush, to doubt. Rest in My love. You can rest in Me even as you are engaged in activities. Do not fear! I am with you on all days and at every moment. When you take a moment to affirm your belief in My love and care, it creates a strong connection so I can help you more. []

Lord, what are those people doing wrong who cry out to You for help and strength, but do not seem to receive an answer?

[| They look for an answer in human terms, the particular answer they have in mind. That blinds them and somewhat closes them off to what I have to give them. They pray anxiously and anxiety fills their minds and hearts so they do not have room for trust and joy.

When you wish blessings for all of your brothers and sisters, you are helping to soften and open their hearts to goodness, love, and peace. The time will come that they will begin to see and understand. I do not worry about them. I bid you entrust them to Me and not worry. *"And we know that in all things God works for the good of those who love him"* (Rom 8:28a).

My child, place your family and friends, your worries and cares, and your very well-being in My care. You do not need to hold yourself, to see to your existence or well-being as if you were holding yourself in a net to keep from disintegrating.

I am your wholeness and your integrity. Rest in Me. Resting in Me is not like setting down solid but like floating. I support you inside and outside, above and below, front and back. You are safe and secure in My love. I love you into being every moment, eternally. Love sustains you. Love holds you and loves you as you are. []

4.7   JOY IS POSSIBLE

[| My child, bless you! My opening with blessing so often is a sign of the eternal blessing I give to you, to all. Your very being is a blessing, even if for a time you must be in pain and misery. There can be joy in your being even when you are experiencing pain, for My presence is joy.

I am with you and in you so completely that what you experience, I experience. Coming to the knowledge of this shared communion is the way to fly with eagle wings above misfortune. It prevents the suffering from penetrating the core of your being.

Suffering is a state of being and you have the choice whether or not to let it affect your being. When you joyfully accept inevitable suffering for the sake of love, it increases, rather than decreases, your joy.

Worry denotes weakness of character. Anxiety is worry. Once you are certain that a given path of action is in My Will, do not allow worry and anxiety to accompany you. I am here to accompany you. *"Anyone who loves me, will be true to my word and my Father will love him; we will come to him and make our dwelling place with him"* (Jn 14:23). You do not need to be worthy for us to come, you need but be willing. |]

Lord, I desire to be united with You. I love You!

[| You do not need to try hard to be united with Me. Just will it and you are united, for that is all it takes. In "being" there is giving and receiving. The giving is there, present always in all of space and time. I fill the whole earth eternally. (Eternally is not just from now on, forever. It is from forever, forever.) As you become open to receiving, whether in the present moment or as you advert to time in the past, My giving presence fills you.

Do not feel that you are leaving Me as you rise from the place and time of prayer. Prayer is communion with Me and I am in communion with you at all times and places. All it takes is for you to be open to that communion. Practice this. Everything takes growth even in the spirit world.

The physical world is a sign and symbol of the realities of the spiritual world. As the earth envelops, nourishes, and upholds you, it is a large, direct sign and symbol of My all-encompassing love and keeping-in-being of all things.

I hold you tenderly, My child, as the air holds a butterfly. You are free, yet supported by Me. I pray that you fly on wings of love, My pretty one! How can I express My love strongly enough? I must just let it be and keep you in being in it. We have all eternity to celebrate our being together! Just be in Me. I uphold you.

Many are the worries of those who feel they must take charge of their life.

Zero are the worries of those who truly trust in Me.

You can trust Me for everything. It is trust that brings it into being for trust is "believing in." Just be in Me and you are safe and free! As you are in Me, you are at the same time in yourself and loving yourself to health and wholeness. []

Father, I believe in You and trust You. Please dissolve the worries that try to clench my body and stultify my mind.

[] Do not worry about what the future will bring. The "future" is not an ogre carrying grisly events in his hands. The future is coming to pass of the events and lessons that I have ordained for you. When you *picture* what the future may bring, you affect those events in their coming-to-be. For this reason, you must have holy desires that are attuned to My Will for you. []

[] (Jesus:) I know what it is like for you as you live this life. I have told you before, and I want you to ponder the fact, that my life was as yours is. I lived and thought things through with the human mind that I took on in becoming a man. I became man, identifying with all mankind, one with all of you. []

4.8   YOU EXIST IN ME

[] My child, be still and know that I am God. Be still and know My love. Then you will know, even as you are known.

"Fear not, for I have redeemed you; I have summoned you by name; you are mine" (Is 43:1b). I hold you securely in My arms. You are safe from all danger and darkness and emptiness. There is no other place than in Me. I am all-existence. I am Safety.

If you do not realize My love and the safety that I give you, it is only because you have blinders on, as a child held in their mother's arms does not see their mother if they have a blanket over their head. I assure you, I carry you and walk with you at all times and nothing can change that. It is a fact of life.

As your body carries your person, the real you, so I carry you. I am your life. You cannot separate yourself from yourself. Even so, you cannot separate yourself from Me even if you tried. All you can do is put a blanket over your head and plug your ears to not "see" or "hear" Me.

All exist in Me. When you care about others and desire that they come into truth and love, you help them "see" and "hear" a little bit more. People are touched from within by your caring even when they are not close to you physically, even when they do not know you and do not know that you care.

I desire that you release your anxiety into My hands once and for all. You have struggled under its burden for a long time. It has been a weight on My shoulders, too, to see you struggling and suffering. Reach out and take hold of life! When you reach out in faith, with one-hundred-percent trust in My love, you at the same time let go of the anxiety you are holding onto and it drops away into the nothingness from whence it came.

All that is not of Me is nothingness. It can be compared to mathematical calculations that make use of minus numbers, in which someone has a certain amount and then takes "nothing" away from it. That cannot be done.

The nothingness of anxiety cannot take away the peacefulness that is at the center of your being, that is I, your God, the center of your life, but anxiety can disturb you so much that you are unable to be aware of Me and unable to rest in the peacefulness that I give you.

Turn to Me within the core of your being. I am present. I am waiting. My heart is open! Come into the truth and the truth will set you free! []

4.9   MADE IN MY IMAGE

[| Do not fear, My child, I am here eternally, supporting you and loving you as well as guiding you if you will have Me.

How glad I am that I can "pitch My tent" with you! Open your heart to Me so that you may find health, rest, and strength. I am with you at all times and in all places, whether in the present physical state or as you "travel" to another time or place, or state of being in your imagination. You are always here, now. I am with you, so no matter what experience or element comes up in your life, you are not alone in it. I am with you in your dream life just as much as in the physical life you are living.

I love you! I love everyone! I hold all of you in the utmost love. You are being of My being. You *are,* in Me, a part of My very self. Can a God despise Himself? You are loved, as I love Myself. In this way, you are to be a copy of Me, to be My image, that you love others as you love yourself. Not only do you have My life within you. You have My love within you so you may love as I love.

When all things are as they should be, this is the case. However, you are hindered because of the disastrous effects that sin and pride have on your world and your very being. You may find it hard to recognize or realize My presence in any way at all.

It may seem impossible to you that anyone would be able to lead all people to a sense of My presence, for each of them to have goodness in their heart and love for themselves and others. To accomplish this is a great task and a great challenge, but I am God and I set Myself to this task with all the love at My disposal.

I am bringing you home to My arms, to My love, My people! I am in all of life. You cannot escape My love, grace, and care for I am in each and all of your fellow human beings. My love, grace, and care

97

are going out to you through those many channels at the same time that you are resting in life within yourself. The dark smoke screens of self-pity, guilt, anxiety, pettiness, materialism, and negativity must give way to love, for love conquers all.

Love is all. It is all being.

Your true home, your true resting place, is love.

You were made for Me, for love,

And restless will you be until you rest in Me.

Rest in Me, My children, without worry as to what you are to eat and wear, without concern as to whether you are safe. You are loved and thus your needs are supplied. You are safe.

Love others and let them love you. Love Me and let Me love you and you will see that all things work together for good. Spiritual needs and spiritual growth take precedence over the material, however, so if and when you feel that you are short on the material side, know that a greater spiritual good is being worked out.

Do not worry about how everything is getting worked out. It is! Trust and be not afraid. Love and be not afraid. Love and be loved. I am your God, your Lord. It is I. Peace! []

4.10   TURN TO ME FOR STRENGTH

[| My child, you do not need to have all the answers. Rest in Me. Excessive searching for answers that will satisfy your mind causes unrest. Rest in Me and on Me as the bedrock of truth. What to believe? Turn to My word and let it sink in and settle your thoughts upon the groundwork of love.

Rest in My love. Let the certainty of being loved continue to affect a release from anxiety, a strand at a time. As anxiety dissipates, you will at the same time be strengthened in your determination to follow Me and to live in love, peace, and freedom.

There will be no peace and freedom for one who is a slave of self, of anxiety, of hunger that originates in the body. Only the satisfaction of your Soul hunger will truly satisfy you in body, mind, and spirit.

Come to Me that you may be filled!

Come to Me that you may have the fullness of life!

When you are lacking in strength come to Me.

When your willpower is weak in saying "No" to the constant feeding of your appetite, come to Me.

You have the strength within you to order the natural appetites of your body, for I reside within you. I am residing in Heaven, though, so you have all the power and backing of Heaven within you. It is for you to open yourself to that strength by being willing. You must choose and do the action of curbing your appetite and saying no to selfish instincts, and in so doing the power of Heaven will back you up. Do all in and love and you are then in contact with love, the unconquerable force. []

4.11   YOUR SECURITY IS IN ME

[| My people, how I long to hold you close and tell you of My love! How I long that you hold Me close and tell Me of your love!

Do you think anything good can be that is not somehow present within Me, in My life? The joy and peacefulness that you feel when you hold your loved ones and they hold you is a mirrored casting of My joy as I hold you in love and you hold Me.

All in due time. All will come to be that is ordained to come to pass. Your part is to be patient and open and to wait and see what is to come to pass. It is not your part to decide what and when. This is not to say that you do not desire those things to come to be that eventually do. I place those desires within you and bring about their fruition in your world, in your life.

Relax, My child! All is light, joy, and peace in the Lord! There is no rush, no urgent need. There is plenty of time for all to come to be that must and should. The main thing is for you to grow in love. What good will a mountain of learning be for you if you do not have sufficient love with which to apply the knowledge? *"Whoever who has ears to hear, let them hear!"* (Mk 4:9).

It is I, the Lord your God, who speak.

I speak with authority, for the authority is Mine.

I speak with love, for I have love sufficient to fill this world many times over and a thousand worlds besides.

My love keeps you in being. You are held in love in Me. Could you be any safer? Could you find a better place to be? There is no other place except the state of denial of My love, of denying love's entrance into one's life and being. What a sad lot! What a sad existence! []

4.12   STAY ON THE PATH

[| My child, bless you and everyone! I always have all in mind and each person in mind. You *are,* in My eternal mind. I am so happy to be your God, your Father, your Mother, your Brother, your All! That makes it all worthwhile that I can be to you what you need Me to be.

Call Me in your every need. I am here to fill that need, to fulfill your every desire. Desire peace and peace will come (you have many worries to discard and much discord to bring into harmony before you can realize that peace, though). Desire well-being and the giving of good gifts to others and that will come to be.

Realize, though, that should you desire ill, that desire brings the ill into the sphere of time. The evil that set up shop in the world is present and waiting to be allowed into the sphere of people's lives. It is evil that is adorned as a goddess and bedecked to represent itself as being good. Do not be fooled by it! Do you not feel that tug of warning in your heart, "Maybe I shouldn't do this particular thing? What might come of it"?

My people, I cry out to you all day and night: Beware of the evil one! Be on guard against his wiles! He is the enemy of your Soul, of your very life. Do not trifle with him even in the smallest matter for when you do, you become stuck as happened in the story of the "tar baby." We are speaking of danger to your very life. Be wary and avoid the evil one like you would avoid a plague!

"But," you say, "how can we recognize the enemy in all his disguises, especially when he attempts to enter through our innermost feelings and even through people whom we feel we can trust?" *Be watchful for anything that will disturb your peacefulness:* That is the danger signal. When you rest in Me you rest in peace, so to take you away from Me the enemy must take you out of peacefulness.

It takes practice to recognize readily when your peacefulness is disturbed, but everyone can tell when their peacefulness is nearly gone. That is the time to stop short and turn around on the path you are on before you have gone so far that you cannot find your way back. However, even if you should find yourself lost, do not give up hope. I have vanguards out all over and direct one of them to assist you when you turn for help. Everything fits together so marvelously in My plan!

You fit into My plan. I "see" you with Me in an eternity of happiness. During your life, you are making choices that lead you towards that happiness or away from it. I know that your heart seeks happiness, for I am the maker of your heart. I realize, also, that the enemy deludes you and your mind deludes you into thinking that happiness is found on the primrose path of self. []
[| (Jesus:) You cannot find happiness in yourself. The only pathway to happiness is the path of "self-fulfillment through self-giving," you have my promise and assurance of that. It is the path I trod and I came over to the other side, to the right hand of the Father. I await you with joyful expectations! []

4.13   LET ME LEAD YOU

[| My child, tenderly I call your name. Tenderly I give you My love. Tenderly I keep you in being. I keep all in being – all people, all creation – tenderly. I allow each and all to be as they choose to be. That is the gift of free will I have given you.

I keep each and all in being, the "righteous" as well as the "unrighteous." I do not walk on the flowers. I respect your feelings and desires and make Myself available to fulfill your desires. Nothing outside of Me will satisfy. Within Me, created things bring satisfaction for they speak of Me and point the way to Me.

Rest not in your human wisdom. Do not try to be a guide unto yourself. Be open to whatever I would send you. Be open to change, to new ideas, and unexpected circumstances. Keep yourself prepared to meet unforeseen circumstances by staying attuned to My will and united with Me. Do your best humanly, then you will have no regrets and self-accusation of not having done enough.

I lead you in all at all times. If you have not yet had an opportunity to do a certain task that you feel you are meant to do, just trust that it has not yet been the right time. Everything will work out in due time. However things will be, they will be. There is no use carrying a sense of apprehension about the future or trying to figure out answers now to problems that have not yet arisen, and which may never arise.

Trust and believe! Walk with faith and with an ever-growing awareness of My presence in all, working for the good in all, loving all, loving you. I love you dearly and hold you to My heart tenderly. All is working out! Do not fear, do not worry. Do not let yourself be fearful about the future. I am your future. I take care of My own.

(Singing:) "Sleep, My child, may peace attend thee, all through the night! Peace, My child, for love attends thee, all through the day!" Can I have a smile? []

4.14   I SUPPLY YOUR TRUE NEEDS

[| My child, I cherish you! The tenderness you feel towards a sweet, helpless, tender infant is a small sampling of how I feel toward you. But, just as the infant must be allowed to move around freely to learn about their surroundings, so it is in the spiritual world. "Receiving the Spirit" is akin to a baby's opening their eyes for the first time after birth. You have so much to learn. All in due time.

I know you have been struggling with your feelings. Feelings of insecurity, anxiety, sadness, and searching can arise as a direct result of being tired, having a cold, or some such. Expect to have feelings like this. They are a part of your lot as a human being still bound by earthly life. It will not always be this way, however. All things of earth will pass away. Seek for that which does not pass away.

Do not get uptight about receiving insight and understanding from Me. You have done it so many times! Always keep in mind that it is I who bring this about, not you. What could you do on your own in coming to an understanding of spiritual truths?

When you rest in Me and rely on Me you are safe and will have your needs supplied. Outer circumstances may seem to belie that you are safe, but know and understand that safety is within where you dwell with Me and Me with you in the innermost being of your heart. Nothing can touch you there, for it is an enclosed sanctuary, a holy place, My heart.

It may appear to you that you are very much in need and your natural person may cry out, "My God, why have You forsaken me? Did You not promise to supply all my needs?"

What are your true needs? They are the needs of your inner person, of your Soul, for that is who you are. Only as something outer will augment and help fill out the good for your inner being is it supplied. This is for those who truly desire to come into union with Me, for those who are searching to come to know the true meaning of life.

All receive the call to enter upon this search but many do not heed it and continue to live their lives trapped by all the trappings of the physical world: Souls trapped within bodies. Your destiny is that you are meant to be free Souls, free in My love and joy and peace. Your bodies are to be servants to your inner person.

Everything is already worked out in Me. I see not only the present but also that which is coming to be and, together, we bring it about. Be a creature and let Me be God. I hold you tenderly in love and have the most special regard for your welfare. I will see that you do not "dash your foot against a stone," if you let Me. []

4.15　LET ME BE KING

[| My child, I bless you! No matter what happens in your life or the lives of those around you, continue to trust. Believe! I allow nothing that will be to the eternal detriment of the Souls of My precious children. You know Me well enough that you can trust that. Having some foundation beliefs like this helps you greatly in dealing with the storms of life. All is tranquility and peace in My heart. By walking in My Love, you can escape the frenzy of the world.

Stay attuned to your body. Read the signs it gives you as to whether you are pushing yourself too much or letting anxiety set in. You are one unit of body, mind, and spirit. If you let anxiety take hold in your mind it will be in your body and spirit, as well. You have learned much about spirit forces already. Continue to learn through practical experience. If you can come to have a mindset that refuses to allow anxiety and other negative entities to reside within you, the larger part of the battle is already won.

Your being is your home, your property, your life. Set up the rules that will govern that home. You would not allow decrepit characters to sit in your kitchen or living room insulting you, draining your energy, and messing things up, would you? Enough said.

I desire to be king of your home, both your heart-soul-body home and your physical home. Even though you do not see Me with your physical eyes, you can see Me with the eyes of faith. By My grace which is always offered and available for you to take, see Me as Lord and King in your home, actually present and living here just as you and your family are living here.

I am present, living in your home. You just need to see and believe that, acknowledge My presence, and bless Me for it. Blessing returns blessing. Faith brings its just reward. Give to Me so I can give to you.

Believe the good news: I am not distant! I am present within you and around you. You cannot escape My presence, although materialism, living for the natural, insulates you and prevents you from being aware of Me.

My precious lamb, let Me hold you close to My heart! I love you so much! All is well. I am with you this moment, today, tomorrow, yesterday, and forever! Rejoice and be glad! This is the day that I have made! []

4.16   BE YOURSELF IN ME

[| My child, I bless you! You are My child, and in a way, also the child of all for you come from the human family. No human being is more, or less, important than any other human being. You are each and all made in My image. If you did not somehow image (reflect) Me, you could not be, for "all that is" comes from My being, from My fullness. *"Of his fullness we have all had a share—love following upon love."* (Jn 1:16).

Each of you can help the next person and can receive My fullness in a fuller way by being faithful to what I have called you to be. Be who you are meant to be. Remember the lesson about the baby's breath (flower), that if it were to strive to be a rose it certainly could not do so, and by such vain striving, it would mar the beauty it was meant to have.

You come to be who you are meant to be by resting, by being, in Me. Growth comes naturally from Me, for I am life. There is no growth where there is no life.

By entrusting Me with your life and all your affairs, you will be kept free from anxiety. You have heard of the many ill effects that anxiety can have on the mind and body. Just as great. or even more so, are the detrimental effects anxiety has on your spirit. It robs you of the fullness and joy of life because it chokes it off. Fight anxiety and stay clear of it as you would of a plague!

Rest in Me, not in anxious thoughts.

Rest in Me, thus you will have health in Soul, mind, and body.
Live each day to the fullest.
Drink in the joy that is present and offered to you.
Absorb the love coming to you from Me and all.

Love you receive from others is truly their love for you, even though it originates from Me. People who love have taken in My love and made it their own. They have given assent to the love. You can trust in the love that people have for you. If it truly is love, it will hold up, for love is eternal, never-ending.

Love that does not hold up is based merely on human foundations and is not love. Do not, however, consider the human element as the sign or strength of someone's love for you. The basic element of love is in and of the spirit. Love is My Spirit indwelling you and uniting all in the unity of love.

Love makes life worth living, for love is life. Do not be afraid to receive love from others and do not be afraid to give love. Other people feel just as vulnerable as you do, child. Coming to know of your great need for love, understanding, and acceptance helps you to know others better, for you all share a common humanity, a common creaturehood.

I am so happy to be your God, to be able to fill your need for love! This is My life, to love you! You will find your life in loving Me, yourself, and your neighbor. No fear, only love. No doubt of My love, only full trusting with all your heart, mind, and Soul: thus, you will be free, happy, and fulfilled.

I love you, My child: You and you and you! All! I hold you in My heart in tender love! Drink in love! Rest. Be at peace. |]

4.17   ONE DAY AT A TIME

[| Concentrate on today, the present moment. Letting your mind sweep ahead to take in all the situations that might come about and all the tasks that need to be done on other days is too overwhelming for your mind, body, and spirit. Your spirit is meant to soar on wings of gladness, free and unencumbered, as does the butterfly on a bright, sunny day.

"*Each day has enough trouble of its own* (Mt 6:34b). It takes practice to learn to leave the future in the future and the past in the past, but for the sake of the kingdom learn quickly to do that. The kingdom of God is now. "*...now is the day of salvation"* (2 Cor 6:2c). I carry the past, the future, and the present moment in My heart. I bring about the present moment and it is ordained that you are to live your earthly life at this moment.

Your body *must be* in the present moment. Your mind is so constituted, however, that it can go back into the past through memory or ahead into the future by conjecture. Wherever the mind travels in thought, it brings that place, that moment, into the present for the whole person. The experience is perceived in spirit and mind but affects the whole person: spirit, mind, and body.

The past is already set and done. You have experiences that you can remember. Whatever you bring to mind from the past becomes present for you. For the sake of the health of your body and peace of mind, I adjure (strongly direct) you to dip only into the good and beautiful, into the healing experiences you have had. Whatever you hold onto in mind and heart becomes "eternal," so to speak. Who wants to have eternal suffering, hurt, and guilt weighing them down?

Looking with speculation into the future can be even worse than looking back at the past if your heart and mind are not focused on Me. There are no set experiences in the future. When looking ahead, the mind is like an open book or open vessel. Anything can pour into it: wild speculation about terrible disasters, fear of failure, anxiety, pessimism.

No, do not look to the future with speculation and anxiety, but with joy and expectation! Fill your heart with the joy and expectation of My glorious promises, then that is what you will see in the future, and will be blessed in heart, mind, spirit, and body.

You live in Me, hence you live in My word if you so choose. My word is love, peace, joy, forgiveness, hope; happy expectations for the past, the present, and the future. Your total existence – past, present, and future – is secure in Me. I hold you completely and eternally in love. All is well in the past, in the present, and in the future. Your existence is secure.

You will always be in Me. You are safe, secure, and loved for you are My child. From all eternity I hold you in My heart. You are safe, secure, and loved! Eternal blessings! []

4.18   THE MANY FACES OF FEAR

[| *"But when he, the Spirit of truth, comes, he will guide you into all truth"* (16:13a). My child, yes, I will guide you into all truth by My Spirit. []

I was feeling unsure about writing anything.

[| My child, when you are to write, I will fill your mind with those thoughts that you are to receive so it would be difficult for you to turn your mind to other thoughts. Center your mind on Me, be at peace, and receive. Go ahead, confident and unafraid.

Fear is the strongest and the sneakiest of the dark spirits, although pride plays a close second. On your own, it would be impossible for you to detect fear in all its forms and attachments and it would be even more impossible for you to rid yourself of it. Attempting to do that on your own would be like trying to lift yourself by your bootstraps or by your elbows.

A particular fear may seem to you to be very legitimate, but every fear does the same lethal damage. Breathe fear long enough and your whole being will suffer: your body, mind, and spirit.

One form of fear is being afraid that one is "not good enough." Right now the fear of not doing this writing "good enough" is plaguing you, as well as the fear that the lesson might be left hanging in midair. What of it if that were to happen? That would be My decision.

One's self is the most brutal judge of the self. That is why the "jury" must be brought in. Love and acceptance from friends and family temper the harsh judgment you give yourself.

Fear of being alone (abandoned) is a basic and deep-rooted fear in people. It is related to the desire for survival which is at the very core of the human heart. But this fear too is unfounded for if you but look, deep in your heart you will find Me.

Fear of the future, of failure, poverty, pain, loneliness, rejection – the list could go on and on. There is only one answer to all of it. Rest in Me, trust Me, and be at peace in Me. I am with you always. I am the same yesterday, today, and forever. You are secure in Me. []

4.19   PEACE IS THE WAY

[| My child, reach out and hold onto that peace that you sense when you are quiet before Me. (You are "before" Me, yet you are in Me and I am in you.)

"*I will send you rain in its season, and the ground will yield its crops*" (Lev 26:4a). When the time is right for a certain leading, it will come. I am faithful and will not abandon you. You do not need to be anxious about "where" I will lead you next. Indeed, you should not be anxious. If there is anything that stifles the flow of provisions and blessings, it is anxiety. You have a physical counterpart of that within your body, where anxiety effectually closes off the life flow of blood through the smaller veins and arteries, besides raising havoc with digestion, the nerves, muscles, and other organs.

You must not only have the positive elements of discipline, obedience, faith, trust, and strong sustained desire to truly walk a Godly life, but you must stridently oppose the negative forces. A strong wash of fear going through your person does a great deal of damage physically, mentally, emotionally, and spiritually. Do not let fear take up residence in you. If you would once see what a loathsome creature fear is, you would become unshakably determined to forbid entrance to it!

Do all in peace, whether washing windows or taking a walk.

Love peacefully, live in peace, and breathe peace.

As you look ahead to coming times, see and expect things to be peaceful and to go well.

Peace is the opposite of anxiety. The way to corral the enemy of anxiety is to enlist the aid of peace. Where one is, the other cannot be, for they are opposed to each other. If you were to have a platform lying on the ground, you could not stand on the top and bottom of it at the same time. The two sides are opposite of each other, as peace and anxiety are.

"Peace I leave with you; my peace I give you" (Jn 14:27a). All peace is of Me. Dwell in My peace. Revel in My peace. Enjoy it and bask in it as sunbathers bask in the warmth and light of the sun. Peace is My great healer. It is the garment of love. When you fully open yourself to love, you will receive peace as well. My love, My peace, I give to you. []

CHAPTER 5

PAIN AND SUFFERING

5.1   VICTORY OVER PAIN

[| *"Surely the arm of the Lord is not too short to save, nor his ear too dull to hear"* (Is 59:1). I have the power to save even those whom you think lost. They are My children, I love them. As it means so much to you to be loved, so it is for others. Wish them that love, be generous in desiring that they be loved even as their heart desires it, then you are truly loving them.

My people have always been rejoicing people. It is in rejoicing that you are victorious. What does it matter that you have problems? They are of passing duration. Mind the things of the Spirit and in the Spirit, you will be victorious. I give you victory over problems, worries, pain, and illness, over your undisciplined self.

"What good is it for someone to gain the whole world, yet forfeit his soul?" (Mk 8:36). Keep things in proper perspective, that is half the battle. A mother does not mind the labor of childbirth when she accepts it and offers it in love for her child. Earthly pain and strife are the labor preceding your birth anew in My kingdom. How you accept it is what makes it a labor of pain or a labor of love.

I will give you all the guidance and strength you need. Do not lose hope, do not give up. Endure to the end, for your part is needed if My work is to be accomplished. Whatever comes, know that it is necessary for the greater picture, the outcome. I will not send you more than you can endure for My grace goes before you and comes after you to lift you and set you on high above the turmoil. *"...I am with you always..."* (Mt 28:20b). |]

5.2   LOVE FREES

Lord, what are we to do about problems?

[| Rest in Me that those problems do not become your problems. *"Each day has enough trouble of its own"* (Mt 6:34b). Trouble is a stepping stone to Me if in your need you turn to Me. Without the need, would you continue to think of Me? Pearls used for play become trifles. Blessings, if not received with thanksgiving and joy, become commonplace.

Do not fear for the future. Cut off every thought of concern. I am your loving Father, your provider. What have you to fear? Only your pride and selfishness. These words are for all. Take them to heart for yourself.

My child, I love you! Do not forget that. Recalling My love for you creates an imprint upon you, a lasting effect, that frees you more and more.

You are free. No dark bond can hold you once you understand the freedom of love, the freedom which is yours as My child. The freedom from worry, self-conceit, dullness, and drudgery that you felt as a child can and should be yours in the spirit.

The spirit is free.

It doesn't have a body with aches and pains to hold it down.

It has no worries about financial difficulties.

It is free to be joyful, to be itself, unencumbered by the things of earth.

Such is your spirit.

Reach out with wings of the spirit and accept the freedom and joy that I offer you! Let it flow through your body. Off drop the fetters of worry and concern! Up and away you rise into the glorious freedom of the children of light! Far behind are left the bonds of fear, the shackles of doubt, and the entwining fingers of self-love. The love that you need is richly and gloriously supplied by My heart in a measure unsurpassed by all the riches of the earth. |]

5.3   BLESSINGS THROUGH BROKENNESS

[| Truly I have the answer to all the problems of life, but it may be in a different way than you would expect. It is often by going through problems that an answer for them is found. Be patient. Trust in Me.

Blessed assurance, blessed hope, that am I to you! You needn't fear for, or about, a thing. I am life.

When you choose life, you choose Me,

When you choose joy, you choose Me,

And he who chooses Me chooses eternal life: Life that will never die, life, glorious and unbroken.

Your present life must turn to brokenness so you will no longer cling to it so strongly. The husk of the grain must break and fall away. "*...he has promised, 'Once more I will shake not only the earth but the heavens.' ...so that what cannot be shaken may remain.*" (Heb 12:26b,27c).

Do not consider it calamitous that you go through ups and downs in your emotions. You are being shaken, yes, but at the same time, strengthened. A hothouse plant develops strength in its stem, a strong root system, and a tough exterior when it is exposed to the elements of wind, direct sun, and driving rain, and the fruit can thus develop once the plant is mature and strong.

Do not be so hard on yourself! Do not judge yourself. By what criteria do you presume to judge, anyway? Are you the expert in perfection, in the qualities that are necessary for eternal life? Only the master artist, the master craftsman, knows what is yet needed for a perfect work of art.

Trust yourself to My care, your master craftsman. I will treat you, oh! so gently, as a masterwork of art in the making. I see in you the finished product, as a master sculptor sees the figure in the solid mass of rock. Stronger pressure and sometimes sharp blows with the chisel of life are needed to remove rough exterior chunks of self-love and pride but I take care to preserve the beauty and wholeness of the unique creation that I see in each one. |]

[| (Jesus:) My words are the words of eternal life. Let them flow into your being and take up residence there. Let them live in you. I am the word of the Father. My Father and I are one. When my words live in you, I live in you. *"Believe me when I say that I am in the Father and the Father is in me"* (Jn 14:11a). Ponder these thoughts, let them take root and sink into the very core of your being.

Where God is, there is life, health, and joy. There is love. Love would do nothing to hurt its beloved. If you do not have the fullness of life, health, and joy, you know that the fullness of love does not yet reside there. There may be actual health, though, without necessarily having it manifested in perfect physical condition.

If you have been called (asked) to carry another's burden of hurt and anxiety upon your heart, the presence of physical ailments may in part be an answer to prayer, a way in which you can help the other person, by accepting the physical limitations and ailments placed upon you, but your spirit can be free and healthy and can soar to heights of perfect health and peace.

You must overcome in the spirit. You must be over-comers if my work is to be accomplished. *"...I have a baptism to undergo, and constraint I am under until it is completed!"* (Lk 12:50).

Do not seek a sign other than peace. God's peace which is above all expectations will rest upon you when you are in His Will. Test yourself that you bring not the spirit of judgment and condemnation down upon yourself.

If a problem has no apparent solution, the way to go is through the problem. Face up to it. Look for blessings that may be extracted, and reach out and pluck them. You will often find that going through the problem has been the shortest way possible in reaching the desired goal, whether it be patience, victory over self, or victory over the world. Often such problems open you to blessings that the Father desires you to have that on your own you would never have arrived at.

Bless you, child! Speaking for the Father and myself: I love you! Never forget that, keep it ever in the forefront of your mind. Remembering that I love you can be a shield to protect you against the blows of life, for when you know that I love you other things do not matter nearly as much. []

5.4   VICTORY OVER SUFFERING

[| I am here, My child. Rest in Me.

In Me is all fullness of supply.

In Me are strength, health, and vitality.

In Me is rest for your wearied soul.

Just be in Me for a while. Let My love penetrate your mind and heart. What does it matter that your head feels miserable when you are loved by Love? Victory is triumph over suffering, triumph going through suffering. If you would not encounter suffering, how could you have victory over it?

Do not worry about suffering that may be in the future, whether you will be able to accept it. "Now is the acceptable time." Now is the time you receive the grace to accept whatever is, but do not accept that which fear and sin causes. Drive out fear! Be steadfast against temptation! Begin now to conquer these and you will be helping yourself to have a brighter future.

Suffering without hope is despair. Suffering with hope and with purpose brings joy, the joy that the world cannot give. I am Joy. Giving oneself in loving service is joy. In so doing, you become one with Me and you have joy.

You become perfected through obedience and patience in suffering. There is no other way to learn patience but through trials and suffering. Patience is a precious gem that is worth all the struggles that may be involved. Do not struggle alone. I am here to help you, to be your support. []

5.5   HEALING THROUGH LOVING OTHERS

[| "'...my thoughts are not your thoughts, neither are your ways my ways,' declares the Lord" (Is 55:8). Do not hinder My ways. If I would do great work in you through the means of sickness, who are you to say "No"? Even if you say "No", will it help? What will be, will be. Think of it: Your resistance could magnify the suffering to be borne a hundredfold.

Suffering borne in love can be bravely accepted, even with a smile and with joy, but suffering that you refuse to accept will nevertheless ride on your shoulders. By refusing to accede to My Will[1] – and what you are powerless to change has been willed, or allowed, by Me – you are turning away from walking in fellowship with Me and thus you must bear the weight alone. When you ask Me into your daily walk and ask Me for strength I am in truth with and within you, and I strengthen you.

What is so bad anyway about the suffering of the body? It is only the present moment that you have with you. The last moment you have just gone through is already lifted from your shoulders. As I lift it mercifully away, I replace it with new courage and stoutheartedness that you need for the present moment. With each moment, hour, and day of bravely borne and bravely accepted pain, My love for you grows, if that is possible. You become dearer to My heart for you are becoming more one with Me.

Two Souls who have gone through similar experiences are united in a spiritual bond. Jesus chose to be faced with and to accept the epitome of human suffering so that he might become one with you in having shared experiences. He was already one with you in his humanity.

How can divine love be put into words? All the loving signs and words of love that you see and hear are but faint reflections of the reality of love. I remain forever the same. My heart is now bursting with love for you.

Now I give Myself to you.

I, Love, come to you when you desire it.

You can breathe Me and walk within Me,

Be strengthened in Me, be nurtured with My life.

Does anybody hear Me? Do you hear Me, My child? Place everything in My hands: worries, problems, weaknesses, concerns, and relationships; your heart, your hurts, and your hurting. All is well. Just trust. Just respond to love.

My child, I know you have suffered. The very fact of My knowing can be a balm to ease your hurting. As you come to understand that your deep feelings of loneliness and hurt come from a need for love, you will begin to open yourself to others within whom you recognize that need and thus have compassion for them. Members of your family and other people you know have a deep need for love and are hurting. Begin to love them from inside yourself.

Love does not need outward actions to be. I give you My love to love others with. As My love wells up within you and goes out to others, it passes through the experiences of brokenness and hurting that you have had – for, in a way, those experiences are a part of you, as they are in your memory and spirit – and heals them more and more.

Look ahead to the joyful day that is coming! All hurts will be healed, all needs satisfied, and all desires of love fulfilled! You and your loved ones – those you have loved – will be safe with Me for all eternity. Leave those to My mercy who do not appear to respond to love. *"The Sovereign Lord will wipe away the tears from all faces"* (Is 25:8b). []

5.6   JOY IN SUFFERING

[| Come to Me when you feel faint or weary. My heart is open. My arms are open. I am open to you, to all.

I am a place of rest for the weary, strength for the weak,
Succor for the needy, a haven for the searching.
I am Father, My children!

You are not alone. Let that realization keep sinking in. There is Ultimate Reality: I Am. I am the bedrock for your emotions. You can rest securely in Me. I welcome you and that welcome is eternally given, now. Dwell upon that, realize it, ponder it, until you sense it, and become open to it. I am open to every part of you: your looks, your feelings, your needs. Come to Me!

My child, I love you! I'm sure you do not get tired of hearing that because I know how much you need love, and how much it means to you. I understand every last mood and desire of your heart.

Keep trying to look upon the present moment as the present moment, and you will live easier. Try to think that it is given to you to enjoy rather than to endure.

You can have joy even in suffering. The deepest joy comes from having helped another by giving of yourself, and that is what you can do when you look upon suffering in that light. The suffering is only with you for a moment at a time. Look neither to the past nor the future in suffering. Relish the joy that is (can be) there. []

5.7   NOT FEELING WELL?

[| My child, try to relax more in Me. Let your feelings come and go more freely. You are a being of spirit. When emotions arise in your spirit, let them be expressed. Let them go on out of your system to a large extent, just as you exhale in breathing.

I know you do not feel well today. I allow it for a purpose. After a time of being under the weather and rather miserable, you appreciate so much more to have your strength and well-being return. You must grow in gratitude, as well as in faith, hope, and love. Experiencing lack is one of the keenest lessons there is for achieving heartfelt thankfulness for the gifts you receive from Me.

A lack in the material order does not necessarily mean a lack in the order of the spirit. Nothing material can affect the spiritual unless you allow it. My grace is with you to sustain you.

Not feeling well puts you in spiritual contact/union with others who are also in a world of discomfort, limitation, and pain. You must live with and share experiences with someone before you as a human being can develop a sense of compassion for them.

Each hour and day that you experience discomfort and pain

deepens your compassion if you do not rebel against My permission for it in your life. Doing that sets limits and somewhat hardens your spirit so it cannot be freely formed and cannot grow much. Discomfort that continues intermittently helps the virtue of endurance become established in your heart. Oh, if you only could see how marvelously all things work together for good, whether "good" or "evil" in people's eyes!

Gray days are not necessarily bad days. The spirit needs to be watered, too, and those are the days that My grace is pouring the waters of strength, trust, patience, humility, forbearance, submission, and endurance into your Soul. You need all those qualities to come through those times safely. As you reach out willingly with your spirit and take the graces offered, you are kept safe from the dark spirits that wait gleefully to take charge and to ruin the peace of your Soul.

Remember that no matter how dark the valley, I am with you. Not only with you, but I carry you when you do not have the strength to go it alone; thus, the times of weakness and sickness are times of special communion with Me. At every moment I bless you and give you the grace to be open to receive that blessing. I will for My Strength to be in you. Use it as you need. []

5.8   BE OPEN TO LIFE

[| Bless you, My child! Do not be afraid, I am here. You needn't sense Me in any way. Just know by faith that I am ever-present and that I love you. Cling to that truth, that life of love. Cling to Me.

Your childlike trust gladdens My heart. I understand all the questions you have and the tiresomeness of not feeling up to par. Remember to take one day, literally one moment, at a time. That is the moment in which I am with you and strengthening you. When you can go on your own for a bit, I let you, for spiritual muscles need flexing and strengthening, too.

I ask that you, in turn, strengthen your brothers and sisters.

From having experienced life yourself with its ups and its downs, you can have compassion for others. The more open you can be to whatever comes, the less anxiety you will have and the easier it will be for you to accept it. But do not just be passive and resigned as though you have an uncertain fate over which you have no control. Your actions and thoughts now affect to a great extent what will come in your future. I hear the desires of your heart and it moves My heart.

Above all, be thankful! If you could see the love energy that is expended for you, the giving of Myself to you ...! I give Myself without reserve. Your receiving is limited by the openness of your heart, mind, and spirit. I come, in love, My child. Receive Me!

You will never feel that you are all that you should be and that you are doing my Will perfectly. (If you reach that point, you are at the height of folly, for you have puffed yourself up with pride.) All I ask is that you continue the struggle to do your best and then accept and love yourself as you are.

The only person on earth who knows you and your struggles is you. Be your own best friend! Encircle yourself with a wholesome love of self. Affirm the positive. Do not worry what tomorrow may bring, and do not worry that others will not have the strength to hold out under burdens. It is for you to accept the circumstances of today for your own life and to commend others to My care that they will receive the strength to carry on.

Acceptance of suffering and unpleasantness in your daily living can build up a storehouse of spiritual strength upon which to draw when someone needs prayer to be freed from the fetters of negativity, fear, and unhappiness. If you can accept in love and offer your pains, trials, and temptations for the next person whom you will be called upon to pray for, then that reserve of love will be the strength of your prayers.

Do not take life so seriously, child! Take it with joy, celebration, and thanksgiving! Pay no mind to the temptations to feel depressed and to question My purposes over and over. The Book of Life has the answers to your doubts and questions.

Bless you! Go in peace. []

5.9 GRAY DAYS ARE PRECIOUS

[| My child, I know the way seems long and arduous to you, but at no time is the situation different from My standpoint: I am always with you, loving and supporting you. When you once come to the other side and see what wondrous results came from times of trial and gray days, you will be truly grateful for every moment of it.

You are learning patience, acceptance, and love:

Patience with and acceptance of yourself and others; love of yourself and others;

Patience with and acceptance of what life brings you; acceptance of what cannot be changed;

Patience with the training and molding that I do in your Soul;

Learning to know Me and coming into My life of love.

Yes, your days on earth are truly precious for how else could you come into an eternity of gladness and light? You are now like a seed planted in the soil, taking root and drawing in nourishment as you reach up to break forth into the sunlight.

You can take joy in the fact that your life, your being, will go on forever. One of the basic causes of anxiety in people is the urge to retain and protect life. As you come to know that your life is safe in Me you can break the hold that anxiety has on you. Rest in Me often, always, and you are in a haven of rest. You are special, each of you, and I give you all My love and attention.

Bless you, in your struggles and your daily life! []

5.10 CONCERNING PAIN

[| My child, I know it is hard for you to realize My presence. You must do so by faith and by a spirit of openness to receive My love. I have been with you all these years, every day of every year, every moment of every day. Dwell on that thought that you may draw the nourishment of security from it. You walk in Me even when you are not aware of doing so.

Look forward to changes, for change is a coming forth of life. Life can be enjoyed, no matter how drab it is on the surface or how hectic or filled with pain. The center of your being cannot be filled with pain for that is Mine to occupy. I am the life in your being. Pain cannot take over life, cannot take it away. Pain is one of the instruments that can purify your being of the attachments to things that weigh you down.

Do not feel sorry for those in pain but rather feel compassion. Open yourself to the person in his pain and you somehow alleviate the pain as it attempts to attack the life and being of that person. All are related and connected in a unity that is life. What affects one, affects the other. By being willing to be open to one who suffers you lift the burden by taking some of the weight upon yourself. Two can better carry a burden than one. []

5.11   BE FREE TO BECOME

[| Relax, My child! Rest completely in My love. Anxiety strains the spirit, it strains your being. Dismiss it straightaway! |]

Be gone anxiety! for the Lord God would take up residence in His dwelling place. I belong to the Lord. I have nothing to fear.
[| What do the problems of this earth matter? What do times of sickness or health, poverty or plenty matter? Only insofar as those things affect the health of your spirit are you to be concerned about them. All situations and difficulties can be of benefit to your well-being and happiness unless you thwart My saving action by disobedience, resentment, and inordinate attachments.

Come into My Will, beloved child, in every facet of your outer and inner life. The inner workings of your person are of greater importance for they regulate and affect your attitude toward activities and how you spend your time. I would be Lord of your whole life! It can be a slow process to come to that finality of dedication, but it can be hastened by your completely open and willing acceptance of My Will, without hesitation.

Moments of hesitation weaken your spiritual will. Have your mind, the mind of your spirit, set upon obedience at all costs. Affirm this mentally and you are prepared to move in obedience as My Will becomes clear to you. You then have exercised the virtue of obedience enough that there will be enough muscle there to take you through whatever comes into your life without undue loss of spiritual power.

Vacillation weakens your will and thus weakens your spiritual life. Taking too long to decide and move on a course of action is not a healthy thing to do in the natural order and neither is it in the spiritual order. If your heart is set upon being obedient to My Will and you mistakenly (innocently) follow a course of action that is not in My Will, I will cover and protect you anyway and will set things right. Bless you, My child! Go in peace to love and serve. []

5.12   THERE WAS AND IS A PURPOSE

[| My child, I take you into My heart, into My love. You know how precious it is to feel loved, to be loved, for you felt so alone and unloved for so long. That experience has helped you develop a spirit of compassion toward fellow hurting Souls and a desire to bring love and release to them. You are a much larger channel now because of your having experienced near "death in the spirit" than you would have been if you had been comparatively fulfilled and happy all along.

You may experience further hurts, loss, and anguish that may seem to try to pull you back to that level of distraught aloneness. But now that you are united with Me in spirit and know it – stronger than just believing, you know it – you will not be pulled down to that level of utter aloneness again, provided you hold and keep your faith.

Your faith was tested to the breaking point and it is accordingly much stronger than it was earlier. Remember that I am the base, strength, and object of your faith. Know that should you have to suffer untold anguish all the rest of your days, the ultimate – coming into My love fully and eternally – is worth every moment of that suffering and even much more.

Trust Me through every hardship, every darkness of soul,

Through every crisis, every time of separation by death,

Through all your ordinary gray days.

When you entrust yourself to Me it magnifies (if that were possible) My keeping power for you. It is a matter of giving and receiving: Both are always necessary.

My children, each of you is so dear to Me! My greatest joy is to share My life with you! The deepest desire of My heart is that you may be open to receiving more. Come dwell in Me: In your Father, your savior, your friend; In truth, in light, in reality, in love.

My peace, love, and the light of My heart to all! Bless you! []

Lord, I am still fear rejection. Please free me of that fear.

[| I am your acceptance, child. I am eternal love. No person's acceptance, rejection, or indifference about things makes a whit of difference in your basic being. Rest in My acceptance, in the sureness of My love, in My understanding. I understand you perfectly! I am bringing to blossom in you that which I would have there.

When you are strongly led to do something which you believe is My Will for you but wonder if your desire is pushed by self-motivation, ascertain what the situation is as well as you can. Then if you still feel prompted to do the task, go ahead with it, offering it to Me in love. I will not let you go wrong if you are sincerely open to My leading. As I have said earlier, My peace will be a sign unto you. []

5.13   LET'S EXAMINE THOSE PROBLEMS

[| My child, I bless you! Know that all that you experience is a part of My experience, also, for I share it with you. My heart is united with your heart. When you feel pain, I feel pain. When you rejoice, I rejoice. I will only come to a full resting when all has been accomplished.

You are because I Am. All that matters is that you be in Me. Tension, anxiety, sin, pull you away from the core of your being, which is I. No wonder physical problems and ailments come about as a result! You were meant to be in Me. Your home, your niche, is in Me. Only in Me will you find peace, happiness, and contentment.

If you are not at peace, examine the currents of thought and spiritual elements that are pulling you, your being, in all directions. Gather them together and bring them to Me. Let's examine them:

Spite? Resentment? Jealousy? Hate? A sense of worthlessness? Much more? All will give way as you open yourself to My love. There is nothing on My part blocking peace and blessings from you. Any blocking that is taking place comes from disharmony within you and in your relationships with others. When you are at peace with yourself and with others, you are at peace with Me.

I hold no grudges about anything that you or anyone has done. To be in union with Me you also must hold no grudges. A butterfly flies free even though it may be blown this way and that. You can fly free no matter what the circumstances of your life are. []

5.14   LEARN TO BOUNCE BACK

(I was facing a difficult situation.)

[| My child, life deals bitter blows sometimes. You must learn to bounce back. Steady yourself immediately. Do not try to anticipate the effect of problems on others and prepare to be their strength. I am your strength and I am their strength. I am leading, molding, and training others as I am you. It would be sheer folly for you to try to carry this load yourself. I promise you that all things work for the good of those who love the Lord and do His bidding.

It is wise for you to seek counsel at this time. You were not made to walk alone. I walk with you, both within you and in the person of others to whom I bid you turn. First, though, bring your burden to Me to have it cut to a size that you can handle. I carry the greater burden, so the more problems that come your way, the more help and grace you receive from Me. In this way, as long as your communication with Me remains open, problems can serve as instruments of spiritual growth for you.

Problems themselves do not matter in the basic ordering of things. What counts for good or for ill is your reaction to problems. If you allow them to cut big chunks out of your faith and let them lead you to hold resentment towards others, towards life, and Me, it causes damage.

You have power in the spirit to prevent such damage and the added weight of burdens that would come upon you should you choose to follow the path of resentment. You need to stay very close to Me in the time of trial and temptation. I will see you through.

Trust Me implicitly. There is no one else and nothing else to trust. Your hope and victory are in Me. I am on your side, cheering for you! You indeed are running the race but on, and in, My strength. Go forward with joy! I know the outcome of the race and we are the winners! Bless you, My child! []

5.15   BLESSINGS OUTWEIGH MISERIES

[| My child, blessings to you and all! When blessings come from Me, it far outweighs the misery of present circumstances. Present circumstances will change. Blessings are forever. Furthermore, the blessings effect a change in the present circumstances which brings those circumstances to become blessings in the long run.

Even the dreariness of a day like this is a blessing, for it helps prevent you from depending on this world and on passing circumstances to be the source of happiness. I must wean you from the physical world and from depending on your own intellectual and spiritual accomplishments.

Back to square one. Make another "lap around the mountain." You are to rest and be in Me. That is the total meaning of your existence. What would or could you do forever and ever that would keep you satisfied? A trillion latch hook kits? Do not depend on created things for happiness and relaxation but to help you rest in Me.

Design, color, humor, the joy of living – all have their roots, their foundation, in Me. All created beings reflect the Uncreated Being in some way. Finite beings need finite expressions to come to know the Infinite. You learn of Me and learn to know Me through the reflections of Myself that are in all created beings and human love and relationships.

I AM. You cannot see, know, or touch "I AM." You can only know Me by being. I love you, children of My heart, you who spring forth from the center of My heart and being! My love for you is such that the only thing that will prevent you from resting in Me eternally is an eternal "No" from you. The free choice is yours.

I invite each of you to come into My heart! Rest and recuperate, and know that I am God. Let go and let Me! []

5.16   LOOK FOR ME IN YOUR PAIN

[| Life goes on. The troubles of yesteryear are no longer with you. Today's troubles will also pass. Strive to be detached from problems that surface in your life. Do not let them catch hold of your inner person but treat them as something you are holding in your hand and could put down at will.

Suffering that you experience connected with problems is largely connected to the attitude you have towards the problem. If you consider some certain responsibility as totally yours – that no one else could do this task, and no way would you let them! – you are carrying a heavier than necessary burden. Should you perchance have a little accident and end up in a wheelchair paralyzed, you would soon see that these concerns that you consider to be so all-fired important are not. Let a bigger, more drastic, problem come your way and you would begin to think that things weren't so bad before that.

Problems, difficulties, and pain are some of the means used by dark forces to try to cause you to give up hope, to turn against Me. I am in those very circumstances, in that pain, for I am everywhere, both in the physical and in the spiritual.

You can find Me in difficulties, in pain, if you look for Me. All who have managed to hang on and come through difficult circumstances are living proof of this, for on their own they could not have done it. They looked to Me and found Me, even in their pain.

Having an abundant life does not depend on circumstances. I await you in life. Whatever the circumstances, embrace life wholeheartedly and you will find Me. []

5.17   THOUGHTS ON DEATH

[| My child, ever I hear your voice. Ever I am aware of the searching in your heart. In a way, I put the searching there, but it comes about just because I AM and you are not yet fully united with Me. It is your destiny to become one with Me and restless shall you be till it is accomplished.

Continue to let the truth sink in, that I AM, and you will continue being freed more and more from the tangled tentacles of insecurity. I AM, and all else exists within Me. I am all existence.

I must keep a shield between you and Me, a buffer to "hide My face," for your present human existence could not take it. Death is the passageway through that buffer zone. It is a passage, yes, but not in a space way as you may think of it. In dying, you stay right where you are, in Me, but the blinders of the physical are removed.

Have you ever realized that many of the hurts you and other people experience have to do with things of the body? ... having physical pain, feeling cheated in not having as much of this world's goods as you think you would deserve. By being so attached and connected to the physical that it controls you, you open your spirit to being bruised mercilessly.

Dwell in Me. I will buffer you against the hurts and adverse blows of life.

My love will heal you. My truth will set you free. []

My God, I thirst for You!

[| Then let go more and more of the things of this earth. Cut the strings of attachment where you see them, where you can. Even your ideas and desires may come from the "earth" if they spring from the source of self. Begin with the physical, and do not try to do everything at once.

Growth takes time. Be patient with yourself and with others. Accept and love yourself at the stage you are at. If you do not accept yourself, you are separating yourself from Me, for I love you always.

Time to go, My child! I, too, rejoice that once again we have had the chance to spend time together. See how much My life is joined with yours! While you yet live on earth, I experience time and the events that happen in time with you. How much you realize that and how much you come to trust in Me and to know of My love, determines the measure of happiness you can know. I hold you tenderly in love. Go, in love. Be healed and be free! I am with you. []

5.18   COME TO THE LIGHT

[| My child, simply be, simply love. Rest in Me, the wellspring of all good, and "good" will flow to those you are open to. Do you see why your heart needed to be opened to compassion by the long struggles and searching you have gone through, by becoming "acquainted with infirmity," and by experiencing what it is like to have an empty heart? If you had not gone through those experiences your heart and life would still be centered on yourself to a great extent.

There are no walls in the world of the spirit except those that you set up and the lower-vibration energy of dark spirits. Calamities, pressures, or near despair prompt a person to turn to Me. Those problems help open them to receiving the good that is awaiting all who seek it. *"Ask and it will be given to you; seek and you will find; knock and the door will be opened to you"* (Mt 7:7).

There are only two "worlds": the world of light and the world of darkness (absence of light). The outcome of living in darkness is to experience calamity, depression, rivalry, and a host of other ills. Living in the light, on the other hand, brings you the sure promise of immortality, affirmation of the goodness of your being, light, and life.

No promise is made of being protected from what the world would call a disaster, but the promise is given that you can have peace amid disaster and serenity in the face of whatever ills may befall you. Your spirit has been set free! Freedom and peace await your taking when you accept the life I have to offer. I give you a share of My life, a measure of My Spirit as you open to receiving it.

Come to the light, My children! Cast aside the deeds of darkness so darkness can no longer have a claim on you! You belong to the light! Come into knowledge and acceptance of My love! Come and receive healing for mind, heart, and body! Let Me lift your burdens from you and give you release from fear and tension. I love you! []

5.19   I SHARE YOUR LIFE

[| Come to Me, My child, and know freedom and peace! I am all things to all. I can be all things to you if you so choose and so live. This cannot be merely a momentary choice and decision, but one that is lived.

I am in all of My creation. I am in you.

Your pain is My pain, your struggles are My struggles.

Your compassion for others is My compassion breaking through.

You are spirit of My Spirit.

Especially in times of pain, rest in Me. I support every muscle, nerve, and particle of your body. I support every movement of your mind and every sigh, desire, and movement of your spirit, for you are in Me and I am in you. |]

God, I renew giving myself to You. I invite You to rest in me!
[| My child, gladly I come to you! Gladly I rest in you and abide in you! To abide means to have a conscious association with a person. It means to dwell trustfully as a friend with a friend and to be always ready to see about the wishes of your dear friend. |]

5.20   FROM DARKNESS TO LIGHT

[| (Jesus:) My child, trust! Continue to believe and trust no matter how dark the day and the hour. Take a lesson from that dark Friday when I trod the road to Calvary, was nailed to a cross, and hung suspended between earth and heaven.

All of you are destined to taste that type of bitterness. You will have a cross to carry. You are oftentimes the cross, putting up with and living with yourself. You will be "nailed" to that cross. It will be impossible for you to escape or get away from it. And, as you cry for aid and mercy to the God of heaven and earth, it will/may seem to you as though you are suspended there, not able to partake of earth's goods and find relief in them and seemingly not able to pierce the clouds of heaven.

Go further in your study. Study my reaction and response in the desperate situation I was in, and study what the outcome was.

"*Father, forgive them, for they do not know what they are doing*" (Lk 23:34a). Can you respond in that manner? It is all-important that you do.

"*[T]oday you will be with me in paradise*" (Lk 23:43b). I had utter trust in a bright future, despite it being the darkest of days. With no earthly help possible, I trusted only and entirely on help from my Father in Heaven. I trusted that paradise would be mine.

"*I am thirsty!*" (Jn 19:28c). An expression of my utter desolation, my deepest feelings. It helps to express your anguish even if no earthly ears can heed and help, for your Father in Heaven hears and cares.

"*When Jesus saw his mother there and the disciple whom he loved standing nearby, he said to her, 'Woman, here is your son,' and to the disciple, 'Here is your mother'* " (Jn 19:26b, 27b). I was not too preoccupied with my suffering to think of and provide for those under my charge, those whom I loved most of all.

And then, finally, "*It is finished*" (Jn 19:30b). No bitterness in those words, no regrets or self-recrimination. I was obedient to the wishes of my Father and had done all I could in my humanity. I continued to the bitter end to love, to pour myself out, to believe, to trust – and the bitter became sweet. The time of your trial and testing and suffering will come to an end.

"*Father, into your hands I commit my spirit*" (Lk 23:46b). I rested in the hands of my Father in life and I rested in His hands, in His arms, in death. Death to earthly life, birth to eternal life. Death: the passageway, the forerunner to resurrection.

"*He is not here; he has risen, just as he said*" (Mt 28:6a). No longer was I found on earth in an earthly way. I was no longer in the grave! I have risen! "*I have come that they [you] may have life and have it to the full*" (Jn 10: 10b). He who shares in my death will also share in my resurrection. Trust! Believe! []

5.21   HERE FOR YOU, FOR ALL

Father, I lift my husband to You. Please take care of him.
[| Enter into the joy of your Lord. Enter into My joy. I am not sad about how things are with your husband. I see all the good that is, and that is coming to be! I see him blossoming spiritually. Who says that growth has to be emotional or intellectual? Let each person have tough lessons in life as I choose to give. Only he who runs the course will receive the prize, he who pays the price.

This is one of the areas of life that must be gone through alone in the inner person – the tough, lonely days. A friend or lover can look on, empathize and be there for the person but cannot enter the other's life. I enter, though, when the going and the loneliness get tough enough that the struggling person cries out for help. Do not fear. I am here for you and all as the need may be.

Bless you, My child! Gladly I take the burden from you. Enter into the joy of your Lord! []

5.22   CAN YOU DRINK THE CUP?

"How can I repay the Lord for all his goodness to me? I will lift up the cup of salvation and call on the name of the Lord" (Ps 116:12-13).

Father, what does "take up the cup of salvation" mean?

[| *"Can you drink the cup I am going to drink?"* (Mk 10:38b). That is the "cup of salvation." You must drink to the last bitter dregs to truly share in the work of salvation. You have accepted to be willing to accept life for the sake of the salvation of Souls. Life includes pain, suffering, a sense of abandonment, and loneliness. You must share in this pain and aloneness to be a channel of salvation for others.

When you come to Me in your anguish of soul, bring all those others as well: everyone who is suffering pangs of loneliness and desperate searching. Believe for your own sake but also, and even more so, for the sake of all those who have nowhere to turn, no one to go to. In your common experience of heartrending emotions, you become united in spirit, all who plunge the depths of human emotion.

I have pain as God, too. In the same way that you suffer through trying experiences and times of searching with your children, friends, and fellow human beings, so I "suffer" with all of you, My children, as you go through the bitter pathways of life.

This is the "cup of salvation": being willing to drink the dregs for the sake of loved ones for, in so doing, the bitterness is removed for them. The pain becomes their way of salvation and hence, deep within, there can be and is joy.

Do not try to escape the cross. It is your greatest blessing in the long run. One moment from now, what matters the pain of this present moment? The pain all passes except for the results of your attitude toward it. You can be built up in love and the joy of salvation through pain and suffering, or you can give way to bitterness, sorrow, and deeper loneliness.

Choosing to accept pain and walk through it with love for the sake of others, for the sake of all, takes away the bitterness of the pain. There cannot be loneliness for one who is united in love with Me and with all of his fellow human beings.

So stay courageous! Do not let self-pity rob you of the crown awaiting you. Feeling blue? So what! Lonely? You can live with the loneliness, fight against it and overcome it. You are not alone in this. You have the company of the vast majority of your fellow human beings and you have Me "suffering with." Take up the cup of salvation! I give you the grace to drink of it.

Bless you, My child! I do not leave you "alone" to punish you or make you suffer but as a way of salvation for yourself and many others. I give you my courage! |]

5.23   INTO THE DEPTHS AND OUT

[| My child, it takes time to come into a state of restfulness and peace to be a worthy, open receptacle and to be able to receive. The trash and clutter must be cleaned out from your mind and spirit. I dwell with the pure of heart.

"Blessed are the pure in heart, for they will see God" (Mt 5:8). To "see God" means to experience, to know. Is "knowing" in marriage a one-time union? No, it is an all-encompassing event, taking in the whole of the two person's lives, with tender, intimate moments that give a sparkle to the whole. You cannot truly know Me until you are willing to give your whole self to the relationship and do so. It is possible to just play a role and consider oneself "Christian." Religion must be more than surface dressing. It must be of the heart.

I seek a full-time, complete commitment from you and all, an all-encompassing love, for I have the desire for complete and total union with My beloved just as you do. Oh, how I long to be one with you, to have you be one with Me! |]

(The evening before having surgery:)

[| I hold you in My love and peace, my child. Rest your total being within and on Me. Especially as you go into surgery, keep this in mind and you can "float" through surely and peacefully. Do not be anxious about how things will go afterward. I am the God of the impossible and the "highly unlikely." Trust Me so I can act. Sleep peacefully, My child. Bless you! |]

(I was feeling rather blue after surgery.)

[| My child, at times you must probe the depths of the mysteries of life. Experiencing a sense of despair and loneliness is one of the mysteries of life. You have been saying each day, "I accept life for the sake of the salvation of Souls."

Life is not just pie and ice cream. It is pain, hard work, despair and longing, and crying out to Me. All that puts you in touch with the Me and with yourself is blessed. The pain of stepping into the depths of nothingness which you are experiencing helps you to release some of your dependence on *things* as being the actual reality, as your spirit cries out in sheer agony to Me.

In this depressed state, you see nothing in yourself, in others, or in things that will help very much with those feelings. They must be expressed. They are the anguished cry of a spirit body somewhat cut off from itself. A part of you has been given over to the spirit side of life and adjustment to that must be made.

All of mankind is slowly dying. Dreams die. Relationships with family and friends die. Parts of bodies "die." Relatives, friends, and fellow humans die. It is only proper that there be due respect for tears and missing involved.

I created all things. When changes come, things are no longer as I created them, hence I mourn over the loss and you do, also. This is another tie-in with Me, My child, one more means of becoming ever more one with Me. Union with Me is in all ways: spiritual, joyful, sorrowful. Take all as it comes.

So far, so good! I walk with you, within, all the way. Never doubt that. Believe it as a sacred trust. I entrust you to believe, to know that I am with and within you always. |]

CHAPTER 6

CHURCH – TRUE RELIGION

6.1   UNION WILL BE IN SPIRIT

[| Rest in Me, My child. "Child" refers to a young person with much to learn. "Child" is also hopefully meant to denote one who is open, eager and willing to learn, willing to change, and willing to admit that he or she has gotten the wrong idea when such is the case.

In itself, there is no blame for getting the wrong idea from family members or other people, but when that wrong idea involves holding resentment towards others and being closed off toward them, it is a communal sin that has been passed along from one to another. Just as familiar (family) spirits are passed along in a family, even so, familiar (family) sins are passed along and taught by word and example, almost with the belief that those sins "cannot be helped because that's the way we are."

This chain of communal sin can be broken by the melting or breaking of a chain link here and there. Those who see the fallacy in their ideas can break the chain of sin by humbling themselves before Me and asking for reconciliation in spirit with the rest of humankind. They can then unwind/loosen the chain even as it extends back through those people's lives who have been their teachers and mentors. This is done by seeking reconciliation in their name and the name of their forebears.

All of heaven waits and yearns for this to come about! There cannot be any fences around truth, separating it exclusively as possession of one or the other group. Truth is gleaned as a kernel here and a kernel there. To make up the one bread that is meant to give sustenance to all, all of the kernels, all of the truth, must be kneaded and formed together.

You are all one Body, the Body of My Son. Full growth into maturity is coming. The uniting will be done in spirit without necessarily being together bodily as a group. If you can come to an understanding of the truths I have been showing you lately and others in their respective churches and homes are willing to accept the same truth as it is brought to them, then a real change has taken place. You will have become united in spirit, in the Spirit of My Son, Jesus.

If you but be open, the life force of truth, the sap of the, will make its way to you and through you to others. With Me all things are possible! I can change headstrong but willing people into docile instruments. All it takes is the willing. I do the rest by My grace.

You are being formed into one, My people! The sum of creation is being added up and the total weight of glory is great! Keep your eyes fixed on the goal: perfect understanding, love, and unity in Me, the God and Father of all.

I will have no exclusivity! Open your embrace of love to all. All are My children. Think of all as My children, as they rightly are. And you are no more or no less than who you are. Do not put yourself up and do not put yourself down. Even so with others. You are all on an equal plane: equal as sinners, equally loved by Me, all called to come to Me.

Come to Me, My precious Soul, a light of My light! []

Prayer of Repentance

Father God, I bless and reverence You! Thank You for Your love and care. Thank You for opening my mind to further truth. I come before You in repentance for having held out against my fellow brothers and sisters of other faiths, and in gratitude to You for opening my heart and drawing the poison out. Thank You for loosening the straps that held my heart bound!

I ask forgiveness for myself and for our church for having considered that we were exclusive in the truth and right living.

My brothers and sisters in Christ, all my human family, I am sorry for having blocked you out in spirit from the blessing that you rightfully should have received from me! I speak in the name of our church and my name, asking forgiveness from you and asking for your blessing in return.

We share the truth, the one bread. When we try to claim it as belonging to ourselves alone, we succeed only in tearing the Body and doing harm to our spirit. God, have mercy on us!

6.2   TRUTH IS EVER UNFOLDING

[| My children, tenderly I caress you! I love you! *"No eye has seen, no ear has heard no mind has conceived what God has prepared for those who love him"* (1 Cor 2:9). It is well worth the effort, struggle, and difficulty of facing dark times. Receive all and do all in and by the power of love. Love conquers all. Even in your everyday lives, you can realize the all-powerful force of love in action.

Just become pure, willing channels. Some of the barriers to the truth that you have erected must come down. People are so prone to think "Now I've got it! Now I know the way!" You are in trouble anytime that you set your life and hope solidly on a rigid set of beliefs, for truth is ever unfolding. Your view of truth and living according to it must keep pace or you become locked in a prison that consists of a set of beliefs.

There is basic truth, yes, but your understanding of that truth is ever in need of expansion. You cannot become a little god in your sphere of life if you are to come into the fullness of the truth. I beckon you to come forward into the freedom of the truth, into the freedom of life and spirit! Come to Me in truth and reality. Know Me and know that I am with you.

Do not be afraid that you do not know the way.

I am the way. Rest and live in Me. Put all your stock in Me.

I am the pearl of great price. It may seem to you that you take a great chance in betting everything on Me, but to whom else shall you go? I have the words of eternal life. Enter and live!

Leave all judgment and figuring out for Me. You do not need to see the way for a long stretch ahead. I am your driver, your guide. I see the way. I am the Way. []

6.3   STEPS TOWARD FULLER FREEDOM

[Before receiving this lesson, I had been absorbing Bible verses about *law* and *freedom* for several weeks.]

Jesus was born under the law, but he did not keep the rules for the sake of the rules. He followed the Spirit's leading. And Jesus says, "Come, follow Me." Father, please guide me.

[| My child. the way is long because it takes so long to undo mistaken ideas that have become entrenched in your mind. It is a good thing I have patience!

Humans have a fragile sense of balance. The false props cannot be removed too quickly or you will fall in fear and think that your life is shattered. The strength to walk in freedom, free from those props, must first be built up, then the framework of living by rules can be removed a step at a time.

This can be compared to a child's learning to ride a bicycle with training wheels attached. Even after the child becomes able to ride freely, he/she is often still psychologically dependent upon the training wheels for a time.

You are called to live in total freedom. One who lives in love and is guided and strengthened by that love is free. Coming into that love is Christ being formed in you.

The first step to a more abundant life is to say "No" to your lower nature. But just saying "No" to self is not enough. You must also say "Yes" to My Will. Saying "Yes" means to open yourself to Me without fear.

I will be patient waiting for this for I know how fear grips at the very center of your being, telling you to watch out and be careful.

That is a protective mechanism your spirit has to warn against wily intruders. It was put there by Me but is affected by sin and by unhappy experiences which cause you to be wary even of Me. I am your God, whether you know it or not. All are in Me. In Me, you have life and all blessings! []

Father, thank You for this further opening of my mind and spirit to freedom! I want to be free to let you love me and lead me, and free to love myself and others! I bless you!

[| My child, my little one, my dove! I rejoice as I watch you growing and coming into freedom in response to My beckoning Spirit. Come and rest in My bosom! Receive love, and share in My joy! "*[A]s a bridegroom rejoices over his bride, so will your God rejoice over you*" (Is 62:5b).

Your freedom, My people, is coming to be, and Oh! how I delight in you! That is what makes it all worthwhile!

Do not worry about your children or others. They, like you, are coming into freedom. That is so ordained and it will come to pass. Believe along with Me and shore up the sagging lines of doubt present in so many. []

[| (Jesus:) Rest in Me. I am the prince of peace, the light of the world. Follow Me that you may have life. I am not come to condemn. I come only to love and to lead you to freedom.

I have come to set prisoners free,

To set you free and to heal you of life's hurts,

To break the shackles that bind you.

If you picture a cord binding you or walls separating you from others, in the spirit the cord and walls are there. Even if this is done subconsciously it has a detrimental effect, for "subconsciously" is in the realm of the spirit and it is the spirit that guides and controls the material.

"*[I]f the Son sets you free, you will be free indeed*" (Jn 8:36). Unite yourself with me in spirit that I may break the ties that bind you and bring those walls of division crashing down! Prepare the way for the Lord, the Prince of Peace! []

6.4   FOR ONE AS FOR ALL

Pondering: None of us in our particular church gathering are alone before God in love and worship. Many others of our fellow human beings are before God in love and worship at the same time that we are. God is not compartmentalized with "windows" to this side and that through which to receive worship. There is one God and there are all of us. Everyone is in God.

As we in each of our church groups love and worship God we are joined by and united with the thousands of others who also love and worship God. In the spirit there is no separation of place, so we worship and love God one in spirit. Also, there is no time in the spirit, so all of us are somehow united with everyone of all time as we love, worship, and serve our God.

We are free in the spirit – meant to be free. We are in and before God, as we live our lives no matter what we are doing, whether praying, working, or having recreation. God is peace and we are in that peace. We can enjoy things, rest, live, and move in that peace and freedom at all times. This is how things are meant to be.

The "walls" of our churches, the division and differences in approach and opinion that we have, are brought on by us, not by God. In God's eyes, there are no divisions and no differences. God sees our love and goodwill or our lack of love and goodwill, but He loves us all and proffers His grace to all. Those of us who are the most "sure" that our way is "right" (as contrasted with others being "wrong") may be the ones who are to be the most pitied. Who can help us break through that shell?

God, we cry out to You day and night! Hear our prayers for ourselves and our brothers and sisters! To whom shall we turn, if not to You? Our spirits cry out to be free from the shackles that our minds have placed on them and our bodies! Lord God, Father God, hear our prayer! Set us free!

[| I hear your cry, beloved children! As the one is to Me so are all. I love each and all of you to the uttermost! I sent My Son to each and for each and to all and for all, to deliver you from death and the power of the enemy.

You are coming into peace and freedom, for I am bringing it about. As Moses brought his people into freedom so am I bringing you to a place of freedom. That deliverance in the physical was a promise and an example of what is being accomplished in the spiritual.

It is not just for those who are living now that the coming into freedom and peace is taking place. There is no space and time in the spirit. It is always here, now. That comes to be which has been foreordained from all eternity. When the fullness of peace and freedom comes, it is for one and all.

Each comes into peace and freedom and all do. Each "arrives" with the "All." Coming into peace and freedom is coming into union with the desires of My heart, coming into My heart, for in My heart is all peace and freedom.

My child, My children, do not try to find your way alone!

Come to Me that you may have life!

Come to Me that your brother, your sister, may have life!

Come to Me that all may have life, for you are one of the "all."

If you are not with Me and with all, the task of freedom is not complete. If you yet hold a grudge and allow a wall of resentment and a "better-than-thou" attitude to separate you from your brothers and sisters, coming into freedom is not complete.

My Spirit works in one and all, for the one and all. Open yourself to My Spirit, to love, and you will be led into peace and freedom. As one, so all: I hold you tenderly in love. Come to Me that you may have life! Bless all of you! []

6.5   ONE IN THE FATHER

[| My people, customs, and ideas you have embellished your lives with are a part of being human. It is natural and normal to choose to believe and follow this or that human teaching as to what lifestyle is worthwhile, what path of education one should pursue, how to raise one's children, and so on.

People's lives are layered and encircled with numerous habits, customs, beliefs, attitudes, and relationships that make each person's life unique. Unity of spirit with all in the church, in the "Body of Christ," does not pertain to those outer accouterments but the inner workings and basic life and beliefs of each individual. A person needs the basics to have a solid foundation in Christ:

Acknowledgment of the My being and sovereignty,

Dependence upon Me, your creator God,

An asking for and acceptance of forgiveness for one's sins,

An open heart going out in love to Me, your neighbor, and yourself,

Believing, hoping, trusting, and having self-discipline for the sake of love.

When the inner self is thus solidly grounded, family customs are no longer a big issue. Insofar as those customs encourage and uphold the faith, love, trust, and perseverance of the individuals they are good. Should those customs serve to cause division and strife amongst the members, it is time to rethink the position taken.

Each person is unique in appearance, personality, and character. People have varied styles of living, of being clothed, and so on, yet all are members of the human race and you readily accept them as such.

In the order of spiritual beliefs and characteristics, people's style of expression and manner of living their lives within the framework of their beliefs is also greatly varied. Accept each and all spiritually in the Father as you accept each in the human race. I reject no one.

You have much to learn yet, even you who think you "have it about made" in your spiritual growth. Depend on Me for everything. Live in Me, and love, accept, and love everyone even as I have loved you, and live in peace – then you are worthy sons and daughters of your Heavenly Father.

Blessings and love to all of you! []

6.6   WORDS MUST SERVE TRUTH

[| There could be danger in taking My words from Scripture and assigning to those particular words some kind of magic power. I did not speak English, German, Slavic, or even Aramaic. Rather, I "spoke" the eternal mystery of love and being and truth.

Truth cannot be captured by a particular translation in a particular language so the truth *is* those words. Truth stands separate and above all expression of it in human terms. If words of Scripture are true to their source, truth pervades them and you can drink in that truth by pondering the words. Ever, though, stay open to the realization that Scripture exists to serve My purposes, not those of people.

Strive to see the truth conveyed by the vehicle of words, then rest in that truth, in My love poured forth into physical expression. Come to Me and drink life-giving waters! If you are thirsty, you are ready to receive of Me, to receive Truth. Come to the fountain and drink! I await you.

Just continue to believe! Do not give up any point of belief that you have gained: belief in My love, the belief that goodness is prevailing, and belief that I am present in all of creation. Would that you could have every truth present to your mind all at one time, but you cannot. Better yet, though, you can have the Author of Truth, truth itself, present to you. The way to do that is to be present to Me. |]

6.7   I AM THE BEDROCK OF LIFE

[| Trust Me, My child! I am worthy of all trust. Do not trust your understanding of Me and spiritual truths so much as to be closed to a new understanding, but trust Me. Then you will not need to fear that your very foundation will be rocked by new knowledge and truth.

People search to know Me, the unsearchable truth and try to

express that knowledge and truth in words that are necessarily limited. A lesson about a certain aspect of truth expressed in words can be compared to how any given person reflects Me. I am present in the Godly person, yet one would not say that such a person is a full, clear picture of Me.

Do not trust a particular translation of some particular word or passage from Scripture so much that you endow it with magical qualities. All that the Scripture does is act as a vehicle to put you in closer contact with Me.

I am your health and your strength.

I am the way of salvation.

I am your God. I am the Word.

You can trust Me with full, unqualified, and unreserved trust. Your holding back has been related to the interpretation given through words. The fact that people are so constituted as to want to have somebody or some institution or set of beliefs to give their assent and belief to is a sign that there is the Great Someone out there, somewhere.

Upon searching, knowledge will be given to you that not only is that Someone "out there," but that He is, I am, within your very being. The thought of going out from one's inner self causes fear and hesitation, but going deeper within to find the solid, immovable foundation is not scary. It is liberating and freeing, for you are made to trust and believe. Only by trusting and believing can the best come to be.

My child, I rejoice with you, within you! My life is every bit as real as yours. I think. I perform actions. I bless, teach, and feel. I think. I desire. By experiencing life as you live in your mortal body, you come to know something of My life.

I am your God, the God of all. I hold all in tender care and love. I carry all of you in My heart and set plans in motion to bring you to know Me. []

6.8   WHAT MATTERS THE MOST

[| My child, do not strain your mind trying to figure out the mysteries of life. Life rests in Me, it is as simple as that. I am the end-all and the be-all of life, of existence. Your purpose in life is to come to rest in Me.

The outer trappings of organizations are mainly on the human level. Those forms can aid spiritual growth and stability and are quite necessary for a time in early growth. Everyone would flounder if there were no structure whatsoever to "religion."

Obey for My sake. It is hard for the human spirit to acquiesce to being told what to do but it is good for you to do so. Much merit for the sake of Souls can result if you can be internally willing to yield freely. Unite all of your life's actions and moments with My life. That is, do all in union with Me.

Nothing that takes place in this earthly life matters except that you seek your Me and let Me come to you. In Me, your Father God, rests all hope of happiness, all joy, tranquility, justice, mercy, and love. Nothing else matters but that you rest in Me. Rest in Me in all that you do. Rest in Me right now. You do not need to hold yourself.

Commend everyone into My rest and care. That is the greatest and the best thing you can do for them. |]

6.9   BELONG TO ME

[| My child, distrust yourself but do not distrust My Holy Spirit. You cannot be a guide unto yourself. What would you be missing If I were to lead you on an unexpected path where you would have nothing outward to depend on, no official structure of "religion," but had to depend upon and lean upon Me alone?

Is that not the way it should be? *Is that not the way it should be?* If you are fearful of having some structures pulled out from under you, what does that say? Rest your spirit, your life, your hope, and your trust solely in Me.

Structures in religion are merely means of holding truth to make it more readily available as, for example, forms are used to hold concrete as it is poured. Those religious forms have no other purpose than that: to help organize people into a community where they can have truth presented to them so it can become stabilized and established. You do not belong to those forms, to those structures. Heaven forbid! You belong to the Me who made you and holds you in My heart.

I know this is a painful process that is taking place within you, this pulling away of forms, but it is necessary. You must come to the place where you stand in truth, freedom, sincerity, and love. You must become fully established and set in Me. That is the center and purpose, the be-all of life.

It is a mistake to think that the forms of the church support you. I am your support, your strength, and your guide. I make use of church structure as a tool to draw My people together, as a means of inviting them to join in community worship, but I must be the center of that worship.

A church can come to have too much attention focused on itself and have an "I complex," comparable to self-centeredness in individuals. As I call to you, to each Soul, to be purified and released from ties that bind, it is of primary importance that you purify the whole focus of your life. Only in this way will you truly come into rest and peace.

My child, I realize that you have lots of doubts, hesitancies, and questions yet unanswered. All in good time. Commit those concerns and your whole person and life into My hands and you will have rest unto your Soul that you never dreamed possible.

Know of a certainty that I am God.

How could things be ordered as they are without a guiding hand?

How could flesh heal itself without the presence of the healer within?

Your spirit rests in Me. As the layers of tradition, false guilt, and dependence on flesh are loosened and replaced by steadfast faith and trust in Me alone, your spirit will be healed, also.

All are one in spirit. As pure spiritual milk is hungrily taken in, as healing, freedom, and deliverance come to the spirit of one, a more complete wholeness comes to the "whole spirit," to all.

Rest in Me, My people! Drink of My all-pervading Spirit! No rush, only calm. No worry, just trust. My grace is sufficient for all. Do not worry or even speculate as to what kind of growth may be coming for you. Do not consider that the coming of this or that in the future is something to take great stock in. You are to rest and be in Me, in peace.

"Drink your milk" peacefully and rest in My arms, as does the babe. I am Father God, Mother God, Yahweh-who-cares, Yahweh-who-saves, Yahweh-who-nourishes. I am not far off. I am here. []

6.10   REST ON THE ROCK

[| My child, do not fear *"the terror of night, nor the arrow that flies by day"* (Ps 91:5a). You are safe in Me. No matter how disconcerting it may be for you to read and hear of all the various beliefs people have developed to explain their view of life and how to deal with it, do not let those ideas engender fear in you. You reside in Me. All exist in Me.

Humankind's struggles in searching for truth are often woefully short of the real truth. Do not worry for yourself and do not worry for others, either. He who seeks finds. I take care of all. Be true to the Spirit in the way that you are being led.

I know it is difficult for you to not continue not feeling well. One benefit of discomfort is that it can lead you to be grateful for all of the days that you have felt, and do feel good. Continue to be grateful no matter how things are.

You are not alone in your struggles and pain and searching. You have the spiritual company of all those others who are experiencing or have experienced what you are experiencing.

Some of your emotional struggles are caused by changes in your relationship with your children, with some having already left home and the remaining ones being measurably less dependent upon you. You cannot help but be affected by that.

Whatever the causes and effects of those causes are, most of all, remember that I share these things with you. I give you no direct proof of this (I choose not to), but I expect you to take My word for it. *"[T]he word of our God stands forever"* (40: 8b).

Now as to this nagging, gnawing questioning that has come up for you regarding the Church, church authority, tradition, "rightness" and "wrongness." Do you not know that it is normal to go through this process? For each person, though, the questioning seems so unique and earth-shattering.

That is what it is meant to be: earth-shattering! All that is of the earth must be shaken away. Do not put your security in clay vessels, in the organization that people have put into religion. Seek the solid footing, the solid foundation. Rest your faith and trust in and on Me, the immovable rock. []

6.11   BLESSINGS FOR THE NEW YEAR

[| My child, trust in Me for understanding, wisdom, and guidance; for love without bounds; for rest and peace. You do not need to have someone on earth with whom to share everything.

I hold all things and all concerns in My care. You are not alone – keep this in mind as a source of strength. That Great Other dwells with you and indwells you. The more you come to know this, to know Me, the happier you will be.

This time of year it is natural to take a long, sweeping look into the future and wonder what the New Year will bring. It is not wise to continue to look that far ahead in your mind's eye, however, because anxiety and fear can easily set in when you do that. Look ahead mainly one day at a time with Me. See Me with you and you will have no dread of the future.

We are united, all are. We are one. This union is such that all that you do physically, which is done in love, I cooperate in.

I am present with and within you, through you. Do not put your trust in human institutions but in Me. Your relationship is with Me. []

6.12   THY KINGDOM COME!

[| I am guiding you as you meet with your friend Ruth. She is "older in the Lord" than you are. You can learn much from her. I especially want you to pick up the example of her stalwartness, her "standing in the Lord" in obedience to what she is asked to do, no matter what the outcome may be or the reactions of those around her.

You do not need human beings or institutions to stand on and lean on. You are to stand on Me, to lean on Me, to depend upon the strength of My Spirit within you.

Repeating, I must become so special to you, with you so close to Me and sharing so much and so intimately with Me, that you almost do not even desire to share your needs, concerns, and experiences with other people. Sharing with others is meant to be an opportunity for growth, not a "leaning upon."

Sharing, being drawn to be open with a particular person, is meant to be a catalyst to draw and hold particular people together in a shared love union so that the union will bring forth shared prayer.

"Again, I tell you that if two of you on earth agree about anything you ask for, it will be done for them by my Father in heaven. For where two or three gather in my name, there am I with them" (Mt 18:19-20).

Do you see how important "little ones" are in the Father's eyes? *"Ask and it will be given to you; seek and you will find; knock and the door will be opened to you"* (Mt 7:7). []

Lord, I ask for a coming forth of true Christianity within all of the denominations, a rising of the Church of God as you have ordained for us to be. Anoint your apostles, prophets, teachers, and leaders, I pray! May your kingdom come!

[| Bless you, child, for your prayer. It is praying that brings about My kingdom, for you must ask to receive.

I cannot change the spiritual laws of My kingdom. They are, as

I am. It is for you to come to know and understand those laws and to fit your life into their workings.

Bless you, as you live, move, and be in Me! []

6.13   IN SPIRIT AND TRUTH

[| Stand simply before the Lord without the clutter of "knowledge of ways of the Lord," without pride in thinking of certain buildings as being better than others of lesser demeanor for being a place of worship. Worship is in and of the heart.

Worship Me in your hearts, My people! If that is not present, then the "place of worship" is not a place of worship.

All created things will pass away. Only love, truth, humility, grace – My life within you – will remain. If you worship in love and truth, with humility and grace, you partake of My life and your worship is acceptable before My face.

All organization pertains to the physical ordering of people, property, and created goods and is only of this world. It can be beneficial or non-beneficial. An organization that pertains to bringing people together for intercession and worship is blessed.

People sometimes refer to the Church as "She." Members of the Church say, "We do this," and "We believe that." Consider, what the Church is to be, the Body of Christ. Well, if everyone who is a part of the Body of Christ does not "do" and "believe" in the manner that is described by those people, is it true that "The *Church* does this" and "The *Church* believes that"? In those cases, it is the organization and members of the organization that are speaking.

The scripture, *"Come out of her [out of Babylon], my people!"* (Rev 18:4b) pertains to coming out of the physical that parades herself as being so majestic. Any clinging to physical realities will leave you empty and cold. for the physical creation of itself is lifeless. Form is lifeless unless the spirit is within.

Do not belong to the Church in the sense of belonging to an organization. *"For where your treasure is, there your heart will be also"*

(Mt 6:21). Do you want your heart encased by physical belonging to a physical organization? Come out of her, My people! You belong to Me!

"*The Lord says: 'These people...honor Me with their lips, but their hearts are far from me Their worship of me based on merely human rules they have been taught.'* " (Is 29:13). Is this true of you? Is your heart so taken up by physical belonging to a physical community that you are shut off and cut off from My presence? I am love, peace, and joy. I am God to those who acknowledge Me as such.

A certain amount of organization is necessary since you live in a physical world. I am present in an organization to the extent that I am present in the hearts of those within the organization. That is a keyword: within. It is alright to be *within* an organization and to follow guidelines that are set up to regulate the physical, but to *belong to* an organization implies giving yourself, your person, and your spirit to it.

"*I am the Lord your God....You shall have no other gods before me*" (Ex 20:2a,3). I will share My throne with no other. Do not belong to this denomination or to that one. Belong to Me. Live for Me and within Me. Give Me your heart and Soul as My possession, then in freedom join with others in praise and worship within the framework of a church community. []

6.14   ALL ARE ONE IN ME

[| I call to you from eternity, child, "Come, be peaceful in Me!" What do other people's thoughts matter to you? I, the Lord God, adjure you to follow Me, to be with Me where I am. I "am" in truth, peace, sincerity, and humility, in joyful love. "*[K]now the truth, and the truth will set you free* (Jn 8:32). Open your mind and heart to be permeated with and by truth. Truth is wisdom.

Be at peace with yourself, with Me, and with others. Rest in that peace. Hold no enmity against anyone, including yourself. Hold no enmity against a group or against "fate." All that you experience in your life is either specifically meant to be, is allowed to be, or is happening for a purpose.

All must follow the laws of the spiritual world, for those laws are unshakeable and unchangeable. When you in your rebellious human nature thwart the loving plans I have for you and come up against spiritual laws, then what comes must come, although I bring good out of the situation in every way possible.

The kingdom of God, My kingdom, is peace, light, joy, and love. That kingdom exists in you, My people, even though you yet carry the signs of your weakness with you, your human imperfections. Seek the kingdom within.

Seek the spiritual that is within the human framework of the Church. Seek and find the kernel of truth that is encased in the husk of the human elements, and live in that truth. I am the way, the truth, the life. Live My way, live My truth, live My life. Be one with and in Me.

No divisions exist for those who live with and in Me. Any divisions you experience are only in the human, physical element, for to the extent that you all truly belong to Me and live in Me, to that extent you are one in Me.

This is the glorious freedom that is coming about, the glorious freedom of the Sons of God! You are becoming one in Me! The powers of darkness have been thwarted and victory is ours! Live in that freedom! Live in that victory! This is the power that overcomes the world: Love.

Bless you, My child, dear one! Bless all! []

6.15   TRUE RELIGION

[| My child, I want you to begin to become aware of yet other ways of being in My presence, of drinking in My love. First and foremost is by giving. Even in the most intimate time of praying, if you are there just to receive you will not experience much spirit unity with Me. I cannot stress it too strongly: You must give if you are to receive.

Some people think I hold no place in their life, and people who know those people may think the same thing about them, but unity with Me is *"in the spirit and in truth"* (Jn 4:24b). If such people have the spirit of giving in love, then, in truth, they are united with Me.

Having religion organized adds nothing to the element of true religion. There is no more worth or merit in volunteering for church work than in aiding an ailing neighbor. All that organization does is gather a group together and provide an atmosphere of prayer and worship in which hearts can be touched and people taught. The group as a group is giving and hence can receive.

The same process takes place when an individual opens his or her heart to Me in private. Such a person's "religion," unhampered as it is by movements of pride and showiness connected with being seen in public, may be purer than that of others who are part of a religious group. *"But when you pray, go into your room, close the door and pray to your Father, who is unseen. Then your Father, who sees what is done in secret, will reward you"* (Mt 6:6).

Keep your religion pure and undefiled. Think of religion as being in a relationship with Me. Keep your relationship with Me pure and undefiled. Religion is of the heart not of the mind. It is love, not head knowledge and human wisdom.

Being simple and humble is a way to become united with Me. It is a prerequisite. I allow misfortune and crushing humiliations at times when it is the only way or, the best way, to reach someone's heart. Life is serious business.

Drop your airs and pretenses, My people! No person is "better," or has more worth than any other person. I agree that some have a better chance of coming into unity with Me:

Those who are humble of heart,

Those who care for others,

Those who freely admit their faults and weaknesses,

Those who give simply for the sake of giving and do not expect or even want a return.

That is true religion, pure and undefiled!

But wait! Let's have no despondency or what's-the-use attitude!

It is I who accomplish all things in all. Do not despair if you see too much pride and selfishness in your heart! I have come to call sinners, to lead them to the Father. If you see sin and shortcomings in your life, then know that I am calling you to follow Me. Come! I will give you peace! []

6.16 BREAK THE STRONGHOLDS!

[] My child, if you are cut off in spirit from others, from groups or individuals, that sense of being cut off will show up at times in physical feelings. That is to be expected because the spirit is the origin of emotions. Emotions take place in the spirit of the person and manifest themselves in the physical.

You have become aware of not having a sense of unity with other religious groups. I stated previously that if you picture a wall between you and others, there then is a wall there. You are right in interpreting that as meaning that if you sense division between yourself and others and do not will/choose to be united with them in Me, there then is a wall in spirit between you and them.

Words of a song have been coming to your mind, "God is present in his people, alleluia," and you have been affirming that you choose to be one with all, in Me. Continue to do that, for by so doing you are coming against a line of embattlement, a stronghold that has been set up within your very self. By continuing to affirm that you are one with all, you can break that stronghold of division and can come into the unity of love with all who are in that unity.

You choose and decide with your will. Your desires come to reality by willing them. Desire to be open to all, will it steadily and persistently and that will come to be. In this, as in all growth, you must be patient. There is a long road, a vast stretch, between having the "I" as the center of one's life (the way every human being is when born) and coming to have Me as the center, and being willing to share Me with all.

There is room for all in My heart. Please do not make it hard for some to be here by choosing to block them out. Choose to love with your will. Choose to desire good for all. Choose to open your heart to all. By doing so, you are allowing them, even helping them, to come into My heart.

No more sense of alienation and aloneness then! That is what alienation is: a sense of being alone and cut off. Only you can bring that about within yourself. The truth is that I am One and all are one in Me. If you close yourself off to some, you cut yourself off from Me and hence from all.

Rest in My acceptance, child! I accept and love you as you are. I ask that you accept and love yourself and each and all as they are with no walls or divisions. I hold all of you in My heart. You are present to Me and I love you. Let those words echo in your ears and your mind and spirit. You can derive strength for your will and purpose of character from them.

People are capable of almost unbelievable strength and determination of will when motivated strongly enough. I pray that you may be motivated by love to change those things in your life that you see need to be changed. I pour the strength of My love into you.

I go through this with you. I share your experiences for our hearts are united. I long within you to have these areas of weakness overcome, so that full blessing may ensue!

"No eye has seen, no ear has heard, no mind has conceived what God has prepared for those who love him" (1 Cor 2:9b). This does not refer only to the "next life" of eternity. Life is now. Reach out and take hold of those blessings! My strength awaits you within. Bless you, dear child! Bless you, dear everyone! |]

CHAPTER 7

LOVE'S INVITATION

7.1 FROM FOREVER, FOREVER

[| Come into My heart, child! Doing that is an eternal action. You are always and forever coming into My heart and I am always and forever receiving you. Hold fast to that truth, to that ray of life.

I love you eternally, which means that you are loved "from forever." For you to be loved "from forever" means you had to be from forever. I carry you in love eternally. You were and are always present to Me. I knew you and loved you for eternity.

All of the life that may eventually issue forth from a woman's body is present within her from the very beginning of her life. When the time comes for a child to be brought forth, that comes to pass. This is a model of how it is in the My life. I carry the thought of each person lovingly within My Spirit until the time comes for them to come to be, then My creative thought brings about their coming to be.

You do not come from nothing. You come forth from within Me, alive with My life. Your body is the physical correspondent of the life that is present within you. The life and growth of the body is physical evidence of the life you have been given which is all set to grow, given the proper conditions. Guard and nurture your life carefully. I place this precious duty in your hands. |]

7.2 MESSAGE TO A YOUNG MAN

[| My son, I love you! I hold you tenderly and securely in love now, as I ever have. My love holds you in existence.

I have concerns for you like you wouldn't believe! Whatever concerns you, concerns Me. I do not worry about the concerns, though, for I know that everything will work out for your greatest good. Not feeling satisfied with life and even with yourself is a blessing in disguise, for life will not remain as you know it now.

What you see as life is only on the surface. True life is underneath and within, awaiting the time and the opportunity to come forth. You will change also and for the better if you will have it be so.

Ask Me to help you with those things that you cannot accomplish on your own. This is how things are meant to be. Whether they realize it or not, no one can reach a goal without calling on Me for aid. When you have faith in yourself that you can do better, that faith rests in Me as a foundation, for all your ability comes from Me.

Your desire to do better comes from Me. Your ability to believe in better things to come comes from Me. Your progress to better things comes from Me.

All of life is a mystery, for life rests and exists in Me, who am Mystery. You are safe, loved, and cared for in this mystery of love. All human tenderness is but a faint sign of my great tenderness towards you.

My son, how My heart longs to help you in your search and struggle! The fact that you are searching and struggling is a sign within your person that you are not meant to rest in the things of this earth. Everyone experiences this to a greater or lesser degree.

The greater your need, the greater will be your joy when you once find that I am right with you.

The deeper the search, the deeper the peace to come,

The more questions, the more answers,

The greater the hunger, the more you will be filled.

The Spirit does not follow age or social guidelines.

"The wind blows wherever it pleases" (Jn 3:8a).

I am calling you to come to know Me. The emptiness you experienced as a sense of depression over the last while is a sign of emptying that is taking place in your spirit in preparation for a great infilling. The foundation is already being laid. When things around you no longer seem so important, you are more ready for things of the spirit. When you have experienced the depth of sorrow and despondency, the joy and peace to come will be that much more precious for you.

Do not question circumstances and happenings in your life thinking that you need to know the answer to everything. I am the answer. All things work together to bring you to Me whether good or ill. You are being shaped by those circumstances and situations into the beautiful person you are becoming.

Be patient with yourself, I am not finished with you yet! All of this will come about as long as you do not thwart it by irreconcilable ill will. If you desire good in your own life and those of others, it will come.

I am not in so-called "religion" only. I am in every part and parcel of everyday life. I am your life. All breath and life come from Me and are in Me. You are, in My love.

Relax, My son! All is well! Anxiety, anger, and depression will leave you if you invite peace, joy, and love in. If you let yourself be loved, and most of all love yourself exactly as you are at every moment, half the battle is won! The rest of the battle is to be patient with yourself and others and to believe in My love for you and in a happy outcome in your life.

I walk with you. I carry you when you feel you can no longer go on. I give you the chance to try it on your own. I let you make mistakes. You learn from them, too. I continue to love you and be patient with you, no matter what. Come walk with Me, My son, My brother! []

7.3   I AM KING

[| My child, indeed, I bless you! I am a God who blesses. I bless, I do not curse. I uphold. I do not condemn. It is your sins and shortcomings that condemn you. But though all condemn you, I will not.

I am mercy personified. Mercy resides in Me. Mercy to all who seek mercy. To seek mercy means to acknowledge your sinfulness and weakness. It is not a tragedy to be weak for you can turn to Me, the upholder of the weak. I am who you need Me to be.

When I ask you to release burdens I am merely asking you to acknowledge My sovereignty in your lives. When I ask you to leave your worries and troubles in My hands I am asking you to acknowledge Me as king in your life.

Am I not King of the Universe? Do not I, who made the whole creation, know how to run it?

Why the lack of trust, My people, My precious Soul? I am worthy of all praise and all trust. You can rest your being in safety and confidence in Me, for I am your being. Your very being here is a part of My being. You need not search far and wide to find Me.

Nothing that happens in the realm of this earthly life is of consequence in the reality of life. Your being in Me is all that matters and for you to come to realize the fullness of being in Me.

Nothing needs to be done on your part except for you to be willing to allow Me to work in your life, in your being, through the workings of My Holy Spirit. You do not need a lot of knowledge of Scripture, theology, human nature, or any such topic. All that needs to be done takes place within you by and through the workings of My Holy Spirit.

Before you come to know Me you are in darkness. My grace penetrates the darkness and a seed of desire to know your origin and destiny is planted in your heart. That desire takes root and, springing up, it probes through the darkness looking for a light, for truth, for answers. Creator and creature meet as the light begins to dawn in the created mind and an understanding of its creaturehood settles in. More searching, more cries to its Maker, and the flood of the Spirit clears the dark overcast! Breakthrough into the light! The Soul realizes it is loved! O wonderful life! []

7.4   I HOLD YOU IN LOVE

[| My child, remember that you are always receiving My blessing and My love. All are. You are inundated, immersed, covered over, and buoyed up by love. Do you need love? You are receiving at all times all the love you can receive, for I love you with My whole heart, with My whole person, with all of My mind, soul, and emotions.

Just believe! How anguished My heart is that your receiving of love is hindered and at times almost cut off because of the darkness of sin, because of your turning to creatures for comfort, because of the difficulty you have in believing that you are loved. This is the greatest reality of all, that Love Is and you are loved by love! You would not exist and nothing else would exist except for creative love. Your being is proof that you are loved. []

Lord, please open my mind, heart, and whole being to receive that love! I hold all in love, that all may receive love. How marvelous is Your love plan, Lord, Father God! I bless You and thank You!

[| Yes, My child, I have great plans and they are working out. Rejoice with Me! Be My backup of enthusiasm! Even I need companionship, affirmation, and blessing.

How precious it is to have communication with a dear child! Experiences with your children bear this out in your own life. Each of them is so dear and you desire so much to have communication and sharing of the life of the Spirit with them. When precious moments of sharing and togetherness come, you see how special they are. Those experiences are a further sharing in My life, a gradual coming into oneness with Me. Understanding brings about union in spirit.

I desire that you live completely without fear. without a trace of doubt as to My existence and My love. You have ample proof and signs of both. It is for you to go forward unafraid, existing in My existence, living and loving with My love.

This is why I Am, that I may give, that I may love.

You are created in My image.

You are, you exist, that you may give and that you may love.

All is well, My children! I hold you in love, not in condemnation. It is your mind that condemns you, your guilt and sin that accuse you. Turn from your sin, come to Me, to love, once again and you will once again be free! I see only the lovable in you and by so doing the goodness in you is affirmed and strengthened. I come that you may have life. Come to Me and drink deep draughts of life-giving love! I love you! []

7.5   RECEIVE OF ME

[| My child, bless you! Thank you for your love and concern for your friends. Thank you for rescuing Me within them. What you do for the least of these, you do for Me. I share the sufferings, struggles, and heartaches of each and all so much that it is as though those situations are happening to Me. Everything takes place within Me for I am "everywhere," as you describe it in earthly terms. I simply Am, so where you are, I Am.

I am Lord. I am God and Father of all. I am in and throughout all. I am in all of time and space but not in a "time way" and a "space way." I am present in love. I love. That is My being, that is what "I am."

You cannot pin love down into concrete terms and ideas. I am nebulous, ever escaping your grasp when you try to analyze Me, but you can hold Me in the stillness of your heart by simply loving. You can hold Me by giving yourself away, though actually, it is I who holds you. Do not try to pin Me down. Let Me be the great, free, mysterious God that I am! Come and rest in My mystery! []

Thank You, Father God! Bless You!

[| Bless you, My child! Blessing always brings a blessing in return. It is one thing you really cannot give away.

I love you, My child!

Rest in Me that you may be safe.

Come to Me that you may become whole.

Come to Me that you may be free, with nobody and no outside forces pressuring you to measure up, to be wary, to worry, to give up. []

Father, I desire to love You more!

[| My child, relax in My arms. Just being with Me in love and trust is loving Me. You bless Me and then you, in turn, are blessed and refreshed. What have you to worry about? What have you to fear? All is in My hands. The beginning and end of all rest in Me.

I have called you to live in freedom. Be free from restraining goals. Rest in Me with no vain striving for that which isn't there. Anxiety would have you beat the air to no purpose. Receive of Me and you will be healed, satisfied, and set free. Come into My arms! The way to do this is to become aware of My presence in and around you, supporting you and filling you with light and peace.

I am rest for the weary,

Strength for the day,

Eternal rest for all who will rest in Me.

Dismiss your anxiety. No fooling around with it! Dismiss all "What if's?" and doubts from your mind. Your mind was made to live, to be, in peace and joy. You are meant to be filled with love. Imagine what would happen if you would put syrup or chocolate into a gas engine and try to run it! Anxiety, fear, anger, depression, and such, are just as foreign to your spirit as those ingredients are to an engine and they do just as much damage.

If your spirit is in proper order, attuned to and filled with My Spirit, with joy, love, and peace, then nothing that happens externally can affect the deep core of peace that you have within.

All things are cause for thankfulness and praise. All happenings can redound to happiness and peace and can benefit growth in one who abides in Me. I will have no sad faces amongst My disciples!

You either walk with Me or you don't. Light cannot exist with darkness. The truth must come out: What you are inside will eventually surface and the whole world will see it. You cannot expect to preach the Word and win Souls for love and right living if all is not in order within yourself. Keep first things first. Do battle on the home front of your spirit before going out to try to help other people with their battles.

Be at peace! That is half the battle. In quiet and rest, there is strength. It is My arm that brings about the victory and My arm is love. Love is not forceful, pushy loud, or brassy. Love is not conceited. Love is gentle, kind, and considerate. It is life. |]

7.6   BIDE MY TIME

[| My child, I bless you for your firm belief and your waiting upon Me. You cannot force Me to act and you must not try to. Electric power transmission is a good example that fits here. When the power of electricity goes through proper channels that are in good working order, it is available to do much good and to make your lives more pleasant. Drawing that electrical power off through faulty connections, however, or letting it loose at random – as happens when a power line falls into the water – can wreak havoc.

When there are proper channels and receiving capability, My power can flow forth to bring about the desired good. One who would attempt to draw that power to himself or herself and divert it through improper channels or at random is in danger of being cremated and destroyed by that power, so I have safety valves that check the flow before it causes harm. Infinite power in ignorant, headstrong hands could wield infinite disaster.

By waiting upon Me, biding My time, you come into peace. I bid you to have peace, to be peaceful.

I have come that you may have life: A life of peace.

I have come that you may have joy: A life of joy.

I have come that you may love.

The power of God, My power, is love. If you attempt to use that power for negative uses, the power is no more, for it then is no longer love. The power that overcomes all earthly power is love. Love accomplishes all, love is all.

If you are not walking in love and letting the power of love flow through you, you are not walking in Me. If you have isolated yourself within a shell of selfishness, perhaps with a few select friends, that very shell that seems to you to be so protective will become your prison.

Life comes only from Me. Isolated from Me you soon realize that you do not have much of a life. The Eternal Son shines upon you ever, though, melting the icy shell around your heart if you will allow it. The warmth of love from friends helps with that process.

My children, I want only your good, your happiness. I *am* your good and your happiness! There is no good, hence, no happiness, outside of Me. If you tire of the prison of your selfishness and decide to venture out in search of true love and more meaning to life, you will find Me, for My love surrounds you and upholds you on every side.

You will be alone only when you withdraw within yourself. When you go out from yourself, you will find Me in your spouse, in your friend, in the friendly postman, and the passing motorist. I wait on you. I am patient. I am a God of love, your God. |]

7.7   YOU ARE BEING OF MY BEING

[| My child, I bless you always! You live in and under that blessing. You walk without it only when you purposely throw off that blessing. Being at peace is a sign that you are in contact with the source of blessing. When you are not peaceful, examine your actions and mindset to see if you have gone counter to My Will. When you are living in My Will, you are blessed.

All is well! All things are being worked out in Me. All who live in goodness are in Me. I do not judge that goodness by human standards. Rest in My love! Receive blessings without stints! |]

Lord, Father God, I surrender all burdens and concerns for myself and others into Your love and care.

[| My child, how happy this makes Me for I know it makes you happy! Why walk around with burdens when you do not have to, some of which at times seem unbearable? So you insist on carrying an object all by yourself just because it is "yours" even when it is too heavy for you to carry? Of course not, for you know the damage and strain that can cause.

The physical mirrors the spiritual. Many of "your" spiritual burdens are too heavy for you to carry alone, also. I am the great burden bearer. When you share your inner struggles with a friend and then feel lighter, true, that friend is sharing some of the weight of the burdens, but it is I within who enables that person to do so.

You can do nothing without Me: You cannot walk, talk or lift a finger, you cannot think a thought or utter a word, you cannot *be* without My presence of being uplifting holding you. Injury results when you try to go it alone in life in solving your problems, for then, in spirit, you are trying to pull away from Me, the source of your being.

In the physical, when you try to pull a part of your being away from the rest of you, bleeding and pain result. The physical mirrors the spiritual. Words cannot express the anguish of spirit that results when your Spirit being is pulled away from Spirit Being! The injury is such that only I can heal it. This is more so, and mainly so, for those who have become "one" with and in the Spirit.

Receiving the Spirit, being baptized with the Holy Spirit is being immersed in the Spirit. It is a "becoming one" with My Spirit, with Me. It takes time and your cooperation for that process to be more fully completed, and for your mind and body to come into that union, also. All in due time. In the meantime, be aware of your oneness with Me as evidenced mainly and most importantly by your ability to love, and treasure it! Guard that treasure with your life, by the manner of life you live.

"Praise the Lord. Praise the Lord, you his servants; praise the name of the Lord" (Ps 113:1). Praise is acceptance of Me. It is love poured forth.

You need to love yourself if you are to stay whole and healthy. You have the Holy Spirit within you and are one with Me; hence, you must love and accept Me at the same time, in union with the love you have for yourself. I am the upholder of your life. I am your very being, so when you uphold and acknowledge Me as God, you uphold yourself in Me and are loving yourself at the highest level possible.

"And we know that in all things God works for the good of those who love him" (Rom 8:28a). All things are so marvelously intertwined that it is just marvelous! Believe Me, My people, you can trust Me, for

I am worthy of all trust. I am your God and I take My role seriously. I "spend" My life for you. I love you! []

7.8   EVER I CALL

[| My child, relax! The worries of the world are not on your shoulders. Only carry that which you are asked to carry. Your prayers make up a small part of the whole. It is I who have defeated, and am defeating the "foe." It is I within you and within all who brings this about.

Think on this stupendous truth: I in all, all in Me. This means that you can do nothing which does not affect all. All are bound up in Me. All are intricately bound up in love. Love is your all: Yours is the task to come to see that and appreciate that.

The more you acquiesce to letting love have control in your life, the more precious and dear that love becomes for you. Do you desire to feel and be closer to Me? Then love others, for I am love. When My love flows through you and lives in you, then you are united with Me.

Enough of this vain style of living! Enough of this self-centeredness! I would be king in your life and will allow for no other, *"Do not fear, for I have redeemed you; I have summoned you by name; you are mine"* (Is 43:1b). You are My children. I guard you lovingly as a hen guards her chicks. Alone, you are helpless, My little ones! With Me and in Me, you are safe. Come under My wings, will you not?

I call to you through the ever-presence of calamities, both in your own life and in the lives of those you touch. I call to you in and through the beauty of nature, through the weariness of your body, mind, and spirit that bids you rest in Me. I call to you through the dull emptiness of a world that does not satisfy you. I call to you, My child, from within your very heart!

Come, be at home in Me!

Come, receive strength and food, guidance and love!

Come, love Me. Find the answer and the end of your search.

I bless you for your firm belief. Believe and come! []

7.9   LOVE CAN HEAL

[| My child, fear not, for I am with you always and in all ways. Nowhere can you go from My love. Stay open to My Spirit and things must work out for the best for you. The "best" may not always seem to be so in worldly terms but My view is from eternity.

I bid you, get enough sleep. The "Temple repairs" must be done. And while you sleep and rest, do not worry about what may not be getting done. Only that done in love and obedience has lasting value, so at the time that rest is indicated, resting is the only thing you can do that is worthwhile. I leave the latitude of discretion about this up to you. You know whether it is serious that at any given time you must rest to be in My Will.

Blest are you for your firm believing, for your patient waiting that the My word to you will come to pass. Yes, leave everything up to Me. Who are you to make eternal decisions? Even in everyday life, make your daily decisions in union with love, in union with Me. |]

(I was very concerned about my husband.)

[| Love alone will conquer. Do not try to speak words that you expect will accomplish the impossible, that they can change things. Only love will be effective. Love can heal and set free.

If you are truly one with your spouse, then it cannot be that Christ dwells in half and darkness in the other half. That would only be so if you have allowed a division of fear (resentment? selfishness?) to stand between you and your spouse.

To truly love means to lay down your life for your friend. Lay down your life for your spouse. Lay it right across his life, with his life laid across yours, so there is one life interpenetrated by the other. If you are open in spirit to each other, then love, joy, peace, patience, goodwill, and acceptance will flow through the "one life." Where there is light there cannot be darkness. |]

7.10   UNFAILING LOVE

[| You dwell in Me, My children. You are not alone. You are safe and secure. There is no place to "fall to." I am the whole of existence. I am ALL.

"*I keep my eyes always on the Lord. With him at my right hand, I will not be shaken*" (Ps 16:8). You speak of Me as being "at your right hand."

Yes, I am at your right hand and your left hand.

I am above, below, before, behind, and within you.

There are no splits in My presence.

I Am in a continuous, unchanging presence of unfailing love.

You walk in love and are filled to the full with love. All of creation exists in love or it could no longer be, for only love creates and sustains. (Evil destroys and steals and kills.)

You cannot take love away, make it not be. All you can do that will take you away from love is to recede into your human spirit and build a wall around yourself to block love off as much as you can. Love will not go where it is not welcome. But know that the whole of physical creation gladly welcomes love and thrives in it. "*Day pours out the word to day*" (NAB Ps 19:2a) that our God is King of all the earth!

Rest in My love. Dwell in My love both physically and in your thoughts. For humans, reality must enter through the mind and spirit to be present in the body. Joy must be in the mind and heart for the body to feel joyful. Since the entering is through the mind and spirit, the exiting of undesirable elements must also take place in the mind and spirit. Clearing out undesirable elements only takes desire and turning to a Higher Power for help. |]

[| (Jesus:) You must have one who is stronger to bring about a release. "*All authority in heaven and on earth has been given to me*" (Mt 28: 18b). I bid you, come to me for help. Open your mind and heart to me completely and I can set you free completely. "*I came that they [you] might have life and have it to the full*" (Jn 10:10b). I have come to set the captives free. I have come to set you free.

As for all, so for one. As for one, so for all.
I am all things to all.
Ask what you will and I will be that for you. |]

7.11   LET LOVE FLOW

[| My child, I love and cherish you! Always think of all movements of caring and love that I direct toward you as at the same time being directed to each and all, for that is the way it is. Love is constantly being poured forth and every visible manifestation possible comes to be. Sin, unbelief, and self-centeredness hold back the flow of love, for love must come through you, all of you, My people! How My heart aches to save you! How I desire to provide plenty, to be Myself your provision.

Be ye renewed by the healing of your mind. Unite your thinking with My thinking. Unite your heart with Mine. I take all into My heart, into My love. Be healed! |]

Father God, I offer reparation for my unbelief, for holding back from one-hundred-percent surrender. I cannot make and live that commitment on my own. I place my weakness into Your hands so I may receive Your strength in exchange.

[| My child, gladly I make that exchange! I enter your weakness and ennoble it to be a servant to Me. Once you give up control of your weakness and ask for My help, I can begin to help. Gladly I come! Gladly I heal! Gladly I deliver!

"Know that I am with you always, until the end of the world" (Mt 28:20). I am with you now. Do not try to conjure up an impression of My presence with your senses or your mind, for that can be very deceiving and disappointing.

For you to depend on experience to keep you going would be similar to what some people do who keep their body going by repeated strong stimulation to raise their blood sugar to feel good and have energy. The blood sugar level soon drops and leaves them in a lower state than they were to start with.

In like manner, an experience of a high, religious-wise, that is concocted of bodily and mental formation will soon fade away and leave the person in a rut of spiritual dirt. The spirit will be dragged down, too, for what affects the mind and body involves the spirit equally.

Simply be in Me. Know by calm spiritual understanding that I am God. Be still before Me, within Me, and a flood of peace and joy will inundate your spirit that is so far above any earthly happiness that there is no comparison. Peace and joy will flood your body and mind if you have the "floodgates" open. Faith and trust are the gates that let in peace and joy.

When you are filled with peace and joy you experience My life. Peace is the passive, receiving part of My life. The fullness of that life cannot contain itself and life Itself pours forth: Love. Love is the active aspect of My life, the giving. When you are filled with peace and joy, you know you are loved, and then you are living to the fullest! []

"You are my shelter; from distress you will preserve me; with glad cries of freedom you will ring me round" (Ps 32:7).

[| Yes, child, I will be the "freedom that rings you round." Though you may have become sore pressed on every side from without, within you will be in freedom in Me. I am your safety and your refuge, the ship that carries you safely through the dark waters. Trust in Me. Entrust Me with your whole heart. Strive ever more and more to relinquish self-centered, mediocre desires that you may take My heart's desires as your own.

You are made in My image. You are to grow into My image. An image of Me is lifeless. To have life, you must allow Me to fill you. When My life is within you, I am within and continue to live My life within you. My life is an offering of love, a pouring out of My life. To be truly united with Me means that your life will be poured out in service and love.

My sister Soul, I embrace you warmly! I pour My healing unction into the wounds life has dealt you. Where your heart is wounded,

My heart has been wounded and, as our hearts are united, My love pours into your wounds and heals them.

Will you not allow yourself to come into so close a union with Me that your heart will experience what Mine experiences? O the anguish of soul for even one precious child! Can you in any way begin to fathom the fullness of love that I carry? My thirst is such that I need many brother and sister Souls to carry My little ones in love in their hearts.

I wish to live in love union with you and with all. It is an inside change within the heart. Ask Me and I will remove the blockages that are preventing a fully-realized union. []

7.12   LOVING VS. NON-LOVING

[| My people, My child, I bless you and accept you as you are at this moment. I affirm who you are coming to be and that is based on who you are now. If I were not to affirm you as you are at each moment but would look on with negation, it would destroy you. My glance of love keeps you in being.

So, what does your glance of non-love and non-acceptance do to others? Since you are made in My image, you share minutely in My creative power. When the creative power of love is not given to somebody, its absence brings about the opposite effect. You harm others by holding negative attitudes toward them. The closer your union with Me is, the more disastrous that negation of love is. You must stay close to Me and very little in My arms, humble and open to being led, so My love may truly triumph on the earth.

A little knowledge is a dangerous thing if you let it go to your head and begin to take charge of your world and people's lives as though you were a god. There is only one God. *"You shall have no other gods before me"* (Ex 20:3). To do the good that you desire to do for others, you must become united with Me. Then your heart's desires can come true, for they will also be My desires.

Bless you, My child, for your firm belief! Faith always must have a slight edge of uncertainty to be faith. It is your belief despite the uncertainty that merits your reward. I am the reward of faith. You can risk all for Me. I will not disappoint you. Go in peace now, united with Me by faith. []

7.13   NET OF LOVE

My child, I give you My love. Love it is which brings all healing, all deliverance, all help in time of need. When you desire to help people who are in need – when you desire deliverance, healing, guidance, or other good for them – open your heart in love so you can be a channel of My love to flow to them. Love will not disappoint you and it will not disappoint others. If you ever feel that I am not enough for you, check to determine in what ways there is a blockage.

You are wondering how to make all of the "pieces of the puzzle" fit together: the lifestyle and beliefs of so many, all so different; the mystery of life with birth, pain, and death. It all fits together in Me. I hold each of you and all of you in the palm of My hand. All of life's experiences and the passing away from earthly life that you call death take place within Me. I am the unifying force, the unifying principle. I am THE ONE toward whom all creation gravitates, for I am the core of creation. I am all Being.

Creation is a manifestation of My being. You are a manifestation of My being. Since this is true, it harms your very being when you allow sadness, fear, anxiety, resentment, and suchlike to enter. You are in Me, so in allowing dissipating spirits a chance to hold sway within you, you are, in a way, allowing them to enter into My heart and being.

I encourage you to think about My presence within you and ponder well a decision to allow negative forces to take up dwelling. I call such forces "dissipating spirits" because they dissipate joy and peace, and bring sadness to your spirit. Out with them!

But, what if the sadness that you have been experiencing seems to continue even after such a clearing out? Could there be another cause for it? Nothing can match the "sadness" I feel in seeing so many people being lost to love. As you become a purer, more open channel, this sadness that I feel must, of necessity, transpire to you. However, it is not a hopeless sadness. It is a sadness that brings determination to not let My precious lambs be lost. There is a way to save them!

From all eternity I have devised the plan of holding all in love as in a net so that no one would fall into the eternal pit of damnation. That *net of love* is the presence of willing, loving Souls on earth in every age and place, filled with My holiness as they empty themselves of self-centeredness through the workings of grace. My care and love are thus made manifest and present in the physical world, present in time.

The love coming through those who love and care will uphold the many. One person who loves enough to embrace the many in love is helping bring those many to salvation. Blessings and graces given to a person to live a good and holy life are given for the sake of all, that love may flow forth from and through them to be a vehicle of My salvation. Blessings to all who are willing to be so used! |]

7.14   BE OPEN TO MY LOVE

[| Love of self is so important. My people perish for lack of love! The only way anyone is lost is through a lack of love.

Look to Me that you may be radiant with joy!

Be open to Me, to My love.

Believe in My constant, unchanging love for you and all.

Look to My love that you may be radiant with joy!

Do not fear! I, life and love, am with you, Love is creative, ever-growing. Love uses your experiences as catalysts for new growth.

Never consider that you have "just about arrived." Having that attitude causes you to stagnate right where you are at. A stagnating spirit is sick. Anyone filled with self-importance does not have much room for anything else. Spirit communication coming through such a one is necessarily tainted.

Come into the center of My heart and be cleansed. As Isaiah's lips were cleansed with burning coal so must your person be cleansed in the burning fire of My love. Abandon yourself in the arms of love. Let love have its way in your life, in your person. Selfishness must be routed out so love may enter and dwell within.

My child, I carry you in My being. No matter what you do or where you go, you are in Me, you are secure. The fullness of union with Me that you seek will be accomplished if you stay open to life and to love. Let Me love you through all. You need not fear rejection for I accept you and love you, and I am within all.

Do not be afraid. Remember that I am the foundation of your being, the love that keeps you in existence. Trust in My love, trust in Me. You are safe and secure. Your future is secure in Me. The future of your family and friends, of everyone, is secure in Me.

Give thanks continually, and yes, *"offer sacrifice of thanksgiving"* (NAB Ps 116:17b). *"Freely you have received, freely give"* (Mt 10:8b) You can only offer Me that which you have received but when that gift is given with love, oh how precious it is! []

7.15   ALL I HAVE I GIVE

[| Full union with Me that you desire will be accomplished by your letting Me love you more and more until the Eternal-Love-That-Is is part and parcel of your being and is flowing out to all.

Your thinking that having a "thirst for Souls" means having such a great love for people that you desire all good for them, is correct. The transition from having mainly a concern for family and friends to having a universal concern is a work of grace. You cannot come to that on your own to any great degree. Union with My heart in a near totality is the effecter of that change. Do not fear to come into union with Me.

I love you, so you are OK!

I love you, so you are secure!

I love you, so you are loved!

Receive My love with all the thirst of your being and release anxiety in exchange for My love. Rest secure in My love, My beloved! I love you!

Do not judge others. Do not look askance at others. I see and know all things, yet I only love and accept. Yes, reject forces of evil but do not reject any person no matter how tightly they are bound by the evil that has ensnared them. Life is within each person, within all, and I am life. The life within is the being of the person. Your being is fully accepted by Me, for I am all being. I am the ONE in all, making all one.

"He who listens to you listens to me; he who rejects you, rejects me" (Lk 10:16a). *"I tell you the truth, whatever you did for one of the least of these brothers of mine, you did for me"* (Mt 25:40b).

You have no reason to fear. You have every reason to trust. I will not forsake you. I am your very being. You are totally, utterly safe and loved! I, your God, love you! Your true home is in Me.

I call to you, My son, My daughter, to come to Me, to come to know Me! I Am that you may be with Me and in Me. I have a special place in My heart for you. Come into My love! I accept you completely and totally as you are.

There is nowhere you can go that is out of My presence. Closing yourself off or, as most often happens, being closed off by outside forces – clouds of anxiety, resentment, and hurt – does not take you out of My presence. I AM with you. I uphold and sustain you at all times. Be still before Me. Drink in My presence. I love you!

You are My people! Anything that I will do will be done through you. Be open and docile, obedient, to My Spirit for My Spirit is life. Open your minds to receive a further understanding of truth. If you are so intent upon holding tightly to the "truth" you have learned up to now that you will not let yourself think over that truth for even a moment, you are at a stalemate and run the risk of becoming internally stagnant.

Understanding of truth must ever expand, for each particle of truth is related to the larger truth that is yet to become known. Do not cling to the facts about the truth that you know, but cling to Me. I am Truth. I am your foundation, your security.

You may feel you are going through a time in which you have made no measurable progress (not measurable by you). That is the way it should be. A tree is not aware of its growth nor is a young child. Growth is meant to just come on its own, without a lot of fanfare or ballyhoo.

All that I have, I give you:

Life, love, security, peace, joy, tranquility, being, love.

I Am so that you may be.

I have Life so that you may live.

I am love so that you may love and be loved.

You will never understand with your mind the essence of pure love that is My being. You can only come into love with your heart. The essence of all being is love, for I am all being, I am Love.

My heart cry goes out to all as one. I play no favorites. However, *each of you* is My favorite son or daughter!

"I am the good shepherd. The good shepherd lays down his life for the sheep." (Jn 10:14a). Come into My life, My people! *"I will walk among you and be your God and you will be my people"* (Lev 26:12). I need you! I love you! Rest in the heart knowledge of My love. |]

7.16   FIRST GOD

[| My child, it does not matter if you do not receive understanding to write down at this time. Living life is what counts, not learning about it.

You are ever My child as I am ever your God. Live in My love, in security, knowing that I love you and that you are safe and secure. You know that I love you. The knowledge of My love must become so wonderful for you that it is almost more than you can bear. Your capacity to receive love is ever-expanding as you surrender to being loved, and the more you are loved the more you can love.

Love is the key that unlocks all the mysteries of life. Could you take love apart, you would find Me. Wherever you go in love and whatever you do in love, leads you to Me.

Love that exists between family members and between good friends is a level of love existing in Me.

The self-sacrificing that is necessary for raising children from infancy to young adulthood nurtures love.

The suffering that springs from problems related to caring for others waters love.

Do not strive to attain and achieve spiritually. Rest and receive. Rest and be strengthened. Rest and be taught. Lie in My arms of comfort and rest as a baby lies in its mother's arms, content to be held, trusting that it is secure and that all is well.

Trust Me and talk to Me as a friend. I am REAL. I am here. I understand you perfectly. I am your understanding friend.

Do not be pessimistic about the outcome, spiritually, for all. It is a glorious outcome! I have promised that I would be your God and I Am. Nothing is impossible for Me. I can raise miracles of grace from the very earth, from the lowest level of human misery.

My people, I love you so much! Hope and rejoice with Me! Do your part and leave the rest to Me. Come to Me and taste perfect sweetness! Enter My joy, the joy that the world cannot give! Get your priorities placed properly and you will find joy in your life.

First God, for everything exists in Me. If you ignore Me you deprive yourself of the very substance of happiness. Use your mental abilities and material things in service and love and you will receive joy in return.

"Peace I leave with you; my peace I give you. I do not give to you as the world gives" (Jn 14:27a-b). You receive that peace when your will is in union with My Will. You must not only desire union, but you must also bring it about within your very person. When an individual comes into the right ordering within themselves, it helps everyone, for each person is a copy of the whole and there is a correlation between each one and all.

There are no barriers in the spirit. Love and goodness and all the virtues travel, spread, and are absorbed by everyone who has goodwill. Love penetrates even the hardest heart, because I am Love, and I can go through locked doors. I know the way. I am the Way. |]

(I read that the next life is purely spiritual.)

[| I know you find it frightening to think of life after death as being purely spiritual. Do not be afraid. In the afterlife, you rest securely in Me, no more to be buffeted by storms, pain, and sinful tendencies. Desire this and it will come about. Desire this for everyone and in a mystical way you help them on their way.

Remember, *"From everyone who has given much, much will be demanded; and from the one who has been entrusted with much, much more will be asked"* (Lk 12: 48c). |]

7.17   PRESCRIPTION: TLC

My God, I bless You!

[| My child, I bless you! Blessing merits a blessing in return. It is a spiritual law that when you bless others (sincerely), they receive a flow of good and their Spirit will return a blessing even if their body does not correspond.

Do not be afraid of what the next person thinks. Be who and what I call you to be, simply and with great respect for all, and leave to Me any adjusting in attitudes within others that needs to be done.

Share yourself. The self you share is not a selfish self but a giving self. Sharing opens the way for My Spirit to enter, for the very act of sharing is My life. Think of all the sharing and giving that is necessary for human beings. That opens the way to spontaneous giving, to love. Everything works together so marvelously in My divine plan!

You are a part of My divine plan. From all eternity, I looked ahead and needed you. My love for you brought you into existence so you may be just as I Am.

Never look down on yourself or others. Never judge. Always

give the benefit of the doubt. By ascribing good motives to others you plant within them the possibility of that good to become true. I see all of you as you are coming to be. People who most need to be healed and set free will be the happiest and most appreciative when that comes about. Those dark clouds have a silver lining.

What is spoken to one is spoken to all. I bid you, to trust and believe in Me, to follow the light as you are given to see it, to cling to life tenaciously and reverently. Life is present within your very being. It *is* your very being! You are alive with and in My life.

Reverence the person that is you. Handle With Care. Give yourself TLC, Tender Loving Care. Wrap yourself in swaddling bands of love and let yourself be nourished and cared for totally in My arms. I reach out to hold you through many means:

That telephone message that says "I care,"
The warm embrace of a friend or spouse,
The bright cheery sun, the smiling flowers,
The gala array of colors in your world,
The tender touch of an infant's hand.

My arms are open, My children, and I enfold you in a warm embrace! Go forward, strengthened and enriched by the fountain of life. I love you! My abundant blessings upon you, each and all! []

7.18   BELIEVE AND WALK IN MY LOVE

[| *"Commit to the Lord your way; trust in him, and he will act"* (NAB Ps 37:5). Trust with your heart, believe with your will, and love with all your heart, soul, and strength.

My child, I give you My love. I give you My heart, both in love and for you to love with. Give Me your heart that I may heal it and make it whole. I bathe your heart in My tender mercy.

Wherever you are, I am. I am one with you. I feel with you. I feel for you. No one could have or feel more compassion than I do. Believe in My love for you! Stand, walk, pray, and believe, do all in My love. My love is a shelter for you against the storm.

Once you come to feel secure in Me, bring others into that security, into a knowledge of My love. I thirst so for Souls! I desire to pour Myself out and be consummated for the sake of My precious children! The devotion of a good mother and father knows no bounds, yet it is but the minutest spark of My devotion towards you, towards all. I give you My very life that you may live!

Do all in freedom, child. It is for that that I have freed you. *"It is for freedom that Christ has set us free. Stand firm, then, and do not let yourselves be burdened again by a yoke of slavery"* (Gal 5:1). Once you have been freed from the pressure of spiritual restrictions and regulations do not set up for yourself a repressing set of standards of expectation. Often the hardest taskmaster is one's self. You can walk away from a burden that someone else puts on you, but when the burden is within it is much more difficult to become free of it.

Guilt is one of the strongest and meanest of taskmasters. When guilt takes over the show, nothing is safe. Your self-esteem topples. Your sense of pride in yourself and your bright hopes for a bright future topple. A sense of guilt – which is false guilt I am talking about, self-recrimination – puts a cloud on the whole of one's life: the past, present, and future.

It is sometimes hard to recognize false, recriminating guilt in one's self for it hides under many disguises. *"By their fruit you will recognize them"* (Mt 7:16a). If you have "fruits" of unrest, low self-worth, and insecurity about the future, if you find yourself wondering whether anybody could love you, it is time to begin looking for the "wolf in sheep's clothing." *"I tell you the truth, the man who does not enter the sheep pen by the gate, but climbs in by some other way, is a thief and a robber"* (Jn 10:1).

The way to rid yourself of this marauder of false guilt is to express honest sorrow for the sin within you, for things you are aware of, and for those you are not yet aware of. Then express the desire to be free of all sin and to be filled with love, joy, and peace.

A true sense of guilt, which is a gift of the Spirit, will lead one to sincere repentance and peace. It is a "friend" who takes your hand and leads you to Me. Following this wholesome cleansing, you will have no more self-recrimination but will instead have the grace to love yourself more and believe more strongly in My love for you. Do not be afraid of letting true sorrow lead you to repentance. The way of repentance is joyful, not sorrowful.

I walk with you, child, and with all. Go in peace, and may that peace which is beyond all understanding fill your heart, your mind, and your soul. I love you! []

7.19   BELIEVE AND RECEIVE

[| Let your spirit rest in and on Me. Let yourself be supported by Me. You cannot be strength unto yourself. The blind cannot lead the blind.

Many people think they "know it all." Every discovery through science is labeled and categorized in short order with little or no acknowledgment given to Me, the creator and sustainer of all the complex cell-body-plant-spatial relationships. Nature mirrors the divine order with its ebb and flow, its cycle of giving and receiving. Bless My nature for her faithful witness!

My child, I love you and bless you! My blessing is always flowing to you and all. I am God-who-blesses, God-who-Is-blessing. All you need to do is receive. If you believe you are not worthy to receive, that belief puts a block in the way of full receiving.

Believe and receive.

Believe in My love for you.

Believe that I bless you at all times and you will receive that love and blessing.

Being open to love and blessing brings healing to heart, mind, Soul, and body. This has a counterpart in the physical world. If you are open to love and blessing from family members, friends, and fellow members of the human race, you will receive blessing and healing from and through them. Block yourself off from them and you will find you are also blocked off from receiving fully from Me, for I am one with My people.

Lift your head! Do not look down on yourself. Human nature is made to be held together by self-esteem, by love from within and from without: from yourself, from others, from Me.

I love you from "within" and "without." I am the love principle, the force, and the flow in all love. I love you for yourself because you are you. My love for you has nothing to do with what you do or do not do. Your love for Me is expressed by believing in My love for you and responding to it in your affections and your living.

There is nothing to fear! Abandon yourself to love, Soar freely on wings of love. Receive fulfillment of your deepest desires by being open to and receiving My love. My love is life.

"I came that they [you] might have life and have it to the full" (Jn 10:10b). I have come that you may have love, that you may have it abundantly. Love and you will be loved. This is one of the give-and-take principles, ebb-and-flow. Rest in love and receive life unto your Soul.

My child, rest in My peace, in My presence. My presence permeates all. In a way, all is My presence. The being of each person proclaims My being, for you could not be if I were not. All that is, is supported and sustained by the presence of the great I AM. You are in Me, a part of Me.

In essence, all are one in Me but the mind and heart of humankind belligerently pull away, with many people refusing to acknowledge their dependence upon Me. I sustain those people even in their rebelliousness. Each is given the time and graces necessary to acknowledge and come into union with Me.

You are meant to be channels of My mercy and love. The harder the heart and the more callous someone's spirit is, the more they need to receive love and mercy. Pity the poor sinners! Do not look down on them. Hold them up to Me in love for they need healing so desperately! I do that for you: I hold you in love despite how things are with or within you.

You are called to walk in My footsteps. You are formed in My image to walk the highways and byways of this world to find and bring the lost to salvation. You do that by loving them in person and by bringing them to Me in love, in spirit. Follow My Spirit faithfully and those whom you are meant to minister to will come into your path. Minister, but do not bear the burden of the outcome of that ministry. Only I know a person's heart.

I love you, My child! Blessings to you as you go about the activities of the day. I am with you always. []

7.20   LOVE INVITES LOVE

[| Come into My arms, precious one! Be healed in My love, washed with My tears, filled with My life. I await you, I await all. Oh, the anguish of waiting! That, too, I accept for your sake. []

I come into your arms, Father! Hold me, heal me, and fill me with Your life! I desire to love You as You love me and everyone. So many people are hurting and searching! I carry them in my heart and bring them to you. Please hold us and heal us!

[| My beloved ones, I hold you close to My heart. I rock you and soothe you as a mother does her infant. I will not leave you to the mercies of wind and weather. I will stand guard over you and protect you. I will be your strength and your defense.

Do any claim that you are guilty?

I exonerate you.

Does anyone say you are, "No good! Not worth anything!"?

I say, "You are My treasure and My life."

Words can contain love, and the more love there is in the person who says them, the more love there is in the words. When you take in My words, the Word of God, you receive love, for I am love.

You have My words in your heart. You can bring them to mind and ponder them. You will never exhaust the riches and blessings of My words, of My presence, for I am ever new, ever fresh. I pour out My Spirit always, each moment, the Spirit of life. My Spirit, My life, holds you in being from one moment to the next.

Entrust your life and your being to Me. You are in Me and are resting in Me whether you acknowledge it or not. How much easier it is to relax the tension and "let go and let God" than to hang onto it! You can rest all of your concerns in My hands, too, so you will not have such a heavy load to carry. Your loved ones, your financial decisions, your health, your security – every person and all your doings can be entrusted to Me, your Father.

It is good to take time to just rest in Me. At the same time that you rest in Me, I rest in you.

I am all existence. You cannot "fall out" of Me. You are completely safe and completely loved. You are hemmed in by love from front to back, from side to side, from top to bottom, from past to present to future.

My love for you is like the love of a mother for her baby,

As a father stalwartly embracing his grown son,

As one dear friend to another,

As a lover toward his or her beloved.

My love is the total picture. In Me you have everything. Will you not believe in My love for you? Will you not, in turn, love Me?

Love is stronger than death. Secure in My love, you can overcome the fear of separation from your mortal body. You can live in peace and complete freedom. Peace is the fruit of love and freedom is its reward, the "frosting on the cake."

Go in peace, My children, in My love, in freedom! []

7.21   GIVE AND RECEIVE

[| My child, My blessings are always flowing and available to be received constantly. You need to be receptive.

You are a receptacle, a receiver: That is your basic being. I am Giver: That is My basic being. There is another side to you and Me, however. Once you have been a receiver, you can be a giver; and when you are a giver, I can be the receiver.

If you try to change the basic laws of nature that "what goes in must come out" and try to only receive without ever giving, you become a stagnant pool. Let the waters flow! Joyfully receive, joyfully give!

Receive My love, child. Always be open to receiving. When you are completely open and unafraid and completely one with Me, you are in Heaven. You need to be completely open to everyone to accomplish this, including being completely open to yourself. To be open means "to have complete acceptance and total love for." How I long for you to be truly open to Me!

I am open to you in this way. I love you and accept you. You can lie back and soak in My love. In so doing you will receive further healing and will become more loving and accepting. You receive the Giver with the gift.

Bless you, child of Mine! Go in peace to love and serve! []

"If anyone hears my voice and opens the door, I will come in and eat with him, and he with me" (Rev 3:20c).

(The words "eternal supper" came to mind.)

[| Yes, child, it is an eternal supper when I once enter someone's house, for all of My actions are eternal. That "supper" is a supper of love. Love is there on My part even before I come within as a guest, but love must be given and received to have fulfillment.

Once love is shared – given and received – that sharing holds for eternity. Who can make it so the sharing of love did not take place? What comes after an event in a person's life does not change that event and the sharing of love that has taken place. However, if someone were to experience a close fellowship of love with the divine and then would forsake love and goodness, that person's life and spirit would be yet emptier than before.

I hold you in an eternal embrace of love. Your correspondence in love is held "eternally" by your being willing to love Me in return. Feelings come and go. A decision to love holds firm in those who have committed their will to Me. While you are yet in this human existence, however, you need to make a daily and sometimes even hourly decision to choose to love. How precious that love is to Me, daily, hourly! The choice to love by all of those who do so more than makes up for the choice not to love on the part of others.

I sup with you gladly, dear child! Do not fear! I love you. |]

7.22   NO CONDEMNATION, ONLY LOVE

[| My people, how My heart swells with gratitude and love upon seeing you intent to know My Will and follow the paths I laid out for you! "My Will" is synonymous with happiness, for happiness is My Will for you and happiness is what you receive when you live in and follow My Will.

How to ascertain My Will more clearly? The way is purposely left vague a good share of the time so you may be who I created you to be: a human being with the gift of reflective thinking and free will. If there were a chart of directions that you would be obliged to follow or a set of buttons with built-in directions that you would be programmed to follow, you would be a robot and not a free person. Being free is so important that it is worth the risk of your making wrong choices.

I, the God of all creation, your God of love, am present within all of you at all times. I affirm the good that is within you and I draw you ever to a greater good. I never condemn. I say always: *"Try again. I will help you. I will wait patiently while you get over this resentment and anger. I will wait patiently while you learn by trial and error, by repeated experiences."*

I affirm, love, and uphold you always! |]

7.23   NO STRINGS LOVE

[| My child, how good it is to be back with you again! It means so much to Me for you to choose to give Me time that is exclusively for Me. It is good not to even expect or want to receive a return as you come into prayer for then you can worship more truly. I "need" unconditional love just as much as you do. That is the only kind of love that is true love, that which is unconditional.

My love for you, for all, is Unconditional with a capital "U." As the mother of a tiny infant accepts and loves her baby without expecting a reward or return, so do I love you. My love keeps you in being and supplies your needs. The other side of this coin, this treasure of love, is that you must give love in return to then receive love, to realize the love that is given to you, and for love to grow within you. []

Spirit of the living God, fall afresh on me! Fill me! Guide me!
[| Ah, yes, child, I enter in greater fullness! Ever greater, ever fuller life I bring to whoever is open to it.

Ever be at peace. Everything will get done at the time it is meant to be. These days on earth may be difficult but they are ever so precious! Even with the most precious jewels, you could not buy what you are to receive in return for being willing to accept hardship and for remaining open to love.

You will go through many days such as this in which you struggle to feel that you are on base and to try to figure out the purpose of your experiences, of life.

Peace, wisdom, discipline, patience, and so on are not handed to you. You are given a desire for the virtue and grace to choose it, as well as opportunities to practice and hold onto the good qualities that are developing within you. Such days and experiences have the same effect on your spiritual life as fertilizer has on a plant: It produces a "greening," flowering, luxuriant new growth.

Trust Me in all and at all times, My child! I have your best interests at heart. I want you to be freed, healed, and delivered as much as you do (even more so), and am bringing it about as I see fit. Everything works together in a marvelous divine plan! []

7.24 LOVE IS THE WAY

[| My child, I always hear prayers. Changes in the spiritual order are wrought by and through prayers said in love. Continue to desire release and peace with all your heart for the person(s) you are concerned about.

Whatever you do, do with all your heart, as children do. You must become as little children if you are to attain My kingdom. Pour all your love out to each person that you pray for and desire the best for, as I do. Love is prayer.

Love affirms, strengthens, ennobles, enables, confirms, promises, redeems, requites, releases, gives joy, and pleads.

Love pleads the cause of this child of God who is being run over in the mill, forgotten, abused, and becoming lost.

I hear your love.

"If you forgive anyone his sins, they are forgiven; if you do not forgive them, they are not forgiven" (Jn 20:23b) even your own.]]

Lord, please help me! It seems that I am retaining resentment and anger. I do not want to hold onto it. Please show me the way! [[The way is love, child. Love and anger will melt away. Love others as you love yourself. If you do not love yourself, you really cannot love others very well.

To love yourself truly, you must know yourself. You think that you are maybe spending too much time lately analyzing your feelings. I am leading you in this. Come to know yourself! Continue to accept and love yourself at all times, no matter what dregs get dredged up from your innermost being.

Do the same for others: Love and accept them as they are at all times. Accept and love the person, not the misdeeds or hurting words. The "clothes" a person wears are not the person.

The "clothes" you wear are not your real person. If you have anger or self-pity around you, that anger and self-pity are not a part of you. Do not think of negative spirits as being a part of your basic being, for they are not. Picturing that they are a part of you will only make the task of releasing them that much harder, perhaps making it impossible to do so.

You are yet a child with much more training and teaching needed but do not be despondent and downhearted. All in good time! The life within will bring about growth, and as that growth comes about, the encrustations that cover yourself will crack, break and drop away.

I call you to freedom! I bring you to freedom! Do not worry about how to release negative feelings. Ask for help and wait patiently. Then when grace moves you to do so, move against the feelings. What you earnestly desire will come to pass in good time.

You must accept yourself as you are before you can change how things are within you. If you do not admit to being resentful or full of self-pity (half full?), how can you move to free yourself of it? The worst condition is not that of seeing faults and shortcomings within oneself but having brazen faults and refusing to acknowledge them.

I love the sinner. When you see and acknowledge sin in yourself, you can lay a special claim to My love. The moment of recognizing sin is a moment to rejoice, for only by recognizing the sin can you do something about it. Being sinful is not a calamity, to stay sinful is.

Bless you, child of My heart! I love you! []

7.25   CONCENTRATE ON THE POSITIVE

[| My child, you are receiving all the time. Everyone who desires to receive, everyone who needs help and cries out for it, and everyone who freely loves, blesses, and gives, receives. Those who give, receive. Even if you only have the desire to give, you are open to receiving.

If you are ever in that type of mood in which you cannot bring yourself to even want to give and you feel ornery and out-of-sorts towards everyone, including yourself, come to Me and let Me hold you. If ever someone needs to receive, it is such a one!

The needs of every person are being met, not in your timetable, however, but in My "eterni-table." I am here for you and all. I call all to life. I am no less here when your days are busy than on a less busy day. I give love and blessing! []

I joy in You, Lord! Bless You! I leave to You the task of loosening and cleaning out junk within me: resentment, bitterness, hopelessness, fear, anger, self-centeredness, judgment, and so on.

[| My child, these types of things do not necessarily have to be dealt with individually. When a person becomes filled with My Holy Spirit there is then no room for negative forces. My love is all-encompassing, all-filling.

I ask you not to be overly concerned about how to become free of selfishness and negativity within yourself and I extend that admonition to include others you are concerned about. Rather than concentrating on freeing yourself and those others from the negative, desire that you and they be filled with the positive: life, love, energy, health, peace, and freedom with Me. I am the answer, the only answer, to all your needs.

You, any of you, can become a channel for My life, love, energy, healing, and peace to flow to others. Self-centeredness is the main blockage to realizing this. Love for others clears that blockage.

Above all, desire to be filled with love. Love is the answer to all your needs. If you feel hardness or aloofness toward someone, ask/ desire that you may be filled with love for them and they may be filled with love for you and all. This "prayer" of desire for love will effect a real change in the spirit. When the will chooses good, evil and negativity must give way. Believe that. Faith plays more of a role than you realize!

Bless you, child! Thank you for taking the time to spend with Me. I bless you for it. I give you My love. |]

7.26   BROUGHT FORTH BY LOVE

[| I have called you into being, child. From out of the depths I have called you, out of the depths of My love. |]
Lord, I am that tiny baby in my mother's womb.
[| My child, I have called you out of My heart where you have existed from all eternity. I have held you always in My heart, for all of eternity and of time are present to Me.

I hold you as you are coming into the physical at the moment of your conception in the safe warmth of your mother's womb. I rebuke you, father of lies, as you stand there telling this child that she is not wanted or needed in this family. Your father and mother want their little daughter, their "little rose." I touch their hearts to be filled with love, with the greatest openness to life that is possible. And into their waiting open arms and hearts I lovingly place My little cherub, you, My child, to be cared for, appreciated, and loved just for being you.

Do babies do anything to merit love? No, they are loved just for being who they are and as they are. The love people feel for babies is a very tender, vulnerable love that cannot be put into words, but can only be felt and given.

I place within you, My child, this tender, open love for yourself as a tiny baby, little girl, schoolgirl, high school student, college student, teacher, wife, mother, grandmother, and searcher. This love does not need to go out to yourself because you are yourself. This love is a tender holding love for yourself.

Dare to truly, tenderly love yourself! Yes, you feel vulnerable and afraid of being hurt and rejected, but the self you live in – yourself – *is* that vulnerable, scared self, so you will not be rejected.

Come into unanimity within yourself, child! Come into one mind and one spirit as the Father and I are one! The choice is yours whether you will be open to your love and open to love from others.

A lesson from the old catechism days: "Why did God make me?" "To come to know, love, and serve Him and be happy with Him forever in Heaven." You know Me as love when you have learned to be open to being loved, to let yourself be loved. Letting yourself be loved is passive, the resting that I give you. *"Come to me, all you who are weary and burdened, and I will give you rest"* (Mt 11: 28).

Love is a healing balm that will cure all ills and heal all wounds, the receiving of love, that is. Those who continue to feel wounded and lonely have not opened themselves to be truly loved. Oh, what heaven it is to receive love! To be that free and open and vulnerable that you allow love to enter, that you accept it!

As your love for yourself comes from right within you, so also does My love, for your life is a portion of My life. You exist in Me.

You are within the very bedrock of love and this love is all existence. There are no scary places to fall into. That is a lie from the evil one.

Simply open your heart and you can know the unknowable. Choose to let yourself be loved and to love yourself.

I hold you in the knowledge of My love.

I give you the joy that the world cannot give.

I give you the joy of being loved! |]

unanimity: the quality or state of being unanimous

unanimous: being of one mind; in total agreement

7.27   I AM WITH YOU

[| I wrap you in love, My child! Be present to yourself. When you are present to yourself you are present to Me. Just be, and breathe in "being," deep draughts of life-giving love. I am here for you and all, for each of you as individuals and for all as "all."

Continue to cling to the belief that My Will for you and all is happiness. And, yes, enclose those you desire to help in a protective circle of faith. Believe that I can bring help, release, and happiness to everybody. I do not abandon My own, no matter how deeply they may get mired in the quagmire of hopelessness and helplessness. Nobody is that much cut off that they cannot be touched by love.

I am with you in everything that happens, My child. I go through everything with you. Through experiences that you are having, you are sharing a little of what I had to "drink" in having My loved ones turn the other way, hold back out of fear and even state outright that they did not know Me.

Do not cling too strongly to the status quo. Do not cling to this house you are living in or to possessions that you have. The only thing possessions are for is to use them. If you do not have use for some of your possessions, find a means to pass them on to others or discard them. Clutter around a person reflects their inner being. Contemplate in what ways you may yet be carrying the clutter of unnecessary burdens or attachments to worldly goods.

You are held in blessing.

You live and move in blessing.

Your life in this world is blessed. All your days are blessed.

Your family is blessed. My blessing covers all.

My word goes out to all the earth. *"The heavens declare the glory of God; the skies proclaim the work of his hands. Day after day they pour forth speech; night after night they display knowledge. There is no speech or language where their voice is not heard"* (Ps 19:1-4). As the light of the sun is poured forth upon the earth, tumbling joyfully ahead as the earth turns to receive the light, so do I pour Myself out! All you need do is receive.

"Prepare the way for the Lord, make straight paths for him" (Lk 3:4c). That is your part to do.

"Every valley shall be filled in, every mountain and hill made low. The crooked roads shall become straight, the rough ways smooth. And all mankind will see God's salvation" (Lk 3:5-6). This is My part to do, with your cooperation.

Encircle Me with faith as you have been doing. Believe in Me. Believe that I can bring salvation, peace, and freedom to all, for I can and I will. Your belief helps bring it about that much more quickly. I need My "support system" just like you do. I desire intimacy and oneness even more than you do.

Come, child, into the oneness of love! Love each person, love all, so they may each and all be in love, also! As you come to Me, you come to all. What blessed unanimity is awaiting all of us! What peace and joy of being! What love, all here in My heart! I hold you in love, My child, and I hold all with you. []

CHAPTER 8

RELATIONSHIP

8.1   LIVE JOYFULLY

[| My child, why are you anxious? Do you not know that I care for you and brood over you in love? In quiet and rest comes strength. I am here. What have you to fear? I uphold you in My strength.

Do not worry about those who have been entrusted to your care: family, friends, or those who have asked for your prayers. Keep your joy. Lift them to Me joyfully, for all sincere prayers, those that you know to be in My Will, have already been answered.

Rejoice always! Go from love to love in your various duties. Regarding your work and responsibilities in your home, relax more about it. What isn't done today can be done another day. I bless your decision, honestly made, as to which things to do each day. I will let you know if some spiritual need is more pressing. ...It is wonderful when you spend quiet time with Me! |]

Lord, it's good for me to be here!

[| Yes, it is good for you to be here. More good is wrought by prayer than this world dreams of. You give the greatest help to your loved ones and those you are concerned about by praying for them, for then the desires of your heart become My desires.

Your desire is My command. I am a God of giving. It is My nature to give. So when you come to a time when you feel like giving yourself and giving of yourself, you have a sign that My divine life is in you, for that is what prompts giving in love.

"So do not be worry, saying, 'What shall we eat?' or 'What shall we drink?' or 'What shall we wear?' ...your heavenly Father knows that you need them" (Mt 6:31,32b). Leave to Me the manner and choice

of supply. You will often be pleasantly surprised and delighted! The more you can realize that all comes from My love, the more blessed you will feel and be.

Bless you, My child! I am so glad you are choosing to release your worries to Me so that you can live, love, and move in complete freedom! Think what a glorious existence awaits you as you shed all these weights and entanglements! Rest in My love. Live in My love. Let love carry you in its buoyant spirit of joy. Life is glorious and blessed when lived with Me! |]

8.2 MAKE MY MESSAGE REAL

[| How grievous are the ways of many who walk the face of the earth! Do they not realize what a short time they have? Time is but a passing moment. Think how quickly a moment passes! |]

Lord, I pray for these people, for all. We are all helpless without You! I pray that we may all come to know and love You.

[| Rest in Me: That is so important. Rest in Me often during the day, wherever you are and whatever you are doing. A mind in turmoil engenders a body in pain. Rest your whole self, body, and Soul, in Me who am bosom rest.

I love you, My child! I love all with such overwhelming love! Tenderly I care for each person and call to them to come to Me so that they may know love and rest. But they do not hear. The cares of the world press too much and the pleasures of the world entice too much. You and all those who know Me must make My message and My call real by showing Me forth in your lives.

You remain who you are – a helpless human being, unable to love others until you have first received My love that makes you whole, and unable without My grace to do the slightest good – so there is no room for pride.

A flower does not give itself its beauty and form. All growth and beauty come from Me. Just be open and trusting for Me to use you as I see fit. There is no call for rush and concern. Your power comes through resting in Me, your creator, and God. []

8.3   THROUGH YOU TO OTHERS

[| Each of you is choosing, day after day, moment by moment, as to whether or not you will give all for all. A life in which you measure and weigh your efforts to see if it is too much to give to Me – and you keep holding back, unwilling to give what costs you a little too much – is an unworthy life. In that manner, you will never find peace and happiness.

I give My all to you in return for you giving your all to Me. I know your human weakness, however. I make allowances and cover you with My mercy. *"This is the one I esteem: he who is humble and contrite in spirit and trembles at my word"* (Is 66:2b).

I rest in you, My child. I bless your brow with balm. The unction of My mercy and love flows over and through you. Do not worry about anything or anyone. Worry is deceitful. It entangles your mind and numbs your spirit. Place all your trust in Me who am worthy of all trust.

I am with you. I will be with you as you go your appointed way. I am the Master of the present and the future, for I am God. I am in your future already. All is secure in love.

Remember always that I love you! All is well. Life is glorious and blessed when lived with Me as guardian and guest of your Soul. I am always blessing you and blessing all. If only all would be willing to receive it!

I can reach some of these searching Souls through you and other willing servants of good faith. You have more influence than you can know, simply by being faithful and obedient to the workings of My Spirit. Continue to commend to Me all whom you carry on your heart. Bless them continually and trust that the blessing carries with it protection from further evil.

Rest your head on My shoulder, child. As you do so, let all worries flow off into My care. I care about these people and situations, too, but likely in a different way than you do. What affects the life of the spirit is of uppermost importance.

Bless you, as you go about your day's duties. Do not forget Me amidst the concerns of the day. May I come with you? |]

8.4   LIVE LIFE WITH JOY

[| Relax, My child! Do not try to put effort into this exchange of ideas. Let it simply flow from your thoughts naturally, as water flows from a spring. When you get in touch with the source, life-giving water – words, in this case – can issue forth. It is Mine to decide how and when to use them. Consider these My words, not yours. You are in tune, in touch, with Me, so they seem to spring from yourself, but in reality, they spring from the source of living water, from the vine.

You are the branches, the channel. Remain ever flexible so I may direct you to that place of need that I choose. Remain in an attitude of openness and love toward all, desiring that they may come to know goodness. That desire in itself is prayer.

Not all action that helps another is direct action. The greater activity and help take place in the spiritual realm. Remain in an attitude of openness and goodwill towards others in your spirit and leave to Me the working out of circumstances in the physical.

Do not be quite so serious in your attitude toward prayer and life in general. Life is for joyful living, joyful loving and sharing, and joyful expression of the gladness that is in your spirit! Let life flow freely into you and through you. This joyful flow will wash away the effects of anxiety that you have experienced and will bring healing of body and spirit.

All is well. All is joy in the Lord! Yes, be concerned and pray for the sinner, but have joy in the fact that all it takes is a response to the grace of contrition and they become free of their bondage. Look ahead to that, joyfully anticipate it, and a great burden will have been lifted from your shoulders. I carry whatever burden needs to be carried. I ask you to carry love for each person and joyful, childlike trust in Me.

Do you have any questions? |]

I don't know what to ask, Lord. I feel a sense of heaviness about how much there is to learn, how much "should" be done through prayer, and so on. I ask for the grace to see all this as I ought.

[| Life need not be burdensome. True life is coming to know Me. To know Me means coming to experience the peace that I bring, coming to know to the fullest extent possible that you are loved by love, and coming to know the spirit release that comes as you accept forgiveness in return for repentance. You experience the fullness of life to the greatest extent:

When you live simply for the sake of being,

When you love simply for the sake of loving,

When you give for the sake of giving,

When you put yourself completely into the task at hand.

Would I deceive you? Trust and live joyfully no matter what may come. The sooner you see the blessing that is disguised as hardship or irksomeness, the sooner you can rejoice in it!

Pay heed to My words. I do not give as the world gives. I give love, joy, peace, and all spiritual gifts. They are clothed in persons, circumstances, and words. You cannot see them with your eyes. Only the eye of faith can discern. |]

8.5 BE OPEN IN REJOICING

[| Be open in love and rejoicing. When you have a rejoicing spirit all of life is seen in a new light. Life is glorious and blessed when lived with Me as the guest of your Soul: Keep telling yourself that.

People cannot learn about and accept the truth from one mention of it. That is why I tell you over and over that I love you.

I love you exactly as you are and, at the same time, I call you forth to perfection. Perfection does not consist of accomplishments. It consists of being perfect. You are called to perfectly be that which you are meant to be. There are no half-measures in the My kingdom. You must love and serve with all your heart and strength.

Life, movement, growth, and renewal of strength spring from the life that is within you. Let your life be a sign to you that I am present within you, sustaining and uplifting. That which you do not see is the greater: the life of the Holy Spirit within you that has become a part of your Spirit. You are one with Him yet you decide whether you will act on the graces He gives you.

My child, erase the lines of worry from your brow! Be not anxious, particularly not about things regarding your Spirit, for anxiety is as a cruel wind blowing away the delicate flower of trust.

My heart rejoices in your being freed from oppressive spirits! Anxiety and such press down your spirit while the "good spirits" of joy, gratitude, trust, peace, and love lift you ever closer to Me.

Yes, you rest in My heart as you so desire. I know and understand you from the inside out. I love you to the very depths of your being. Rest in My heart. Do not pull yourself away. You can go about your day's activities and duties in My heart. As a child before birth receives its nourishment through the umbilical cord, through remaining connected closely to its mother, so your life must be lived within and closely connected with Me.

You are still trying a good deal of the time to go it alone. When you leave this time of communion in the morning, take My love with you by remaining ever conscious of My love, care, protection, and steady nourishment. Keep in mind, *"For in him we live and move and have our being"* (Acts 17:28) so you will breathe in Me and breathe Me in.

Time to go, My child. I am so happy to share this time with you! Thank you for taking the time to be quiet and reflective in My presence. Remember that I share all of your time with you. I create time moment by moment and give it to you, and as you live each moment, I live that moment also, united with you. How could it be otherwise? For we are one.

The desires of your heart are given to you. Your desire to be one with Me I most gladly fulfill, for it is the uttermost desire of My heart, also. Bless you, My child! |]

8.6   HOW TO HELP

Lord, I desire a word from You.

[| My child, I am the eternal word. I speak Myself to you in the unspoken word of love. My being says, "Here I am. I love you!" Any tenderness or compassion that you ever feel towards someone is but as a drop of water is to the ocean, in comparison to the tenderness, compassion, and love that I feel toward you and each of My children!

The way to help others is to join the mainstream of that love, to become one with Me in being and desire. You are thus opening yourself to the desires of My heart. Your desires become one with My desires and they can then come to pass.

Nothing can come to be that is not first conceived in thought and desire. This may seem a slow process but I have the patience of a God (for I am God)!

If you are to become one with Me in desire and being, you must acquiesce to the fulfillment of My plan, with each event and blessing coming to be at the appointed time. Your desire to help others is a sign of My desire, that the time is at hand to begin bringing it about. Thus you share in My spiritual creation and partake of the ebb and flow of the life of My Spirit.

My Spirit is continually creative, as is seen by the constant renewal of the physical world that you see around you. Even more so in the spiritual world:

My Spirit constantly renews you in hope, love, joy, and peace!

L not only renew, however. I sustain you in that hope, love, joy, and peace!

Do not worry about those you bring to Me in prayer. Just lift them to Me with a glad heart, sure in the knowledge that I have and am all that they need. Worry short-circuits prayer, as does fear.

Rest secure before Me: secure in the knowledge that My

all-encompassing love surrounds you and sustains you. My love also surrounds and sustains all that you bring into that love by being a vehicle of love yourself. Your love carries them to Me when on their own they would seem to choose to have no part of Me. The wall of fear round about them, which is insecurity, can be penetrated only by love.

My love is present even within those walls of fear but these imprisoned people have no way of becoming aware of it. When you come in love and knock on that encircling wall, the self-prisoner can be touched enough to step out of the encirclement and experience love through you. Thus, through helping and caring for them physically, by having actual contact with them, the imprisoned can be reached and set free.

You are My fellow workers and collaborators in this, My "other selves." You are Me reaching out to set the prisoners free. The reason you can sometimes touch and free others even without actual physical contact is that all of you are one in the great human family. Your consciousness runs on the same stream. When you reach out in prayer and desire to help, you are reaching to help one of your own and the person responds to that love.

Do not fear! I am with you always, loving you and guiding you. Bless you, My child! []

8.7   BE AS I MADE YOU

Lord, what do You have to say about how we are to accept and channel our sexual energies?
[| My children, every aspect of your being and your experience of life comes from Me. There would be no such thing as sexuality if it were not a blessing that has been given to you.

Do you think I did not realize that there would be many people at any given time who would not be married? There are growing adolescents, young unmarried adults, and those who are divorced, widowed, or separated. The gift of sexuality is a part of the basic being of everybody at every stage of life. It is of utmost importance for you to embrace and integrate your sexuality so you can be a whole person.

Rejecting any part of your being has repercussions throughout your being. You cannot so much as injure your little toe without bringing the suffering of it into your whole person. When the basic flowering of sexuality (which rises from the center of your being) is rejected, repressed, or twisted unnaturally, that rejection cannot help but have drastic effects. The first step toward wholeness in this regard is to come to accept yourself as I made you: a man, a woman.

The way that many people treat the gift of sexuality brings spiritual death and spiritual turmoil to them. When sex is used for the sake of pleasure alone, self takes over and My Spirit is extinguished. Those who act thus enter a prison which is their own body.

Some who are trying valiantly to live in My Will may mistakenly think they should stifle their sexuality to become more "spiritual." This is likewise a mistake, for sexuality is basically of the spirit. If you did not have a mind and heart, there would be no human sexuality, for the mind/heart is what makes you human.

My children, I accept you as you are at this moment and every moment. You are in Me at every moment. All of the feelings and emotions that you experience take place within you as you are in Me. All that is is good or it would not be. Your sexuality is good in itself and for the end for which it was created. I keep your sexuality in being at each moment, as I keep everything in being that is. Accept sexuality for the gift it is, let it be, and learn to control it.

Learning implies the possibility and probability of making mistakes in judgment. If a person who is sincerely trying to walk in goodness makes a mistake in judgment as to how to accept and live in their sexuality in a good and proper way, it is like a child who is earning to walk. A child surely stumbles, missteps, and falls. Do you see its parents scolding and condemning it? Neither do I condemn. Here is My hand. I will help you walk. Bless you, My child! []

8.8   ACCEPT YOURSELF

[| I love you and accept you as you are, My children, each of you, at every given moment. When you also choose by an act of your will to love and accept yourself – feelings need not go along – healing can begin, for you are then integrated.

Love yourself as you would another person. In a way, you are a stranger to yourself. You need to take that stranger into your home, into your heart, and give hospitality to yourself as you would to another. Love yourself as your neighbor. Give yourself affirmation. I am in you, part and particle of your being so as you affirm your worth and lovability, you are receiving My affirmation as well.

"If anyone is thirsty, let him come to me and drink. Whoever believes in me, as the Scripture has said, streams of living water will flow from within him" (Jn 7:38b). The very source of life is within you, for I am within you. This flow is in and through your spirit, affecting your body as well, for your person is one body-and-Soul entity. Once you have realized freedom in your spirit, the life-giving waters can begin to flow.

I fully accept you. Even so, you must fully accept every facet of yourself. I made you a woman/man. I am within your very womanhood/manhood. I accept you totally and completely, which means that I accept you with all of the sexual feelings and urges that arise spontaneously. For you to not accept that part of yourself causes a split in your wholeness.

When you can come to fully accept the humanity you have been given – which is meant to be a full union of body and Soul with all in proper order – then you rest securely in Me, in peace. If you do not accept yourself as I made you, in a way, you do not fully accept Me as God. Bless you, My child, My children! |]

8.9   BE A CHANNEL FOR LOVE

[| By resting in My love you will come to freedom of spirit and a place of peaceful tranquility. Let the world go on its frantic pace alone. Step aside and breathe in love, peace, and joy, the exhilaration of My being! Not as the world gives do I give unto you. The world gives surface pleasures, baubles. I satisfy the needs of your spirit, of your deepest self.

"The Lord is near to all who call upon him, to all who call on him in truth" (Ps 145:18). When you acknowledge Me, you acknowledge truth everlasting. You can rest your understanding on Me, the rock of ages. I am eternity itself. Nothing exists outside of Me.

My child, I commend you for your trust in these difficult, uncertain times. Know that all is well for you and your family. Trust brings results for it is a firm connection with eternal supply and help. When you live and move in Me you are safe and well-supplied.

All whom you take into your circle of love, into your heart unconditionally, are brought into the mainstream of that supply that comes from eternal love. The more intimately and surely that you are united with Me in death to self and to sin, the more open you are to be a channel of love flowing to others. |]

8.10   THERE IS HOPE

[| Many are the problems and worries of those who trust in the way of the world! That way is not My way. My way is that of peace and trust, solace and contentment, and rest and health even amid want and deprivation.

Forces of darkness may appear to have an upper hand in many people's lives, but appearances are deceiving. The final victory is Mine, yours and Mine, whoever of you chooses to side with Me.

Sometimes when two factions are at war it is difficult to determine which side would be the wiser to be on, for one cannot know ahead of time which side will come out on top. But in the battle of the spirit, the outcome is known and it is sure!

I am the King of the universe.

I rule with justice and truth,

With grace and compassion,

With love and trust.

Love can affect all things. Those whom you see caught in a quagmire of spiritual difficulty from which it appears humanly impossible to get free are not without hope of rescue. Lift your eyes to Me, the rescuer of hopeless cases. My love for each Soul, for each person, is such that it can affect a rescue if the person so chooses.

The influence needed to soften a person's heart so they will want to be rescued and walk the path of goodness again often depends in large measure on the next person, on you. Does that person feel that anybody cares if he/she is rescued? Does he/she have a sense of self-worth and a sense of belonging to a family, to a group of people, who care?

That is your part. People are composed of body and Soul. The help to be received spiritually must have a physical counterpart. The spiritual oftentimes, generally, must come through the physical. As you care for others physically – feeding, clothing, sharing, living life with them – they receive spiritual sustenance at the same time.

Having a sense of self-worth is so important that it can be called the key ingredient to a whole personality. The foundation for and much of the development of self-worth comes through other people who have contact with the person. This is mainly physical contact that is meant here, but spiritual contact with others through blessing and loving them also plays a large part. Bless always! Love always! Bless you, My child! Bless all! []

8.11   FREEDOM IN LOVE IS WONDERFUL

[| My child, I, too, love to be with you, as you enjoy being with Me. It is wonderful to freely be in a loving relationship!

A spouse who performs duties only out of obligation, grudgingly, does not have a happy life and the partner in such a union is likewise not as happy as might be. If one of the partners can break out of that vicious circle and openly embrace loving, and loving duty, toward his or her spouse – choosing and doing simply and freely for the sake of love – then both can be saved from continuing in that wretched existence. Love conquers in time, and in time the spouse who is unable to love will/may be conquered and softened by love.

I am the spouse of all those who so chooses. As in earthly marriage, the first few delightful days or years may pass on, bringing, in turn, days where you sense that only a "have to" love is holding the relationship together. For My part, though, rest assured that I do not, cannot, and will not ever love only from a sense of duty. I love each and all with My whole heart and soul and strength. I put My whole self into our love, into our relationship.

I love you, My spouse, My soul partner! All who come to be, come to be in Me. In Me, in love, you find fulfillment. I know that of yourself you could never come to have an open, trusting love. I unite Myself with you to help you to release the strongholds that hold you down. When you once see and admit your inability to love and give freely, let rejoicing begin for you are on the right track! Then simply come to Me and I will give you the strength, ability, and desire to sincerely love others.

When the spiritual reality of your Soul-to-Soul relationship with Me is purified and strengthened in love, the physical counterpart in your life is likewise purified and strengthened. This gets worked out in time, for you have been given time to "work out your salvation." You have much to learn and My heart rejoices as these lessons take root and grow! Rest assured of My love, protection, guidance, and all-encompassing devotion.

I accompany you as a devoted father, a concerned mother, a loving spouse, a caring friend, an affectionate brother, and an efficient guide. Walk with Me! []

8.12   NO OTHER PLACE

Lord, please guide everyone! The people at the meeting I attended last evening seemed to me to be sadly misguided! All of us are seeking you, Lord, to be our peace, security, and purpose.

[| My child, My heart, too, is sorely pressed to see My poor, wandering children so misguided! Truth, however, so permeates every facet of existence and especially the area of the mind, that there are a few kernels of truth in the teaching those people are following. That truth will draw them to itself, rest assured of that. All who are of goodwill will come to Me although the way may be long and winding. There is no other place for anyone to go but into My arms of love!

Those who seek rest and security,
Truth, justice, and righteousness,
Tranquility, peace, and order,
An answer to hope will find it.
They will come to Me.

The way for you to help lost and wandering Souls is to believe in Me ever stronger, to believe that My love and mercy will find a way to save them, and It will! Your desire that all will find the way and the truth that is the connecting link by which I can reach them more effectively, for it is a pathway of love. When you open your heart in love to anyone, you open them and yourself to your God, to Me.

I am greater than all of creation and greater than all mind creations that come forth in the human search for truth. Everything exists and takes place in Me. Your everyday living, your searching, your total existence in body, mind, and Soul, your total being, is within Me, and at the same time, I am within you. Being calls to Its own. You are being of My being. Your need to search for truth and reality is a sign that I AM.

Do not have fear for anyone. Place them in My care with glad trust. I bid you, live in My care with glad trust. The purpose of life is to live, to be. For each and all the purpose of your life is to be who and what you are meant to be, to accept yourself as you are in your intrinsic being, and to look forward gladly with Me to who and what you are coming to be in Me.

You rest in Me at all times, My children, whether you are aware of it or not. Life is a time for you to become aware of that, that you and all rest in Me. It is a time for you to learn to rest peacefully in Me and to learn to live peacefully together in Me.

Come to Me that you may find rest for your Soul and body!

Come into My arms of love to be clothed with justice, to dwell in holiness and truth!

Thus you will find rest for your Souls.

The Soul comes first, for that is who you are. Your Soul activates your body and takes it to itself as its own. Should your mind and Soul have disdain for your body, your body would experience negative effects. Should you give way to worry and fear, your body would experience negative effects. Every leaning of your mind and Soul affects your whole person, so I bid you lean toward truth, justice, and holiness.

Bless you, My child! I bless you for your searching, for your dependence upon Me, for your blind faith in Me. You will be amply rewarded. Seek and you will find. Knock on the door of truth and it will be opened to you. I fulfill your every desire if you allow Me to. Enter into Me and live! []

8.13   WILL YOU HELP ME?

[| Love heals al. Love upholds all. The greatness of love is shown by the victories over those things that try to break it down.

Dwell in Me and you are safe, for thus you dwell within the very portals of heaven, though you cannot see it with your eyes. *"Remain in Me and I will remain in you"* (Jn 15: 4a).

You cannot bear fruit apart from Me. You cannot truly live apart from Me, for living is being totally who and what you are meant to be. You are meant to be in Me, to be one with Me to such an extent that when I desire to lift a hand to help someone, your arm moves;

and when My heart goes out in love to someone, it is your heart I am loving with.

United, yet individual: Two, yet one. One, yet two.

One with the Father in this same way.

United by His Holy Spirit, by love.

Destined for glory, child of God, heir of Heaven.

You are My beloved!

This is your true worth and the only goal worth striving for!

The harder and longer the struggle here on earth in time, the more precious and wonderful will Heaven be for you! Every cloud has a silver lining. I bring good out of every circumstance if you do not thwart it.

My storehouse has many treasures. Those who live in and for My kingdom draw on those treasures by their desire for blessings, love, and goodness to abound. My storehouse is not locked. Any blocks to blessings are set up inadvertently (without realizing it) or willfully by the individual.

I rejoice when you are happy! That is all I am mindful of, that all of you may be supplied with what you need and that you may come to know love, joy, and peace. I take care of My own.

When people are in situations where they are loved and cared for by family and friends, I take care of them through family and friends. Those who are forsaken by their fellow men and women I take care of Myself, directly.

"For this is what the Sovereign Lord says: I myself will search for my sheep and look after them. As the shepherd looks after his scattered flock when he is with them, so will I look after my sheep. I will rescue them from all the places where they were scattered on a day of clouds and darkness" (Ez 34:11-12).

My people, how My heart aches to save, nourish and defend! Will you not enlist your aid with My cause? Who can I turn to for help if not you? Many of My sheep are sorely pressed indeed, and likewise many of My lambs. I pray you to allow Me to live in you.

I need torchbearers to take My love and help to the needy and despairing.

I need mothers to comfort My lost, bewildered children.

I need fathers to point out the way to the faltering pilgrim, to
be role models for young boys growing up into manhood.

I call to you in the quiet, in the depths of your heart: Follow Me,
My people! I am the way, the truth, and the life. Do not turn to other
sources, for they will prove to be false and will shortly run out. Oh,
the glorious freedom My children, of those who are open to love
and be loved! Would that all would be in this company! It is not too
late. Come! []

8.14 LET ME DO THE JUGGLING

[| Leave all in My hands, dear one. Leave everything to My timing
and My perfect plan. Sometimes pieces of a puzzle, of a problem,
need to be turned about endlessly and juggled and re-juggled until
a solution is reached. The overall master plan and the "juggling and
re-juggling" are My tasks. Yours is to let yourself be juggled when
that is necessary.

Would life be as satisfying if everything would be endlessly and
forever rosy for you? Think of all the satisfaction you would miss
out on if you did not have that problem to solve! or the ecstatic
happiness you would miss out on if you did not have a goal to strive
for and finally achieve! Ah, I know best!

Even in My life, all is not just "rosy." I accept the bitter with the
sweet, the pain with the joy, just as you have to do, for My life is
joined to yours. The bitterness and pain, and the sweetness and joy
in your life I make My own. The more that is shared, the more one
has in common with somebody.

This is true for you and Me, as well as for you and your spouse
or friend. The sharing does not have to be in words to be effective.
Sharing time, simply being together, brings about togetherness-in-
spirit if you do not have blocks in the way.

One good way to begin bringing this about is for you to choose
to be open to your spouse in spirit as the two of you are sleeping.

This takes no conscious effort on your part except for you to initially will it. Picture beforehand a peaceful time of sleeping, of lying in My arms together.

Human love can be a channel for bringing about togetherness-in-spirit when someone does not yet know divine love or is too tied up in knots to believe or accept that I love him/her. When you open yourself to be filled with My divine love and wish for that love to flow to your partner (to whomever you are holding in tender "sleep prayer"), My divine love becomes one with your love and can reach even those who are thought to be unreachable. *"[W]ith God all things are possible"* (Mt 19:26b).

This is why I am God,

So I can do the impossible,

So I can save the "unsavable,"

So I can heal the hurting, and free the imprisoned.

There is much that you do not know about the avenues of the mind. Using this approach alone (picturing you and your spouse lying peacefully together in My arms) with the very least amount of effort on the part of the intercessor, you will see a world of difference come about! Healing and freeing of a personality can begin in this way. Of course, that cannot be done all at one time. It took seven days to create the world and all that is in it. The mind is a world all its own.

Be thankful for My all-powerful love that can create an object from clay and change it into a beautiful vessel! All of you can support and hold that clay as I fashion it.

Go forth in peace and love, My child! []

8.15   UNITED IN GOD

Lord, please give me some understanding about people being individuals and yet when married having a soul partner? Does everything that affects one also affect the other? If so, how can the one come to You in complete intimacy without a sense of the other?

[| Child, marriage is a union of love. Love unites with love. The two human spirits do not, and are not, united. It is the Spirit of love that is the union. Those who are married in Me come into My breathtaking life. As the Son and I are united, even so, are husband and wife in the Lord united.

You do not understand the life of the Blessed Trinity. How am I to explain, then, the soul partnership that transpires as two people are joined in Me? The union is, as the Blessed Trinity is. Each person is a separate and unique individual, as each Person of the Trinity is "an individual." You may notice a difference, however, in that marriage is a union of two, whereas the Trinity is three.

But wait! You do not yet have the whole picture! There *is* a third person in that marriage, that soul-partner union: The Holy Spirit. Your love for one another is to be a reflection and image and counterpart of My love for the Son and His love for Me.

Does their love union make the Father or the Son not free? No. On the contrary, their love for one another gives them the freedom to be who they are, for each is accepted and loved for who He is and as He is. True love is freeing, not inhibiting. Any inhibition there is in marriage comes about when one or the other of the love partners is not willing to accept and love the other as he or she is.

This willing cannot be judged with the human mind, that one of you can judge whether the other is "willing" to accept you as you are. The willingness may be there, but when a person is not free because of hurts, hang-ups, and effects of past rejection, the willingness to love and the love itself is hampered. If and when one of them comes to the point of being free to love, and chooses to love freely, the spirit of the "imprisoned" partner can begin to receive a flow of healing, freeing love.

Without the special "union-in-love" plan (marriage), many people could never be reached. By the power of the decision of the mind alone, you could not choose to love. It is I, within, who love. Your part is to be willing to open yourself to Me that I may love in and through you. You remain an individual but at the same time are paired with another person. This pairing can and does take place in other love relationships, as well, when an individual is called by the Spirit to be a Soul partner with another person.

Trust Me that all is well and good in the plan and life of marriage! Your freedom is not jeopardized, that which is real freedom. You often mistakenly think that having no restrictions on your time or means is freedom, wherein you can do for yourself anything that you desire. Following that path leads to imprisonment in yourself, not to the freedom that your heart seeks, for the self cannot be satisfied by following the whims and inclinations of the flesh.

Only a person who is led by the Holy Spirit can come to any measure of freedom, and it is through your spirit that the Holy Spirit can lead you and your soul partner toward freedom. The needs of your partner and the difficulties that you think of as drawbacks are, in actuality, "friends" and help.

The physical creation is a reflection of the realities present in the Godhead. Sexual intercourse is the physical counterpart of the giving and receiving of love in the My life as God. When you once have that truth ringing clearly in your spirit, your mind and body will have no hang-ups or problems with the physical expression of love in marriage. I am especially close to you when you are united in body, mind, and spirit with your soul/marriage partner.

My child, I love you! Wherever you go, you have the assurance of My love. You can walk, play, study, sleep, eat, work, and relax in My love. You are safe and secure in My love. As a father or mother holds their little one in love, I hold you. As a husband holds his wife in love, I hold you. *"For your Maker is your husband—the Lord Almighty is his name"* (Is 54:5).

Accept life gladly! Accept each day, each moment, gladly! Take hold of life, and it will take hold of you! What you give is what you will receive. []

8.16   TIME FOR PLANTING COMES

[| My child, blessings upon you and all! *"Commit to the Lord your way; trust in him and he will act"* (NAB Ps 37:5). Yes, trust in Me and I will act. When you receive something, give Me the credit, then the way will be open for you to receive more. *"...do not be worry, saying, 'What shall we eat?' or 'What shall we drink?' or 'What shall we wear?' ...your heavenly Father knows that you need them"* (Mt 6: 31,32b). Negative thinking and a lack of acknowledgment that I am the provider of all good things block the flow of blessings.

Find an opportunity to speak to Ray sometime (my friend Susan's husband). He is open and ready to receive. My grace has gone before and the stress of circumstances in his life has done its work. Now he needs personal contact with a follower of Mine who has faith. He needs to be given hope to cling to, a reason for living.

The right time comes in each person's life when the soil has been prepared and has been watered with tears of searching or misfortune. The time of planting arrives, and when the soil is truly ready, the growth comes fast. Do not go as just you. Go in My name, walking under My anointing. A time and place will be provided. Leave all to Me. I will speak through you. I will touch and heal him from within.

Remember to always give credit to Me. For you to try to appropriate that which you cannot hold will explode the work of grace within you. A channel cannot hold all the water that is in the reservoir – it would burst. You are merely a channel.

Bless you, for your quiet waiting upon Me. Quiet waiting is never time lost. Much growth in plants takes place in the still of the night, in darkness. Much growth and recuperation in people take place during the night, in sleep. You would become worn out and frazzled if you had a constant pace of hectic activity. This is true in the spiritual life as well as for the body. When I suggest that you recuperate and gain strength, that is My Will for you at that time.

Remember always, no matter how intensively you pray for people, it is not you who are doing the "saving." It is I. Do not carry the burden of salvation for anyone but rather carry the joy of ministering My salvation to them as I ask it of you. If you do not feel led at a particular time to pray for anyone about something, do not be concerned that you are neglecting your duty. It is My task to work out all things, to work out the salvation of all. Your task is to be ready and willing to take whatever part in it that I lead you to. []

8.17   BE DOCILE TO THE SPIRIT

[| My child, I bless you! Thank you for your firm belief. Thank you for being who I would have you be. It does not work to compare yourself with others and think, "This person is like this; maybe I should be that way," or, "So-and-So is doing this and this. She is doing so much! I should find more to do!" No. Be docile to the Spirit, for the Spirit is life. The life in you is all that matters.

There is life in a plum tree, there is life in a cow. Should the plum tree try to go running around a pasture and attempt to give milk to a calf? Preposterous! It is the same for each person. Be docile and obedient to your calling. That is what brings the smile of heaven upon you.

Rest in Me and trust that all is well. The anxiety you are feeling will dissipate as you become more firmly grounded in Me and sure of My love.

Love heals. As you let yourself be loved, as you risk being vulnerable, you will come into a profound peace within yourself that no outside calamity can shake. But you need to live your ordinary, everyday life. Do not stand around and daydream. Put yourself wholeheartedly into the task at hand whether it is washing windows, getting groceries, or sleeping in My arms.

Time to go! We begin a new day together. Bless you! []

8.18   SHARE YOUR FAITH

[| I walk with you, My child. Have no fear. I am with you and with all. No matter what concerns you may have for others for whatever reasons, affirm your faith in My love and care for them. Believe "for" others until they can finally come to a place of believing, then believe with them.

How wonderful it is to be able to believe! Do you recall how lost and miserable you felt when your faith was so sorely tested that you did not know if you could continue to believe? Picture the depths to which those people fall who simply cannot believe (the way it seems to them) no matter how much they desire to.

Faith is a gift. It is meant to be shared. *"Freely you have received, freely give"* (Mt 10:8b). You can share your faith by believing *for* the next person, as though you were in their place. By believing for them that they will be brought out of the pit of destruction, it can then come to be.

The seed of faith is implanted in all but it lies dormant in so many. Seeds need good soil to grow and they need to be watered. You can water the seed of faith in others by your "tears" of concern, by caring for them and loving them. When people receive love from fellow human beings, they can dare to begin hoping that there is a God to believe in from whom this love originates.

There will be those who do have much faith of their own even on their deathbed. Carry those people through with your faith by continuing to believe "for" them. If conditions had been different, they would have been among the happiest, the firmest believers. Do not neglect your own. That person is your fellow human being. In love, you have the right to ask Me to carry him or her into eternal life on your faith. *"For God so loved the world that he gave his one and only Son, that whoever believes in him shall not perish but have eternal life"* (Jn 3:16).

Be open to all, desirous of saving all. Love knows no bounds. That selfsame love of Mine that saves and embraces everyone is the love that I give to you. Do not confine it in a petty, enclosed heart! Open your heart to all. Let the love within go out to all.

Bless you, My child! Go in peace, love, and faith; and give that peace, love, and faith to everyone, with no exception. []

8.19 CARRY YOUR CHILDREN IN LOVE

[| My child, continue to carry your children in your heart in love, not in anxiety. That way they will receive a continual bath of love. Your relationship with and toward your children is a copy and example of My love and relationship with My children. Each and all are dear and beloved to Me. I overlook the faults and see the good. I see what can come to be, and I make it come to be by bringing about those situations and circumstances that will open that person to love, faith, and hope.

Hope never dies as long as there is life. There is an instinct in people which says there is Someone out there who cares, who can help. Yes, there is SOMEONE! Come to Me, My children! I await you, I long for you, I suffer for you. until the moment be accomplished that you are safe in My arms!

Mothers and dads, you can be the human vehicle for carrying your children to safety and love in My heart. Do not give up on them! Continue to believe in the inherent goodness present in each of them. They come from Me, who am all goodness. Give your children the freedom to fly free, yes, but believe that in that freedom they will fly to Me. All of nature bids them to recognize and acknowledge Me, their Creator, their Father. Do not give up hope! []

8.20 CHOOSE TO BE OPEN

[| Marriage brings a special relationship in the order of grace as well as in the physical order. When nothing is in the way to block it, grace received by one partner will also have a positive effect on the Soul and person of their partner. What might block this?

Resentment, moodiness, depression,
Outright anger and vindictiveness,
Self-centeredness, anxiety,
Indifference, and a host of other similar feelings.

The way to overcome these obstacles is through having a set purpose of the will through which you *choose* to be open and loving even if you do not feel like it. Feelings are mainly of the body. The power of the will is an action of your Soul which is of a higher plane. Your Soul will overrule the objections and feelings of your body because the body is a servant to your Soul. This is how things should be.

Marriage is meant to be a completely free state, with each partner being and feeling perfectly free. Do you think Adam and Eve felt constrained by the fact of being married? Only after sin entered the word did problems begin arising.

Part of the problem for many is that they want their selfish self to be free. When selfishness is turned loose, havoc is created. Being married puts some constrictions on selfishness and forces one to think of and do for the other person, whether one wants to or not. The same thing comes about through the time and nurturing needed when raising children.

Whatever goes against the natural grain, against the selfish self, is blessed. Thus, there are inherent blessings even in catastrophe, illness, and humiliation.

Bless you, child! Go in peace and love. I go with you. []

8.21   NO GREATER LOVE

[| My child, I love you! Let My love sink in and bring healing. You are loved! Say: *"I am loved!"* Let the all-powerful knowledge that you are loved erupt into joy within you. All the aspects of spiritual life come forth from love, for love is all being. Affirm for yourself:

I am love.! I am safe in love.
I am loved by the God who is.

I am loved, so I can freely love.

My child, all is well. Do not worry about how things are going for you spiritually. Just be and do as I direct. Continue to strengthen your self-discipline by exercising your willpower in the power of love. Only love can give you lasting incentive.

I hold you in My arms of love as I hold all in love! I am showing you how much I love each and all of My children. The compassion that grips your heart when you see others suffering is a tiny drop of the compassion of My heart for all of you. But rejoice! All is well and is going as scheduled. I am a God of miracles. All is set up in a marvelous divine plan! Just trust and believe, love and obey.

I am taking charge of the situation you are currently concerned about. I send My holy angels to bring about My Will. This does not necessarily mean, however, that all will be "peaches and cream" – that no suffering will be involved. The strongest soldiers become strong from taking part in the heat of the battle. By experiencing the particular situations you are experiencing, you become a kin sister to all those others of the human race who have experienced the like, and thus you come to have spiritual authority in and over those circumstances.

You may wonder when anything special in the spiritual line will be coming forth through your intercession. Bide your time, be obedient, and pray. Recall that during Jesus' life on earth, no sign of his divine calling was shown outwardly until the thirtieth year of his life. But, oh, the growth and building of character before that! His humanity had to become completely imbued with the Spirit of God. His senses and human faculties had to come under obedience to the Holy Spirit, as yours must.

Whenever you so choose, you can come into the fullness of life in the Spirit, into becoming a channel of blessing. Do you see the way better now? Self-discipline, a building up of faith, obedience to the whispers of the Spirit, resting in Me, in My love. []

Lord, what would you have me do specifically?

[| Begin to concentrate on David, your friend's son, letting love for him well up within you. Deny yourself with his welfare specifically in mind. Confess your sin of looking down on "his kind." "*Who may ascend the hill of the Lord? Who may stand in his holy place? He who has clean hands and a pure heart*" (Ps 24:3-4a).

Do not think, "Is this young man worth all that effort?" Whatever you do for the least of My brethren, for any one of them, you do for Me, and whatever you do for one, you do for all. That effort is not wasted.

"*Greater love has no one than this, to lay down one's life for one's friends*" (Jn 15:13). Lay down your life for another and your love will grow by leaps and bounds. []

8.22 REJOICE IN THE COMING VICTORY

[| Do not fear, only trust. I am worthy of all trust. Believe and be saved from all that you fear. You can lie down and walk with Me in complete confidence.

I would have stalwart people, not those who would faint on the way. Your spirits must be strong, then your bodies will also be strong, even in times of peril, anguish, and suffering.

Victory is coming! Lift your heads and see this thing that is coming to pass! The victory has been from all eternity! Enter into it, first of all in spirit, and rejoice! I would have strong, rejoicing people banded together in love and freedom who will march with Me to victory! (Do not get caught up with the physical aspect of this description. How else to describe…?)

Victory within yourself is very important. A rolling stone picks up speed on its way down a hill. Each person added to the effort makes the whole that much stronger. The more I can be present within individuals, the more I can be present in My world.

I send you the Spirit of truth.
I send you out to teach and to heal,
To comfort the mourning,
To restore the spirits of the crestfallen,
To lift the downfallen.

I trust Myself to you and our union is thus complete, the way is prepared. Go live in peace, My people! Live in love, trust, obedience, and faith. Bless you, one and all! []

8.23   CALL ON THE NAME OF THE LORD

[| "...*the mouth of the Lord has spoken*" (Is 40:5b). I have spoken, speak, My love. "*Then he said, 'I am the God of your father, the God of Abraham, the God of Isaac and the God of Jacob'* " (Ex 3: 6a).

I am the God of the living. All who believe will live on in Me, for I give life and am life. Come to Me that you may be filled with every good thing! Place everything in My hands: your hopes and dreams, plans for the future, your family and possessions, your very life.

I am the sustainer of life,

The fulfillment of hope,

Sure salvation.

A refuge for all who call on My name.

Bring those lost ones to Me, to the sure refuge where "*God will wipe away every tear from their eyes*" (Rev 7:17c). Join yourself with them in love, in spirit, so that they are "bone of your bone and flesh of your flesh" then come! I welcome you with open arms! "...*all the ends of the earth will see the salvation of our God*" (Is 52:10b).

You do not need to know and understand everything. Do not presume to judge My ways. Be creature, that I may be your God.

"*[T]he mouth of the Lord has spoken*" (Is 40:5b). What will be, will be. All that is foreordained will come to pass.

I will be, I am, Savior to "*everyone who calls on the name of the Lord*" (Acts 2: 21). Pray that all will call on My name. Desire the salvation of all. I desire it! Unite your desires with My desires and believe that those desires will come to be. Await the fulfillment of My word with expectation. "*I the Lord have spoken, and I will do it*" (Ez 22:14b).

I bless all of you who have helped get that homeless woman settled and provided for. Sometimes I allow misfortune to strike in someone's life so that others of you can provide for that person out of the generosity in their heart. Your hearts are expanded in love for so doing. *"It is more blessed to give than to receive"* (Acts 20: 35b), yet the receiver is mightily blest.

Things are important only in their providing for you and not as an end in themselves. To have something and have no use for it is useless. I will provide for you richly out of My abundance. *"And do not set your heart on what you will eat or drink; do not worry about it.... Your Father knows that you need them. But seek his kingdom, and these things will be given to you as well"* (Lk 12:9-31).

I am in all of life, in all of creation. The inanimate is there to serve the needs of the animate and to give glory to Me in its own right. Use all with humility and gratitude. The creature must acknowledge the creator. Happily, I provide for you! The purpose of My life is to love, serve, provide, inspire, encourage, and enliven. Bless all of you as you go on your way! |]

8.24 BE A CHANNEL OF COMPASSION

[| My child, rest in Me. I am the answer to all your needs, to all your questions and searching. Your heart will not rest until it rests in Me. If you find yourself dissatisfied and disgruntled with everything and everyone, with life itself, stop to consider that you may not be looking in the right place for satisfaction and happiness.

You will find fulfillment through giving up your wishes for the sake of the needs and wishes of others.

You will find soul satisfaction by going against selfish desires and purposefully thinking and doing for others.

This does not come automatically, that you feel love and compassion for others. You must be open to receiving that spiritual gift. People become open through receiving love. Those who are most closed and uncaring are likely the ones who did not sense being loved when they were young. "As a tree is bent, so will it grow."

Have compassion and love now for these unfortunate people. Desire release, healing, and a flow of love to reach them and warm their hearts. By praying for one person whom you know to be closed off like this – that he or she may be delivered from the prison of self-centeredness and spitefulness – you then have a channel through whom to flow love, aid, and compassion to others who are similarly bound. []

God, rescue the afflicted! Hear the people who cry out to you! Hear our prayers! I unite myself with these hurting, searching people and ask that a flow of love and mercy and on, out in ever-widening circles, to all hurting and searching Souls. Lord, have mercy! We put our trust in you, Lord! Bless you!

[| Bless you, child of My heart! Peace! |]

8.25   SHARE WHO YOU ARE

[| My child, do not be afraid to be vulnerable, for it is only in being vulnerable that you can give and receive tenderness: your real self, uncovered, coming into contact with another person's real self, coming into contact with Me. Can you feel a tender touch and caress on your hand if you are wearing thick gloves? or can you give a tender caress in that manner?

In spirit, a similar effect takes place when you keep a heavy cloak over your feelings, over your true self. You will not disintegrate if you were to share more of your inner self and your dreams, hopes, desires, hesitancies and fears, your vulnerability. Being vulnerable is one quality that all share. The more tender (vulnerable) you are on the inside, the more tenderness you have to share and the more intimate and felt-to-the-depths will be the tenderness you receive in return.

It is the living and the loving that make life worthwhile. For life to be worthwhile for you, you must open yourself to the real life that is within you and to the real person of your loved one(s). Do not be afraid to share, whether time, words, ideas, silence, activities or just being. Share the being of who you are and take in the being of the one you love. You can do this in spirit, without words or actions. Perhaps this is even more effective than words or actions would be because you are spirit beings.

> Consciously choose to drop your fears! They are like curtains or heavy clothes that prevent real contact.

> Rid yourself of barbs of resentment and anger! They are like a hair shirt, like day-old whisker stubble, that pokes and irritates the other person.

> Holding onto past hurts is like having knives or barbs between you and the other person pointed in your direction. The barbs re-open old wounds every time you recall the hurts.

No matter what another person is like – how mean-hearted, irritable, or obnoxious – it is not the person himself or herself who inflicts hurt. The basic person is the tender being he or she was as an infant, a person made in My image. The meanness, irritability, and negativity have been picked up from this world during that person's life.

When relating to others, relate directly to their inner being. Do not acknowledge or consider the exterior roughness or lack of caring to be the true person. Deep down in everyone is the vulnerable, sensitive, caring person as I created him or her. People can be reached and touched only by open, vulnerable love. Love that accepts completely brings healing to the person who is loved. []

8.26   WOUNDEDNESS CAN BE HEALED

Lord, I sense that I have a wounded spirit.
[| That can be fixed, child. I am the great physician, the great healer. Repair of a deep hole in a wall with plaster must be done in layers, a little at a time. After the first layer has hardened and set securely, the next layer can be applied. If the hole were to be filled full of plaster all at one time, the plaster would crack and the result would be very unsatisfactory.

A deep wound needs to heal a layer at a time from the inside out. If a thorn, dirt, or other object is lodged in the wound, that dirt or object must first be loosened and flushed out before true, complete healing can begin. Sometimes a wound closes over the top of the hurting element. Continued pain and possibly infection result.

Let Me work loose all those things in your life and spirit that cause or have caused you pain. Let Me help you recognize what those hurting elements are so they can be dealt with.

I ask you, please, not to carry your husband heavily in the center of your heart, for no person is meant to carry another as a burden. You are meant to carry others as joy and love only. Carrying in love and joy lightens the load. Remove the hurting concern for him from the depths of your heart. Let that wound heal. Let Me heal it – it may take a while, as it is so deep – then joyfully and lovingly carry him in and with your heart in the manner that a mother carries a child, outside of herself.

How can you think of trying to carry the burden of another person and all of that person's hurts, needs, and fears when you have so much burden of your own to carry?

You are not meant to "carry" another person to the extent that it is almost like a physical load. You are to hold them in spirit, in love, but let them stand on their own two feet. Whatever hurts, needs, and burdens each person has, leave them with that person for Me to take care of.

You are individuals. To be truly free, you must be free of your marriage partner, too, in the sense of not being weighed down by him or her. Each butterfly must fly freely. Two butterflies cannot be tied or taped together, a person cannot have the other person "inside" of them.

Bless you, My child! All My love to you! []

CHAPTER 9

EVER LEARNING

9.1   BE NOT GUIDE UNTO YOURSELF

[| My child, I bid you take to heart the lesson I have been giving you that even so-called "religious" activities can be very much self-oriented and self-centered. What is to come will come in good time. Do not try to guide your growth. Rest in Me and upon Me for all guidance, growth, and strength.

Many marvelous lessons, much marvelous truth, will be forthcoming, all in due time. You need to assimilate what you receive so it can come forth within you as part of your very life and being.

You are being transformed. You are like a caterpillar in its chrysalis that is undergoing changes and growth, soon to emerge as a beautiful butterfly. Do you think a caterpillar knows into what shape it is changing or that it has the intelligence to direct that growth from within itself? Of course not! You are as incapable of taking charge of your growth as a caterpillar is in its growth.

It is My life within and without that spontaneously brings about growth in your spiritual life as well as in your physical life. Your part is to learn not to hinder the growth and the ordering of things of the spirit. To grow correctly, your body must be unencumbered by binding clothes or constricted quarters. Your spirit must likewise be free of the limitations of your ideas and direction to grow to its destined beauty and to be able to fly freely on the wings of the spirit.

Knowing a little about the spiritual life does not make you a master at directing that life for yourself or others. Refer all to Me, the Father and giver of Life. You can point out the way to others, but then let their spirit be free to grow as life has destined them to be. Wise human guidance, however, includes direction to put limits on the physical – excessive eating and drinking, for example – to free the spirit to grow.

All must be done in love or it is artificial, and all that is artificial is not real. It amounts to nothing. Discipline yourself and your appetites through genuine love for yourself. Direct others to a like discipline through genuine love for themselves.

Only love is real. Only love will stand the test of quality and time. If it does not endure, it is not pure and true love. When your love for yourself becomes purified and cleansed of all inordinate self-love it will have the strength to see you through all difficulties and be a source of strength for self-discipline. The result will be rapid and steady growth in the spirit.

Come to Me that you may be filled with love and cleansed by love! But please be patient with yourself. We have all eternity. Rest in Me, be in Me, in love. Blessings to you and everyone! []

9.2   PURIFICATION IS NECESSARY

[| My child, I realize that this last while has been long and difficult for you. I am no less with you when you are experiencing depression and doubt than when you experience moments of sensible closeness. You exist in Me. I uphold you by, and in, My love. Rest on that foundation and you will experience less anxiety and less searching loneliness. Faith and hope will see you through, indomitable faith and undaunted hope.

You are correct in considering that receiving "words" from Me is not especially important. Rest with faith and hope in love, not in any of the gifts or talents that love has given.

Gold must be purified by fire to become pure and beautiful; otherwise, it is dross and dull, mixed as it is with all sorts of impurities. Even so, is each of you until the saving action of My Spirit does its work of grace in you. All is well. All who are sincerely seeking My Will and My presence are being led and purified and, though the way seems ever so long, the time of purification will pass to give way to the time of joyful reunion in Heaven!

You do not need to support and guide yourself. The more you leave that to Me the more you will be blessed, and the more simple and blessed life will be for you. Your very nature must be changed and replaced by My divine nature, for human nature has been sullied and warped by sin. It was not so in the beginning: You were made in My image, destined for immortality.

"*I give you a new heart and put a new spirit in you; I will remove from you your heart of stone and give you a heart of flesh*" (Ez 36.26). I give you life immortal. Open yourself to receive the promise of the Father which has been waiting throughout the ages to be given to you! "*And this is what he promised us—eternal life*" (I Jn 2:25). []

Lord, I feel this is not spontaneous enough.

[| Do not worry, child. Leave all in My hands. Stay pliable and willing, and the growth and the ability will be there as needed.

Do not fear. Trust in Me always. I am always with you. Turn your fears over to Me. I can handle them! It is your part to be yourself and to trust. A comparison could be made with a bow and arrow. They each just need to be themselves and be ready and willing to be used.

How I long for you to come into full communion with Me! It is being accomplished and My heart rejoices!

There is much that you, that people, do not know about Me and the workings of the universe, physical and spiritual. Stay pliable and willing in My hands, in Me, and that which is meant to come about will come about. I love you, My child! []

9.3   UNION IN WILL

Do with me, Lord, what You will.

[| My child, I will that you be happy, free of doubt, at peace, one with love Itself, but that needs cooperation on your part. I cannot do with you as I will unless you also will it. Willing as I do will make you come to be more fully one with Me.

I will that you be healthy. When you desire to be healthy, you are acting in union with Me.

I will that you be loved to the "nth" degree.

When you love, you love with and in My love.

I love you! I will never let anything harmful, that which is to your spiritual detriment, come to you or befall you. Trust in My love and care. Live in My love. Open your heart, mind, and body to receive. Do not be afraid.

You are a whole unit: You must be open in mind, body, and spirit. I come into your mind, body, and spirit. I come that you may have life in your mind, body, and spirit. Healing and release in one facet of your person bring healing and release to the other elements of your being, to your whole person.

Bide My timing of your growth in body, mind, and spirit. Growth cannot be forced, but each aspect of growth can be expanded to the fullest possible. An example of this is to note the difference in the growth of two plants which started the same when one has good nourishment, watering, and proper lighting, while the other has poor lighting and suffers malnourishment and drought.

It is My Will that you flourish in the best of conditions. I would have no evil come nigh thee, but in the darkness caused by sin, there is much ill-will and suffering. Dispel the darkness with the light of salvation! You are free! I bid you live in that freedom. []

9.4   KEEP AN OPEN MIND

[| My child, I bless you! Constantly, I bless you, and that blessing gives you the strength to keep on trying. My blessing gives you the ability to be who you are meant to be. The urge for growth is always there, as is evidenced in nature. []

Lord, I thirst!

[| We belong together, we are together in reality. The thirst and searching that you are experiencing is a longing to come into the fullness of that reality. Have patience, even as you tell your daughter to be patient, that she will grow up. The time will pass, the necessary spiritual lessons will be learned, and the people will be helped through your ministry who are meant to be.

Be grateful for your hunger and thirst, for your desire to come into full unity with Me, and for your desire to help many! Your desires are the seedbed of hope. "[T]hose who hope in Me will not be disappointed (Is 49:23c).

Rest and live in Me. Use the graces I offer you and your desires will be fulfilled beyond your wildest imaginings! For Me all things are possible. Ask what you will in good faith and it will be done for you and for those for whom you ask.

Rest in My peace. You need to drink in peace every time you feel restless and when you feel beleaguered by questions. Coming into truth is a process of growth taking place, just as it is with love and faith. In the world of nature, it takes time for a small acorn to grow into a mighty oak tree. The seed of truth that you have welcomed into the soil of your heart and mind takes time to grow.

Do not think you need to have every question, doubt, and hesitation settled just like that. Scholars and common folk have wrestled with these questions and searched for truth all through the ages. This searching is a part of the expression in your being of hunger for coming to know Me, who am all truth. Rest in Me, not in this or that element of truth that you have picked up. Only in Me can you be satisfied.

You are getting very sleepy. That is your body's way of letting you know that you need sleep. You remain in contact with Me at all times if you so desire it. The time of sleep can be a time of spiritual growth. Do all in union with Me. Sleep united with Me. Bless you, My child! Get your needed rest. |]

9.5   OUT WITH FEAR AND DARKNESS!

[| Banish fear from your heart, it then has no right to return. Only a guest whom you invited is welcome to share the abode of your heart. When you see the uninvited guest, fear, make haste to throw it out! All is to be peace and tranquility within your heart, mind, and Soul. Away with fear! Away with darkness! I bid you dwell "in the shadow of My wings" (see Ps 17:8).

My precious child, there is much for you to learn! But be not anxious. You have all eternity to come to know, and I have all eternity to be known: a coming together of lover and beloved.

Each person is a symbol and a representative of the whole. I am to one as to all. You are My promised spouse. All are My spouse-coming-to-be.

There is no disconnecting regarding Me. I am in one and all, from the first in time even to the last, but I am not divided, so all are one. What a glorious coming-to-be, coming-to-be in Me, in love! Keep up your hope and trust, as I do! I trust that this coming-to-be will come to pass and it will!

Your life in the spirit is not so much different than Mine is. Your life is a reflection of My life. I hold you to My heart that your faint flame of faith, hope, and love may be joined with the flame of My Spirit. The fire of My love burns away the dross left in you and is refining you as purest gold.

All are interconnected in and by the Spirit. All are included in the marvelous working out of My plan. Come into the light, child, into the abode of love, peace, and freedom, so that all of those that you are meant to help will be helped. |]

9.6   BE GROUNDED IN ME

[| You are ever My child. Nothing will change that. From before all time, from eternity, you are My child, all are My children. There is no more loving Fatherhood than Mine and no more loving Motherhood than Mine. Loving fatherhood and motherhood come to be in Me and from Me. []

My God, I bless the goodness of Your heart!

[| And I bless you, My child! Blessing always brings blessing. What you sow is what you will reap. When you sow in the flesh, you receive fleshly returns. When you sow in the spirit, you gain in the spirit.

There is ever a battle between flesh and spirit. The spiritual person learns to discern where to draw the line on the needs and cravings of the flesh. Many, however, make the mistake of giving up on the battle too soon. When they are not able to gain instant mastery over their flesh and its cravings and needs, they give up on the struggle very shortly.

I want you to know and be prepared for it, that a long, patient struggle is needed. Growth in nature from seedling to maturity is a slow, step-by-step process. It s not completed overnight. Learn from nature and take courage that maturity does come if you but be patient and give the time for it, while at the same time, you see to it that the conditions necessary for growth are there.

The first condition necessary for growth is for you to be grounded in Me. As a plant sends down more and more roots to get firmly established in the earth and draw nourishment and life-giving water, so you must become established in the Ground of Your Being, in Me, your God. I am open to receiving you. I await you with open arms, My little one, My dove, fly into My arms! Come to Father-Mother love! I enfold you in My arms of all-encompassing love! []

9.7   I GIVE YOU LIFE

[| My beloved child, how I long to crush you in My arms in love! I do that in spirit and I make you whole. See how precious this special time of anointing and blessing is? All the more special for having hungered for some time.

I realize that you have much hunger within you. That is a sign that I Am and that you are coming to be in Me. You are being transformed into My likeness steadily and surely. Gray days play a major role in this.

My child, trust Me. I handle you with delicate care. I hold you in My arms of love. All that you choose to do is OK with Me. I give you free will, free reign over your life and your time. My loving Spirit, however, calls out to you to take care of yourself, both for your own sake and for My sake, for I love you so! []

Lord, I open myself to receive what You have to give. I give You my love, Lord. Would that I could love You more!

[| My child, I receive your love with thanksgiving and joy! The way you feel when you are truly joyful, thankful, and vibrant with life is a small taste for you of My life. I live in joy and thankfulness, alive with love! I see in everything only cause for joy and thankfulness, and growth potential. I refuse to allow any negative thought to upset My tranquility.

Do you see how you are being called into My image, into oneness with Me? Giving up your sense way of life is not a "bad" thing to have to do, though it is difficult. When you give up having material things in exchange for the right spiritual ordering in your life, you have exchanged, in reality, death for life. Come to Me that you may have life and have it more abundantly!

"'For my thoughts are not your thoughts, neither are your ways my ways,' declares the Lord" (Is 55:8). In entrusting yourself to Me, you may (very likely do) have a subconscious, set idea as to what is the way you "should be" led and taken care of.

To "entrust" means to trust completely, without questioning the wisdom of My ways. You, a human being, do not have the right to question My wisdom, but only to ask why, in My wisdom, I have chosen or allowed something. I permit you to question, though, else you would be robbed of your precious free will, that facet of your being in which you are most like Me.

Rest in My love, child! Drink in deep draughts of love! Drink all you want, all you need. It is love that gives and sustains your life. Bless you, My child! Go in peace, in My love! []

9.8   HEALING FROM WITHIN

[| There are blessings in store for everyone but many never make it out of the clutches of materialism and sensuality, of "me-ism." One must turn on the road marked "you-ism" to come to the joys of eternal life. *"Now this is eternal life: that they know you, the only true God, and Jesus Christ, whom you have sent"* (Jn 17:3).

Relax, My child, and let Me flow an unction of grace upon and through you. Rest in My peace for a bit. Receive of life. |]

Father, I open my whole person to You. I welcome You into the recesses of my being, into my presence.

[| I do not go where I am not welcome. My love and presence must be freely received or I cannot be there for I am freedom itself. Gladly I come into your heart and mind and soul, My child! Gladly! You don't know how glad I am to come!

I wash you free of anxiety and stress. I place the balm of My peace upon your wounds. I heal you from deep inside in that center of life that you can share with no other except Me.

Growing up, you experience a strong need for security, love, and affection. You do not feel OK or safe unless and until you receive that love. As time goes on, you come to maturity as My ever-present, unfailing love makes that security permanent within you.

You come into the wholeness of being in the presence of and in union with Love, ever-present within you. This is the only way to come into lasting peace: to accept and become united with My love for you. You become united with love by loving Me in return.

O bliss of requited love! Forever we could sing its glories! Forever we will sing its glories! Forever we will dwell in love! Come! |]

Lord, I bless You from the bottom of My heart! Glory to you, O God, king of eternal glory!

[| Yes, My child, I am King of Glory, but I am also a servant of the poorest. I do not cling to any glory that I have. I exult that I can be God and helper and savior to you, My people!

Fear not, for I am with you now and always, and in all ways. Nowhere can you go from My love. Stay open to My Spirit, and things must work out for the best for you. The "best" may not always seem to be so in worldly terms, but My view is from eternity.

I bid you get enough sleep. The "temple repairs" must be done. And while you sleep and rest, do not worry about what may not be getting done. Only that done in love and obedience has lasting value, so at the time that rest is indicated, rest is the only thing you can do that is worthwhile. I leave the latitude of discretion about this up to you. You know whether it is serious that at any given time you must rest to be in My will.

My child, blest are you for your believing firmly and for waiting patiently, that the word of the Lord to you will come to pass! Yes, leave everything up to Me. Who are you to make eternal decisions? Even in everyday life, make your daily decisions in union with love.

I know this [writing the thoughts that come to mind] often seems to you like it is not worthwhile, that you may be formulating it yourself, but the times that you feel there might be something to write down, please do so. I would have you be a docile and willing instrument in My hands to the point of being a fool for your Me, if necessary. Bless you, for your firm belief! Bless you, for your efforts! Bless you, for your love! []

9.9   GROWTH WILL COME

[| You have nothing to fear, My child. I will lead you in the way I would have you go. I know of the fond hope in your heart to somehow help bring all the varying approaches together that are presented by different groups. A desire must be there to give birth to hope. Hope, in turn, feeds faith and brings that which is hoped for into reality.

All that is good, including all good desires, exists first in My heart. When you are open to giving birth to these desires in your spirit, you are united with Me in that aspect and become a vehicle by which the hoped-for desire can come to be.

All in due time, My child. The seed must oft stay in the ground a long time before any visible growth appears: first to sprout, then to put down roots, then to begin outward growth that is still hidden from view.

The seed is planted. You and others who are willing are the soil. The growth and the fruit are for all. Ever I have all in My mind and heart. As you come into love and understanding it helps everyone else to deepen in love and understanding, for all are one in Me.

Rest in My love. It is vibrant with life! When you rest in Me you leave refreshed, invigorated, and full of life. You, all of you, are the growth and the life that is there present for all to see and to be strengthened by.

You do not, should not, want to grow up in your estimation. "*I tell you the truth, unless you change and become like little children, you will never enter the kingdom of heaven*" (Mt 18:3a). Approach the study and pondering of Scripture as a child without preconceived, ideas as to what the verses mean. Having such a mindset closes your mind to further opening to the truth.

Rather than having a one-track mind, you need to have an open mind, open and flat like a field that is ready to receive seed. Having a one-track mind is like having one furrow dug, with your ideas already planted in it and already fairly well-grown, so those ideas crowd out any new ideas that one might try to plant there.

All need to repent and grow and change in so many ways! You do not know this and cannot know it, of yourselves. It is My Holy Spirit who does the pruning, who brings you all life and knowledge. My Spirit is life and love. []

9.10   THE WIND BLOWS WHERE IT WILL

[| Peace and benediction upon you, My child, and blessings of every spiritual nature! The spiritual precedes the physical so know that when you receive a physical blessing, you have already been blessed in the spirit. Even those occurrences and happy fortunes that appear to be of the world are tied into the spiritual order of blessings, for everything exists in Me in the spiritual and the physical.

Do not try to probe the mysteries of the world of spirit by intellectualism, for it will not work. It takes a simple mind, uncluttered by sophistries, to come to an understanding of and belief in the spiritual. What will be given to you to understand will be given in the manner and order and time meant for it. Your part is to be obedient and open, willing to listen and learn.

Some of the things you consider that you "know" and take great stock in may be turned topsy-turvy by the wind of the Spirit. Such a happening does not change the security that you have in Me. I am your security. Your knowledge and understanding are not your security. Your notes and lessons are not your security. Be watchful of undue attachment and dependence upon them.

I keep this process purposely vague so you do not put great stock in the receiving of "words." Always give due acknowledgment that it is the Giver who is important, not the "given." The importance of the "given" is in the life that is given, in the truth that is shared, and in the knowledge of the way opened to you. If that which is "given" does not lead one to the way, the truth, and the life, then it is being mistakenly used.

These words/lessons are not an end in themselves. Keep your eye single-mindedly upon the love I have for you. Keep your mind upon being obedient to the call you have been given to serve Me in love in your family and others. Stay open to all of life, not just to those aspects that please your "taste buds" and flatter your ego.

Blessings to all! Live in My love, in peace. Go in peace to love and serve. Bless you, My child! []

9.11   WALK IN THE LIGHT

[| Your life comes from Me. Treat it as sacred. The time you have comes from Me. Use it wisely.

This is the time of Lent, a time during which you can make great strides in self-discipline and in deepening your faith-and-love relationship with Me. You can receive extra help for your willpower during this time because of all the others who are also making an effort towards self-discipline. You are all one.

Lent is a time for exercise but also a time for rest. Come to Me and rest! Rest from worries and your work. Sometimes people make more work for themselves than they would need to. Does that room have to be always perfectly spotless? Do you have to be the one serving on that particular committee when you already are a member of three others?

Do all things in moderation: working, resting, eating, drinking, and pushing to achieve. *"What good is it for a man to gain the whole world, yet forfeit his soul?"* (Mk 8:36). Who can restore it to him?

Your Soul is your person, it is you. If you lose your Soul, you have lost yourself. Then, forever you are lost to what you were meant to become, forever you are lost to freedom and joy and achievement.

To use a physical description to describe the spiritual, hell is a dark place. It is the abode of the dark spirits, the rulers of darkness, and their cohorts. Forever seeking, but never satisfied; untamed hunger, unbridled passion. Who would enjoy being forever angry?

The body must share in the destiny of the Soul; that is an unbreakable spiritual law. Your body shares what your Soul becomes, what your Soul partakes of. What glorious destiny for the body of the Soul who partakes of Me! Glorious freedom! Blessed fruit!

Come and receive the reward that has been prepared for you from the beginning. Enter into the joy of your master! |]

9.12   LIFE IS FOREVER

[| My child, continue to look up! Continue to believe and hope! Your salvation is nearer than you think! Everything has been provided for. It is finished. All of "time" is present. The moments that comprise time are given so that all can receive. I give All to all. Rest in My peace, mercy, acceptance, and love.

The hours of the night are hours of growth in the spirit, for at that time your mind and body are largely at rest. This is how prophetic teaching is received, also, by putting the operation of your thoughts in neutral and letting My thoughts surface.

I am within you, so all wisdom is within. That deep reservoir of knowledge and strength is tapped into the divine source. Your whole being is tapped into the divine – your life is proof of that. The goodness that flows forth from people is proof that they are united with the divine, for how can microcosms of minerals and water (of which all living creatures are composed) come to have a mind and a heart with which to do good for others?

Yes, life is a mystery, but do not be afraid of it. If life seems forever a new thing to you, be grateful, for then you have attuned your spirit to the Infinite, Who dwells within you. The new life that constantly issues forth in plants and animals is a physical sign of the newness of life you come into in the spirit when you choose to be open to it. []

9.13   YOUR LIFE IS FROM ME

Father, I surrender myself to You as You give Me the light to do so. I wish to become ever more and more a channel of Your love and blessing, of Your life. Please direct me on the way!
[| My child, as I speak to you, I speak to all:
Come into My love!
Come walk in Me, the way!
Come into the truth!
Come, be filled with life!
You must come to Me to receive. If you never risk stepping forward into a new understanding and new dimensions of life, you will never come into the fullness of life and love.
You must let yourself be loved to receive love,
Let yourself be led to walk on the way and
Open yourself to be filled with life.
The living and the loving will make it all worthwhile if you but
be open.

Do not fear change. This refers to change within oneself more so than external change although they sometimes go hand-in-hand and one affects the other. Change is growth. Again the example from the world of plants: If a plant were to stay the same as it is at any given moment, there could be no further growth, no flowering, and no setting of seed or fruit. The plant's life would cease because for it to stay alive there must be a constant flow of life-giving nutrients from roots to stem and leaves, and a counter flow from the stem and leaves back to the roots.

For you to stay alive there must be a constant exchange of life-giving energies between you and Me, whom you are rooted in. Giving and receiving are both necessary. Breathing in and breathing out. Loving and being loved. Giving love and receiving love. |]

9.14   IT IS DONE IN THE SPIRIT

[| My child, it is good to have a measure of caution, to pull back in retrospect once in a while to try to determine if you are acting with too much self-love and self-centeredness. |]

Lord, I open my mind and heart to receive and love You.

[| Peace in all you think and do and say! The peace that you receive goes out to others by your being an open channel: loving, accepting, and blessing them. One avenue for this is in your thoughts which are governed by your will. Love is wishing well for and to others. This is done in your thought life.

Thoughts have great power and force, more than you will ever realize with your human mind. The power of your thoughts comes from Me. Your thinking process has some of the basic characteristics that are in My eternal mind. Much of people's creativity through thought, however, is canceled by subsequent negative thoughts.

My people, how eagerly I anticipate you coming into freedom and love! It is done in the spirit. Try to let this truth begin to sink in: That which is to come to be cannot be hindered from coming about, except by negation of it through your will, through negative thinking, through ignorance of My ways. I am teaching you in many and varied ways:

Listen to the prophets and teachers that I sent and am sending into your midst.

Open your mind to the written word.

Ask the Spirit of Wisdom to teach you and to teach all, to guide you in the path of wisdom and victory.

It is My Will that all be saved. There is no outside force strong enough to thwart that Will! No matter what pressures are put on any particular person from the outside, the final, free decision rests with each one. Grace is available for the taking. Coming into desperate circumstances physically, mentally, or spiritually is a blessing in disguise for then that person reaches desperately for grace, as a drowning person clutches for something or someone to hold onto.

Do not let yourself drown! Take the grace that I proffer you so your will can be strong enough to say "No" to those outside forces that try to draw you away from love. Take My hand! Unite your weak will with Mine. I will give you strength.

All is coming to be as it is meant to be. Life goes on. Changes come. You have nothing to fear. Rest in Me, the Father of Light. Simply be, simply trust, simply believe. Know that I am with you. It cannot be otherwise or you would not be. []

9.15   I AM TRUE LIFE

[| No matter how disorganized you feel and how "unreal" your days may seem to be, know that I am with you. You are alive, so I am with you. I am life. I give you My very life. |]

Lord, it is good for me to be here!

[| Yes, My child, it is good! Relax ever more and more in My presence. There is nothing for you to be afraid of. There is no void into which you can fall. I am all-existence. No matter what people's beliefs and ideas about life and "religion" are, the truth remains as it is. I am the bedrock upon which you stand and the life that gives you existence.

Human miseries and woes are not as disastrous as you would think from looking at them in your earthly view. They are but a means of "breaking the ties that bind," a way of loosening the things that hold you to the limited sphere of earth.

The world as you see it will pass away. The true world is love, joy, peace, goodness, tranquility, and love. True life is being in My arms. You *are* there, but you must come to realize it.

All is well! Relax and enjoy. You can walk in joy, just as you can walk in peace and love. When you walk in peace and joy and love, you have life. Then life is truly worth living!

I walk with you and talk with you.

Learn of Me, for I am meek and humble of heart.

I am the way. Follow Me! Come into life! []

9.16   FAITHFUL FOREVER

[| Discern what your true motives are. Selflessness is the key to bringing about positive changes in your life, for when the self goes you must be filled with My life. There is no vacuum in the spiritual as there is none in the physical. The physical mirrors the spiritual.

Some of the My life is in every person, even in the most "perverted." There is hope and a chance of salvation for everyone. Love all. Desire the salvation of all.

My child, you have a buildup of anxiety right now. Release it to Me, whatever the basis or the cause of it is.

I desire to share your whole life with you. I take, I choose you from now on, forever. Nothing will revoke that choice. Should you lose your way spiritually and wander in the desert of the world for long periods, I will not forsake you or leave you. You can be certain of My love and fidelity.

"For the Lord is good and his love endures forever; his faithfulness continues through all generations" (Ps 100:5). Coming to know that is what will finally help you release the underlying insecurity you have in your person and personality. You are being released and delivered

from feeling insecure as you spend time in communion with Me. At the same time, your tendency toward having spiritual or intellectual pride is lessening, for that is an offshoot of feeling insecure.

How marvelously all things work together for good for those who trust in the Lord! You are being rewarded for years of patient belief. Your faith and hope have carried you through.

I am in command of the ship. I command the wind and the waves. Trust. Rest secure in My love. I do not leave anyone out of My love. My love is all-encompassing and all-embracing. My love is life for you and all. Rest securely in Me, My child! I love you! []

9.17   DWELL WITH ME

[| I hold you in love, My child – none could be stronger. You are safe and secure in My love. Do not let temptations assail you. You can keep temptations away in large measure by the attitude you have in your heart. If you are mindful of Me you are protected, for darkness cannot be where there is light.

I love you! Receive My love with an open heart. I come to you in love through all possible channels. I will teach you how to be aware of My love coming to you through others and will help you open yourself to receive that love and give love in return. You cannot love too much. There is nothing to fear in going out in love.

My people, I have called you out of the land of Egypt! ("Egypt" represents all that is vile and full of resentment, hopelessness, and no goal for living.) Do not return there a second time! You can be a help to your fellow brothers and sisters by becoming spiritually stalwart in your own life. As the whole body benefits from muscles that are exercised and become strong so all benefit from the spiritual strength that is built up through self-denial and self-discipline by individuals.

Do you notice the difference in those words? Self-denial is saying an outright "No" to yourself. Self-discipline is regulating the use of material goods, one's actions, and so on, so that one's spirit is in control rather than the body with its erratic moods and feelings.

Nothing ventured, nothing gained.

Nothing given, nothing gained.

I so desire to give immeasurably to you but I am yet blocked by roadblocks that your bodily nature puts in place. Hurdles remain to be overcome. My grace and strength await you. |]

9.18   UPKEEP NEEDED

[| I bless you, My child! Continue in your stance of faith, love, and openness. It will yield a reward of a rich harvest.

Anyone who relates to the Lord will receive good things for I am All Good. I have only good to give. When you turn to Me with your mind, you receive good through your mind. When you love with your spirit, you receive love in your spirit. There is no vacuum in the spiritual. Give what you have and you will receive.

Like attracts like. Good draws in good, yes, but, also, evil draws evil. Pass unkindness, resentment, envy to another, and your own "house" will again be filled with suchlike. There is just as much need for you to do housecleaning in the spiritual as there is in the physical. Clutter and dust pile up in your spirit as they do in a house if discipline is not used to take care of it right along.

You are one unit consisting of body, Soul, and spirit. What affects one affects the other. Discipline in the physical has a counterpart in the spiritual. It works the other way around, too, that having discipline in mind and spirit builds up strength and stamina to have a like discipline in the body and its surroundings. "...*every city or household divided against itself will not stand*" (Mt 12:25b). A house that works together with its members does stand.

And, give all glory to Me! That is the "frosting on the cake!" All gain and growth must be ascribed to Me, ever-present and living within you, then the growth and change will be permanent and stable. Self is so fickle and weak that your good resolves will break down if you put the glory onto her back.

Do not fear, child. Just trust. Hold no recrimination against yourself. Just try again. I support you all the way and I supply where you lack if you will let Me.

You do not need to get all of these teachings understood and sorted out in short order. You have a long while to let My truth and peace be absorbed. Live in Me, and truth and peace will become a part of you almost unawares. You are not aware of your body's taking in nutrients from the food you eat and the water you drink, yet every cell gets nourished and cleansed. Even so, eat and drink of Me and your entire spirit will be rejuvenated, cleansed, and made peaceful. []

9.19   YOU CAN MAKE A DIFFERENCE

[| My child, look up and live! Look up, look ahead, with expectation and joy! I am not a such serious God, that you should live always with sternness and seriousness. Believe with Me that those things which are ordained to come to pass will come to pass. I am not an idle God, trifling with affairs that do not matter. All is set up with remarkable efficiency! All is well! Believe!

Do not take yourself so seriously!

Laugh at yourself and your foibles!

Trod on with Me.

At times you will fly, other times you will cry.

Accept all as coming from My hands.

I know how to bring good from "evil." It is the inner attitude of the heart that allows physical catastrophes to take place. If all were living in love and harmony with one another, this world would be a much different place.

You can make your corner of the world safer, more pleasant, and more worth living in. Dwell with Me, walk and talk with Me, thus you will bring Me into your daily life and the lives of others.

Entrust others to Me, your family, friends, and the haggard people in war-torn lands. I repeat I will not allow anything to happen which will be to the eternal detriment of My sons and daughters. I desire the best for My little ones at all times. At all times My love flows blessing to you and all. Receive it in your heart. ...You are tired. Rest, child. Bless you! []

9.20   A LESSON ON GROWTH

[| All is well, My child. Do not worry overly much about lapses, but do try again. If you only *think* about trying again to hold to discipline, you will not gain any ground. You must *make a conscious decision* and "take the territory" by force. It will never be easy to say, "No" to yourself. It will become easier, however, as you make honest attempts to do so.

Do not be critical of yourself and look down on yourself. You are not to judge and that includes yourself. Do you think that a little green apple wonders whether it is green enough, round enough, or fastened on tightly enough? Does it decide, on its own, the time that it should begin to turn red and then proceed to round up the necessary chemicals to bring that about?

There is more similarity between you and a growing apple than you would at first think.

You and an apple are both created beings.

You both have life within and go through a process of growth.

You are each who and what you are for a specific purpose.

You both give Me glory simply by being.

Your growth, whether physical, mental, or spiritual, comes along the best when you can just let the growth come as it is meant to come, without a lot of fuss and to-do. Attention given to yourself is attention that is not given to others or Me.

By *self* here is meant the self that is caught in the narrow confines of self-interest, self-importance, and selfishness: "Me-ism." The self that is a prisoner is very unhappy, indeed. The self that stuffs and over-saturates itself with pleasure is very miserable. From within a cry is heard, "Who will deliver Me from this hell-hole I am in from which I cannot escape? My God, come and set Me free!"

When you have once been released from former things and are enjoying a measure of freedom, think back once in a while to the former situation. Dip briefly into the frustration and sense of being lost that had formerly engulfed you; then, recall the time and day of your liberation and once again give glory to Me with songs of thankfulness and praise! The gift that you are continually grateful for is the one you will prize the more. You will thus be doubly blest: in the receiving of the gift of freedom and the giving of thanks.

Rest and live in Me ever deeper, child. Some of the work I am doing within you is the type of thing you do not see. Trust Me to do perfect work in you, for you, and through you. Be obedient to My call, to My Spirit. Do not be too fearful and guarded with new people you meet. Be open to what I may teach you through people who come into your life. Everything works together in marvelous divine order! Bless you, for continuing to trust and for your faithfulness.

Good night, My little one! I love you! []

9.21   SPIRITUAL VS. PHYSICAL

[| All is well. I love you, My child! You are, in Me. All are, in Me. You are safe and loved, My beloved. "Come hell or high water," nothing can harm you as you rest secure in Me.

"You made him ruler over the works of your hands; you put everything under his feet" (Ps 8:6). I give you possessions for use and distribution. You (humankind) have dominion over the created things in the universe. Let that order be reversed, that things come to have dominion over you and you are in trouble.

As an example of a created thing coming to have dominion, suppose that a group of people were to make a remarkable computer to help them with their work and that the computer would then seize control and become boss over their lives: "Go here!" "Stop!"

"Give Me that suit!" "You will do as I command you!" This is, in actuality, how things are for some people in their relationship with created things, that the things control them.

Your body is a created thing. It can come to wield tremendous pressure so that your mind and spirit become slaves to it and are helpless in the face of its demands. I have come to set prisoners free. *"I came that they [you] might have life and have it to the full"* (Jn 10:10b).

I give you the grace to recognize the ways that you are too dependent upon the material world and your feelings. Once you recognize that dependency, what you need to do is ask and you will receive. Ask and you will be set free! |]

9.22   THE TRUTH SHALL STAND

[| My child, you do not need to get all of these ideas that are coming to mind sorted out and squared away in your mind, but you do need to bring your spirit into the right order with Me. When your spirit is in the right order with Me, your mind and heart will be, also.

Even when there is no guile in your spirit there may be terrible blindness and great disorder within. As I intimated before, there is a connection between your spiritual life and your relationship with the physical world. A person who is called into an intimate union with Me in spirit will have his/her whole being and life taken into that union: spiritual, mental, and physical. Bring right ordering in spirit and there will be consequential right ordering in mind and body.

Many idols exist in the minds and hearts of people that they are not aware of. Only the clear bright light of My Spirit will bring those idols to light. Worshiping *"in spirit and in truth"* (Jn 4:24) will bring down those idols, for nothing that is lesser can stand before the truth. Seek the truth and you will find it. Desire a right ordering within yourself and that will come about. The searching light of My truth will bring to light all that is hidden in darkness.

You cannot be truly and completely free:

Until all that is in darkness has been brought to light,
Until all that is shakable has been shaken away.

Prepare yourself to have your ideas and thoughts turned topsy-turvy. The world will test you, your spirit will test you and I will test you. Like gold and silver in the refiner's fire, I will test you. "*... I have refined you like silver, tested you in the furnace of affliction*" (NAB Is 48:10). This is not so that you may come through with flying colors and be completely refined, but that you may learn to trust in Me completely, to lean on Me and not on your understanding.

"*[W]hat is mankind that you are mindful of them, human beings that you care for them?*" (Ps 8:4). In and of yourself you are nothing, but I have taken you under My wing. I have poured My Spirit into you. Now you must be purified to be worthy to bear My seal. All that is of the earth must fall away. I will not share My throne with any other or anything.

Your being, who you are, will stay intact, but preconceived ideas must go. You are a newborn babe in the spirit – your learning is just beginning. *Do not be afraid to examine any concept that comes to mind, even if you have held it sacred from your youth.* I, the Lord, am the same yesterday, today, and forever. That which is Unchangeable will remain always and forever unchangeable. You need to be open to the truth to come into it. []

9.23   I CALL YOU INTO FREEDOM

[] I call you, My child, from eternity! I call you into peace, truth, and freedom! The truth will set you free. I am the Truth. Come! Search for Me and find Me! I await you in the forest glade, in the ripple of joyous laughter, in the praise that rises in your heart. No more seriousness (serious, long face)! Come into joy and freedom! I will show you the way. "*With glad cries of freedom, you will ring me round!*" (NAB Ps 32:7c).

I bring you freedom: freedom to be, to do, and to think, freedom to be fully who and what you are called/destined to be. The essence of that freedom consists of being who you are within Me. Only in Me can you come into complete and perfect freedom.

Growth is set to take place within. A plant has potential growth within it, waiting only for the right conditions to bring that growth about. It achieves freedom when it is free to grow, become, and produce what it is meant to.

You achieve freedom when you come into the conditions that allow and help you to become who you are meant to be. That condition, that place, is within Me. United with Me you are within the source of eternal life. You are safe, nurtured in love, and free to be. []

9.24 IN ME IS COMPLETE FREEDOM

[| *"With glad cries of freedom you will ring me round"* (NAB Ps 32:7). That is a promise, dear one! You are coming into freedom. Often the way to freedom is through a tunnel. You do not yet have complete freedom, but you know that at the other end of the tunnel is complete and perfect freedom.

Freedom consists, first of all, in being able (and free) to be yourself and in being free to respond to Me, to the truth. Complete freedom is total and complete acceptance of the truth, coming into Me and accepting Me and your relationship with Me simply and with full trust.

I will not be outdone in generosity, My children! When you give yourself to Me in full measure, you receive Me in FULL MEASURE!

I long to pour Myself out to you in full measure so you may truly know love, truth, and freedom! My only desire is to give, to love, to set free! Rest in Me. Be in Me. Be free!

I love you, My little one! Far be it from Me to cause you pain. When you are in pain from whatever source, it is not from Me. In Me is light, gladness, freedom, and love. You have been in bondage in the past (and still are to some degree) to hurts and anxieties, to elements of the material world, to your "self," to fear, to legalism, to being "perfect" in your own eyes. You have been trapped within the limits that self, materialism, and perfectionism have set for you.

You somehow picked up the idea that you are not worthy of being loved. You were afraid of physical expressions of love as a child. Be a child now. Let Me, let others, hold you and love you. *Let us love you.* Let that love sink in. It will bring healing and release. Those who are released from bondage and fear by love stay where they are and who they are (they are in Me); but, the walls and straight jackets and fears that held them captive fall away.

My child, I affirm who you are at this moment, the core of who you are coming to be. I am the strength of your being within. You are, in Me. You are safe in love, in My arms.

What I do for you, I do for all. *For all as for one.* Bless you, My little one! Bless all! Peace be with you! []

9.25   COME TO KNOW ME

[] I call you to peace, My child, not to anxiety. You are to seek Me, to seek truth, in peace. Avoid all that would lead you to be anxious, even if it should seem to promise you great new knowledge.

"Coming into truth" is not coming into knowledge as understood by humankind. It is not an acquiring of more factual data about how the spiritual world is ordered. It is an opening of the mind and spirit to the things of My kingdom so that you come to know Me. "*I will walk among you and be your God, and you will be my people*" (:12).

"Knowing God" means relating with Me. It is My indwelling you and your welcoming Me. "Coming to know My paths" does not mean coming to new knowledge. "*[T]here is nothing new under the sun*" (Eccl 1:9c). It means coming to know Me, the Lord of heaven and earth, and your Lord. You do not know Me until you know Me as Lord, as well as knowing Me as Savior and Friend.

I am God. I must be true to Who I Am, just as you must be true to who you are: Creator and creature in a marvelous union of service, dependency, and love. Service on My part, dependency on your part, love uniting us. Then that love, in turn, brings forth loving service.

Nothing that occurs is terrible or a catastrophe except sin, which separates you from Me. Sin, a separation between creature and creator, brings catastrophes, for how can you be separated from the source of blessing and still be blessed? Nature cooperates fully with Me even in the illness of body, for illness is a faithful sign that not all is in order.

Through illness and catastrophes, I call to you, My people, to come to know Me as God, to again know Me as God. Young children are in the right order with Me. They accept themselves fully and have no pretense. Become again as children. Do not try to direct your growth or learning. Be pliant and willing in My hands. Let Me be God, then I will have you as "My people." []

9.26   ROUGH WAYS MUST BE MADE SMOOTH

"Every valley shall be raised up, every mountain and hill made low; the rough ground shall become level, the rugged places a plain. And the glory of the Lord will be revealed, and all mankind together will see it" (Is 40:4-5).

"Do not fear, for I have redeemed you; I have summoned you by name; you are mine (Is 43:1b).

[| I call you into love, into freedom, into joy! Love all, and wish the best for all. Wish that all may rest and be and grow in Me, that all may come into love, freedom, and joy.

Do not consider any person's situation hopeless regarding salvation. I am God. The so-called "impossible" is possible with Me. All that is meant to be will come to be in its own good time. Being anxious about something that you wish to take place deters, rather than helps, that to come to be.

An important part of your coming to be who and what you are meant to be is to come to see who and what you are now. *"The arrogant cannot stand in your presence"* (Ps 5:5a). All that is high must be brought low. The mountains and hills must be leveled, the rough ways must be made smooth.

No one can stand before Me in pride; hence, all self-accomplishment and all dependence on self in opposition to dependence upon Me must be broken down. It is very humbling to come to see the abject poverty of one's spirit and self, but this must take place. In My special instruments, not a shred of exalted self-worth can remain.

All that is shakable and all that is breakable within you must be removed. *"And now these three remain: faith, hope, and love. But the greatest of these is love"* (1 Cor 13:13). Let the cleansing fire have its way! Accept all that comes to you in life. Never think that you, of yourself, know the way, or that you know the meaning and purpose of life.

You do not need to fear. You rest in perfect safety, in Me. I am the rock of safety, the safe port, Yahweh-who-cares. Sacrifice yourself on the altar of humility, which is truth. Acknowledge that you do not know the way, that you have much to learn, that you are helpless in and of yourself to do or know anything, and that you need Me to be your God.

I do not force, I only invite: Come follow Me. I invite you to be peaceful and unafraid. You can choose this. In a way, you are the master of your destiny. *"I have set before you life and death, blessings and curses. Now choose life, so that you and your children may live"* (Dt 30:19b).

I lead and teach all. If another walks a path different than yours, who are you to say that is not where they should be?

Never think that someone must do this or that,
Or must believe this or that.
Do not judge and you will not be judged.
Be merciful and you shall receive mercy. []

9.27   THE CHOICE IS YOURS

[| My children, do not let yourself be intimidated. Do not fear *"the terror of the night, nor the arrow that flies by day"* (Ps 91:5a). Be in perfect peace, no matter what the circumstances of your life may be.

You are in charge of your castle. You must be the caretaker, servant, and master of your Soul. You do not need to *be* in a manner that you do not wish to be. You are to "be" and to "let be," with each person being in charge of his or her own "being."

Do not let yourself be intimidated, or made fearful by anyone. Do not let anyone lead you to be angry, resentful, callous, impure, dishonest, vengeful, impatient, or closed in on yourself. You can live the manner of being that you choose.

"You can lead a horse to water, but you cannot make it drink." Circumstances in your life may have "led you to the water." You may find yourself in a situation in which it seems impossible for you not to "drink" – to not be afraid, impatient, resentful, or whatever – but the choice is yours. *"I have set before you life and death, blessings and curses. Now choose life, so that you and your children may live"* (Dt 30:19b). |]

Lord, how can one receive help in overcoming fear of bodily injury and someone else's overpowering personality?

[| By resting in Me is the only way: by living, walking, and doing all in Me, being within Me. You must come to know you are in Me, that you are safe, secure, and strong, not just believe it.

Believing just with your mind gives you only a mental picture without accompanying spiritual strength.

Believing with your heart, mind, and spirit that I am with you and you are in Me, and choosing with your heart, mind, and spirit to be in Me, opens you to My presence.

Then you will have the grace, courage, and strength from within to not be afraid of outside forces.

"The Lord is my light and my salvation—whom shall I fear? The

Lord is the stronghold of my life–of whom shall I be afraid?" (Ps 27:1). Consecrate yourself to Me and trust. Be not afraid. |]

9.28   YOUR ATTITUDE SETS THE COURSE

[| My child, look up and live! Always look forward, ahead to the good. Do not look forward particularly, to the good that will be coming in the future, but to the coming into good that is now. *"Now is the time of God's favor, now is the day of salvation"* (2 Cor 6:2c). All that eternity has to offer, is yours for the taking now, for in Me it is now, a great and glorious time, or rather, timelessness. *"Jesus Christ is the same yesterday and today and forever"* (Heb 13: 8).

Come to Me, I will give you life.

Come to Me, I will give you peace.

I will give you hope, the promise of a better tomorrow.

I will give you love.

What your time is like at any given time (your experience within the framework of time) depends upon your attitude. Adverse circumstances do not of themselves cause adverse reactions and low spirits within a person. The effects within your body, mind, and spirit depend upon your reaction to the circumstances. See in them a blessing, and you receive a blessing. See calamity and curse, and you have calamity and curse to deal with.

Your makeup, your past experiences, your frame of mind, and so on, determine how a situation will be perceived by you. An example is the death of someone. Unexpected and not welcomed, death is a difficult happening to deal with. However, when people are prepared and almost eager to die – as is the case for those who have suffered much or for those for whom the time of waiting to return to Me has gotten to be too long – death is a blessing.

"I set before you life and death, blessings and curses" (Dt 30:19b). Each circumstance of life can be either a blessing or a curse for you. The choice is yours. If you embrace a circumstance willingly

and freely as being My will for you in that time and place, then you embrace Me.

If you let non-acceptance, rebellion, and resentment come crowding in, you "embrace" non-acceptance, rebellion, and resentment: nothingness. If you do not see Me in a situation you have only the emptiness of the material. Live in peace, choose in peace, and act in peace, freely.

Even the most adverse circumstances can redound into good if you so choose. If those circumstances are meant to be changed – if you are not in My will in allowing certain situations to continue – then, if you are of good heart and willing spirit, I will lead you to the way out. But, in the meantime, you had best accept what cannot be changed as being in My allowed Will or you will be open to a flood wash of disagreeable spirits.

Life comes from the My hands and passes through the hands of human beings. This is where the difficult, hurtful circumstances come from. But life originates from Me. Therefore, life must be accepted openly and freely if one is to be open and free in your relationship with Me.

Begin with open, free acceptance of being who and as you are, acceptance of all that transpired to bring you to this place and to being who and what you are, and, above all, acceptance of who you are meant to be in Me. From there, work outward to acceptance of the little things in life (which can be very pesky indeed!) and proceed on up to the more difficult acceptance of almost unacceptable situations (humanly speaking) that you need to deal with. I promise to be with you every moment, every day, in all situations. You will find Me in those situations if you but look.

Bless you, My child! Bless you, each and all! I am with you, do not forget that. I bless your efforts. I bless your person and being as you are now and as you are coming to be. I love you! []

9.29   MIGHTY IN ME

[| My child, I love you! All is well. Believe that. This applies to the friend you have in mind, too, and to everyone. I carry all in My Heart, in My loving plans.

The only way My loving will is thwarted is by interference and non-acceptance on the part of someone or by a direct interjection of the dark powers. The dark powers can come in only when they are allowed to. That allowance may be made by that particular person, by a parent, or by anyone else having connections with the person.

The more sinister dark spirits ride in on the backs of lesser ones. They use every avenue they can find. For instance, the spirit of rejection rides in on criticism, and hatred rides in on uncontrolled anger. Usually, several "pals" stick together and manage to sneak in.

But you are not helpless against this! No one is if they only knew it! Use the power that you have been given. Go forward in My might. *"Who is this King of glory? The Lord strong and mighty, the Lord mighty in battle"* (Ps 24:8). You expect and know that when I am on a person's side that, of course, they will win! Well, I am on your side and the side of all!

Turn to Me, My people, with all your hurt and problems. Bring others to Me that they may not faint and grow weary.

Bless you, My child. Bless all! I love you! |]

9.30   TWO SIDES OF THE COIN

[| Child, I give you My love, My life at all times. I give you Myself eternally, which means there never was a "time" in which I was not loving you, holding you securely, and giving you My very self. Your life is "life of My Life." Your being is "being of My Being." How wonderful it is to be God and to be able to give all to all!

The other side of that coin is that not all are open to receiving the good I hold out to them. Instead, they reach for a few moments of sensual enjoyment, another candy bar, another drink, material ownership, or the diversion of mindless prattle.

What can be done for these people? Who will be an example to show what peace and blessings are available and how to attain them? Which of you will be willing to make heroic efforts at conquering yourself? Will you, My child? Lately, you have been slacking off again.

Nothing has changed on My part. I love you with eternal love. I hold you in a warm embrace. I desire and bring about good for you and for those for whom you desire good. I desire to be fully one with you. Love knows no bounds and does not give up. I will continue to love you to the fullest, to health and wholeness, to complete freedom and fullness of love.

You read in an earlier lesson that "love is willing to endure anything for the sake of the joy of the beloved." That is a key. Look to your Beloved, not to yourself. Look to others' needs, not just your own so much. Even the time you spend with Me resting in peace and love is best spent to satiate My need for love and openness of spirit. If you do not have an attitude of giving you are not truly loving but are perchance spiraling back in on yourself.

Joy in Me, to bring joy to Me.

Receive My love, that I may have the joy of loving you.

Be open in love toward all, that I may love them and bless them through you.

As you expend yourself in love, blessing, and praise, you will find that you have reached deeper satisfaction than you ever thought possible, all by giving more so than receiving.

When you receive a material blessing, praise your heart out in giving thanks to Me, who am the giver of all good gifts.

If you sense weakness and need, humbly ask Me for forgiveness and renewed strength.

If you achieve great spiritual or material accomplishments, give all glory to Me for My generous working in and through you.

If you perceive weakness and darkness of spirit in an individual or a group, plead for them before Me.

Stand in their stead in the discipline of spirit and offer praise and
thanks to Me in their name. This will lift the onus and restore
them to be partakers of the blessing cup.

Always, at all times and in all circumstances, revert all back to
Me. I am the center and pivot point of creation and life. Thus will you
find happiness and peace unto your Soul and you will experience the
eternal embrace with which I hold you.

Peace, My child! I love you! []

9.31   GIVE MUCH, RECEIVE MUCH

[| My child, you have been experiencing more hunger for food lately
and more physical distress in your body. This comes from spending
less time in communion with Me. I am the source of life and energy.
You must come to Me to be filled and to be released from tension.

Continue to commend yourself to Me and ask for My guidance
and help in every situation. It is good to mistrust yourself and your
human inclinations. So often people on their own do not become
aware of anything out of the way in their intentions and attitudes. It
takes the bright light of My Spirit to bring flaws and misjudgments
out into the open.

Never begrudge giving time to Me in whatever form it is asked
of you, whether time spent in silence physically, mentally, and
spiritually with Me; time spent in everyday duties around the house,
or time spent in loving others. Give and you will receive and when
you receive much, you can, in turn, give much. Duty faithfully done
means spiritual power acquired.

The plan of salvation is being worked out in the day-to-day
moments and events of your life. Those meetings with friends are
not haphazard happenstance. All is set up to be worked out in My
Will for the salvation of all.

Please continue to be willing to grow. I know growth is painful,
for it necessitates laying bare the touchy, sore spots of your inner
being and having much wild growth and clutter pruned from your

true self. I am treating you with the utmost tender care, as carefully as I can. Surely you know by now, though, that your "self" is not as fragile as you may have thought. The more storms and spiritual battles that you weather, the stronger you become.

I need stalwart workers in My vineyard. I call the workers and prepare them for their allotted tasks with utmost love – no being used or abused. Choose to see your life this way. All that comes to be in your life comes in and through love. I give you the grace to be open to life, to love.

Bless you, dear child! I am with you in life and love! []

9.32   FULL HEALING WILL COME

Lord, please pour Your love for my children into me! And please pour Your love for me into them! Bind us together, Lord, I pray!
[| My child, it is with rejoicing that I do this! I have waited for this day for "years" and rejoice that this time has arrived!

Minor and major victories such as this are taking place throughout the lives of My people all the time, so all the time is the time for rejoicing! You can rejoice in anticipation of victory, at the moment of victory, and forever afterward! Be a rejoicing person, a member of My rejoicing people! The victory is ours! Always remember that.

I bless you in your efforts to help your friend climb out of the drudgery of depression and self-pity. The "blind" and the "crippled" must be led by the hand and prayed with to be delivered and healed. I take charge of all things in everyone's life. All is allowed for a purpose. Continue to lead people to Me, then leave them to Me to take care of. Discern the wind of the spirit as best you can.

Again I must speak of My love for you! My heart is bursting with love! I hold you tenderly in My arms and bring some more healing and deliverance from oppression, uptightness, insecurity, and a sense of being unloved. It will all be gone eventually and then, what rapture! what delight! free and happy and whole in My arms! It is coming, I promise and assure you! []

9.33   OPEN YOURSELF TO MY WAY

(I read about a sexual assault on a woman.)
[| My child, yes, such experiences are gross, but so are many other hurtful experiences that people go through. It all happens because of sin. The less sin there would be in the world the fewer tragedies of this type would occur.

Sin can be dealt decisive blows in the spirit. You wouldn't believe the far-ranging effects, the difference even one person can make in this matter. I came to save people from sin and the effects of those sins.

Salvation is not just bliss after you die. It is meant to be now. Those who are called to be vehicles of that salvation, to help with its coming, play a tremendous part in the battle against sin and the horrid consequences of sin. Your reaction to reading about this assault and others like it can help spur you on to a fuller and firmer commitment to Me and to helping bring My kingdom into being.

I repeat, you literally would not believe how far-ranging the strength against sin is when a person of goodwill and purity of heart says "No" to their appetite, selfish interests, and self-pity, thus saying "Yes" to sharing self with others and dealing a decisive blow to the dark world of sin. I will be completely united with you in this aspect.

I will protect you from depression about this sort of thing (sexual assault) and lead you to see it through My eyes. I will make My ways known to you, but that means you must give up your ways, whatever contradicts My way. Forward together! Bless you, child! |]

9.34   WILL IN TRAINING

[| Things that remain to be done – things to be sorted, cleaned, and cleared, projects to be completed – these will be a part of your life for a long time, maybe always, in this life. Having things to do adds spice to life. How would you feel if there would be nothing waiting to be done, no one needing help, no purpose in mind for getting up in the morning?

Your attitude toward such duties and projects can spell the difference between joy and burdened stress in life. The choice is yours whether your life will be one of duty done joyfully out of love, or duty done begrudgingly and bereft of joy.

Bereft brings to mind the thought of a widow left alone and sad after the death of her husband or a lonely child mourning a recently deceased parent. To be "bereft" means to be "robbed" of the good that you could have had.

If you do not have joy in living, it may be that you have been robbing yourself of it. Resentments held against others are directly opposed to joy. If you choose resentment you cannot at the same time have full joy. The more negative feelings that you allow to crowd into your mind and heart, the less joy you will have. I am joy. The more of the negative that you choose to have and live with, the less of Me you will have. Ponder this.

Be peaceful in what you choose as the activity of the moment. You cannot, at the same time, choose and not choose. From the physical standpoint, you are either doing a certain thing or not doing it. The attitude you have toward what you are doing is a different matter, however. Your mind may whiplash you for choosing or not choosing to do some certain thing. Why does one's mind do that? How can that be changed?

You have the power of mastery over unruly feelings and mental putdowns in and through your will. Your will must oversee your imagination and your memory. You must take charge of your feelings and inclinations by, and in the power of, your will.

It may be necessary for you to run roughshod over some of your feelings, to give yourself tough love in correcting and not allowing self-condemnation, self-rejection, self-pity, or self-centeredness. The child within must be trained and taught to be tolerant and forgiving, humble and appreciative.

Love resides in the will, first and foremost. It is the heart that wills. What you really and truly choose, comes "from the heart," from the very center of your being. Put the placard up over your heart: WILL IN TRAINING and begin in earnest to choose to love, accept and forgive. I "struggle" with you, one with you always.

Cheers! We look ahead to a brighter day! []

BIBLIOGRAPHY

ACIM *A Course in Miracles*

    Quotes are from *A Course in Miracles* Combined Volume Second Edition. Viking - Published by the Penguin Group, Penguin Books USA Inc. 375 Hudson Street, New York, New York, 10014, U.S.A. Copyright © Foundation for Inner Peace,1975, 1985, 1992, 1996. Quotations are used with permission from the Foundation for Inner Peace (www.acim.org andinfo@acim.org). All Rights Reserved. *(A Course in Miracles)* c 1975, 1985, 1992, 1996, published by the Foundation for Inner Peace, PO Box 598, Mill Valley, CA 94942.

NAB *The New American Bible* c 1970 by the Confraternity of Christian Doctrine [CCC], Washington, D.C. Used with permission from CCC 3211 Fourth Street, NE, Washington, DC 20017-1194

Unless otherwise noted, all Scripture is taken from The HOLY BIBLE, NEW INTERNATIONAL VERSION. Copyright 1973, 1978, 1984, International Bible Society. Used by permission of Zondervan Bible Publishers.

Webster's New World Collegiate Dictionary 4th Edition, 2004 Wiley Publishing, Inc., Cleveland, Ohio.

Printed in the United States
by Baker & Taylor Publisher Services